Using Corpora for Language Research

This book is affectionately dedicated

to Geoffrey Leech

by its editors, contributors and publishers

Using Corpora for Language Research

Studies in the Honour of Geoffrey Leech

Edited by Jenny Thomas and Mick Short

Longman
London and New York

Longman Group Limited,
Longman House, Burnt Mill,
Harlow, Essex CM20 2JE, England
and Associated Companies throughout the world.

Published in the United States of America
by Longman Publishing, New York

First published 1996

ISBN 0 582 24877-9 CSD
ISBN 0 582 24878-7 PPR

British Library Cataloguing-in-Publication Data

A catalogue record for this book is available from the British Library

Library of Congress Cataloging-in-Publication Data

A catalog record has been applied for

Printed in Great Britain by Short Run Press Ltd.

Contents

Contributors

J CHARLES ALDERSON, Department of Linguistics and Modern English Language, University of Lancaster

ERIC ATWELL, Artificial Intelligence Division, School of Computer Studies, University of Leeds

TED BRISCOE, Department of Computing, University of Cambridge

JOHN CARROLL, Department of Computing, University of Cambridge

JONATHAN CULPEPER, Department of Linguistics and Modern English Language, University of Lancaster

STEVE FLIGELSTONE, Department of Linguistics and Modern English Language, University of Lancaster

ROGER GARSIDE, Department of Computing, University of Lancaster

SIDNEY GREENBAUM, Survey of English Usage, University College London

STIG JOHANSSON, English Department, University of Oslo

GERRY KNOWLES, Department of Linguistics and Modern English Language, University of Lancaster

TONY McENERY, Department of Linguistics and Modern English Language, University of Lancaster

DIETER MINDT, Didaktik der englischen Sprache und Literatur, Freie Universität, Berlin

GERALD NELSON, Survey of English Usage, University College London

MICHAEL OAKES, Department of Computer Science, University of The West Indies

SIGNE OKSEFJELL, English Department, University of Oslo

RANDOLPH QUIRK, English Department, University College London

PAUL RAYSON, Department of Computing, University of Lancaster

GEOFFREY SAMPSON, School of Cognitive and Computing Sciences, University of Sussex,

ELENA SEMINO, Department of Linguistics and Modern English Language, University of Lancaster

MICK SHORT, Department of Linguistics and Modern English Language, University of Lancaster

NICHOLAS SMITH, Department of Computing, University of Lancaster

GABRIELE STEIN, Anglistisches Seminar, Universität Heidelberg

DELLA SUMMERS, Longman Group UK Ltd

JAN SVARTVIK, English Department, University of Lund

JENNY THOMAS, Department of Linguistics and Modern English Language, University of Lancaster

MICHAEL WEITZMAN, Department of Hebrew and Jewish Studies, University College London

ANDREW WILSON, Department of Linguistics and Modern English Language, University of Lancaster

Preface

Corpus linguistics has now become mainstream. No longer the preserve of the computer 'boffin', corpus-based research is increasingly influential in many areas of language study. The main aim of this book is to introduce the corpus approach to people working in a range of areas within linguistics and language study. The majority of the articles in this book are designed for researchers, teachers and students who have limited computing expertise, but who would like to know what machine-readable corpora have to offer in their areas of interest.

The papers in Part 1 explain in general terms the value of a corpus-based approach and how it can be applied in different areas of descriptive linguistics. Part 2 offers a series of corpus-based case studies in syntax, semantics and stylistics. Part 3, which is more technical in nature, demonstrates the usefulness of machine-readable corpora for people working in speech and language technology. Part 4 explores the ways in which the corpus approach can be extended to wider and more applied areas of language research: machine translation, language teaching, language testing and lexicography.

We offer this collection of papers as a tribute, on his 60th birthday, to Geoffrey Leech, a pioneer in the construction and exploitation of machine-readable corpora. A linguist of international standing, Geoffrey has had considerable influence in many areas of linguistics — grammar, semantics, pragmatics, stylistics (literary and non-literary) and English language pedagogy. It is fitting that this collection explores the application of the corpus approach which Geoff has pioneered, to each of the areas of linguistics in which he is so well known.

Jenny Thomas and Mick Short

PART 1

Using corpora for language research

1 Corpora are becoming mainstream

JAN SVARTVIK

1.1 From corpse on a slab to corpus on the bandwagon

It may not be politically correct to bring up here, in a linguistic Festschrift, the question as to whether research in linguistics can be justified. But in fact, many of us who are engaged in this kind of academic endeavour are all too familiar with negative or, at best, sceptical attitudes to linguistic research (as opposed to, say, medical research) occasionally expressed by members of society outside academia. So, considering that our livelihood and research projects are largely funded by those very people out there, it may not be out of place to pay attention to their views of our activities. Let's face it, in some quarters at least, linguistics has 'a bad reputation as an abstruse subject which has become more complicated than it need be' (Aitchison 1994: 9); it is even considered to be a discipline that suffers from 'a dead-hand legacy'.

But there are enviable, exceptional places of learning that get a good press:

> [Linguistics is] a tradition that sees language as a corpse on a slab, under the dissecting scalpel of the professional linguist. Luckily for Lancaster, however, the past 20 years have seen new life breathed into this corpse. The clinical skills of the pathologist have given way to skills in understanding how real, living language is used in real life situations.[1]

While it would be unfair to attribute to Geoffrey Leech alone, or indeed to corpus linguistics research alone, the Lancaster skills in understanding how real, living language is used in real life situations,

I think it is fair to say that it was he who got the department's bearings right in the first place.

When inviting us to contribute to this volume, the Lancaster-based editors cheerfully stated that corpus linguistics is now 'no longer just an area of highly specialist research, of interest to a few boffins'. Since *boffin* was not as yet part of my core vocabulary, I reached for a dictionary and found that the word denotes 'a scientist who is considered to know a lot about science but who is not thought to be interested in other things';[2] typical collocations are: *a computer boffin, a mad boffin.* Geoffrey Leech was one of those primordial corpus boffins who have been instrumental in advancing corpus linguistics, so that it is now variously described as 'coming of age', 'becoming mainstream', 'a burgeoning field', 'the flower of the decade', 'a buzz-word', 'a bandwagon'...

John Sinclair, another computer boffin, describes the history of corpus linguistics in this way (1991: 1):

> Thirty years ago when this research started it was considered impossible to process texts of several million words in length. Twenty years ago it was considered marginally possible but lunatic. Ten years ago it was considered quite possible but still lunatic. Today it is very popular.

Clearly, if this was madness, there was method in it.

We will now take a historical look and record some of the milestones of corpus linguistics à la Lancaster on its way to rites of passage.

1.2 From TV ads to the British National Corpus

When I first met Geoffrey Leech he spent most of his time watching TV — but it was strictly for business, not pleasure. He was compiling his first corpus, which consisted of 617 television advertisements telecast in Britain in the early sixties. At the time, the combination of advertising on television (then a novelty which carried little weight among academics in Britain) and empirical data (shunned by many linguists as being unfashionable in that heyday of Chomskyan theory) can hardly have been a recommendable platform for an aspiring postgraduate student in an English department. But at University College London, under the auspices of such scholars as Michael

Halliday and Randolph Quirk, corpus studies were fully supported. Of course, he did not have a machine-readable corpus — this was before the electronics revolution, and postgraduate students did not have PCs on their desks, but shoeboxes filled with paper slips. What made Geoffrey Leech different from the rest of us was that, on his desk, he also had a rented TV for watching the commercial breaks from which to extract real English ad words for his first book: *English in Advertising*. Yet, even 30 years ago, its author foresees the prospects of a future computer corpus linguistics (Leech 1966: 73):

> ... counting occurrences, in a large number of cases, is merely a laborious way of coming to conclusions one has already arrived at subjectively. More detailed quantitative analyses (requiring large corpuses and the aid of computers) can be expected to produce results beyond the insight of the native speaker.

After finishing his postgraduate degrees in the University of London (M.A. in 1963 and Ph.D. in 1968) and a first appointment as lecturer at University College London, Geoffrey Leech moved to Lancaster University in 1969, where he has been Professor of Linguistics and Modern English Language since 1974. He has not gone walkabout in search of new academic pastures (except for numerous wide-ranging international lecture tours), but has instead devoted his energies to creating, together with his colleagues, a top-class department. Thus, in the UK Universities Research Assessment 1992, it got the best ranking possible (5A, i.e. research rated as of excellent international standing) and, in a recent survey undertaken at the University of Hawaii, Lancaster was named the best centre for Applied Linguistics in the UK, and among the first five in the world.

Although this volume is dedicated to the use of corpora in language research, it would be a serious misrepresentation to describe Geoffrey Leech just as a computer corpus boffin. His other main academic interests — and in the mainstream linguistics community he is probably better known for these contributions than for his corpus work — include English grammar, semantics, stylistics and pragmatics.

We now return to the historical conspectus of corpus linguistics at Lancaster. In 1970 Geoffrey Leech founded a project under the name of CAMET (Computer Archive of Modern English Texts) within the then single Department of English. The project's aim was to compile a one million word corpus of written British English for use on the computer. It was designed to be a British corpus parallel to the American corpus developed at Brown University by W. Nelson Francis and Henry Kučera — the first computer corpus of English, which set a standard in English corpus linguistics (Kučera and Francis 1967). While the Brown Corpus has been used all over the world for more than three decades, and is still a favourite resource for the study of American English, it may not be out of place to remind latter-day boffins that, in the sixties, anti-corpus attitudes were found both in linguistics and other circles. This was clearly brought home to those of us who had the opportunity of enjoying the dinner speech given by Professor Francis at the 5th ICAME Conference at Windermere, organized by Lancaster University in 1985. Here is the opening passage:

> You probably can't see it from where you sit, but some of you may have noticed that I am wearing a tie clip in the shape of a monkey wrench — or what I believe is called an 'adjustable spanner' in the curious dialect of this country. The story behind this peculiar piece of jewelry goes back to the early 60s, when I was assembling the notorious Brown Corpus and others were using computers to make concordances of William Butler Yeats and other poets. One of my colleagues, a specialist in modern Irish literature, was heard to remark that anyone who would use a computer on good literature was nothing but a plumber. Some of my students responded by forming a linguistic plumber's union, the symbol of which was, of course, a monkey wrench. The husband of one of them, being a jewelry manufacturer, had a few of these clips made. I cannot say that they have become collectors' items, but I would certainly not part with mine.[3]

The parallel British corpus was completed in 1978, in Norway actually, thanks to the contributions of Stig Johansson, Oslo, and Knut Hofland, Bergen — hence its name: the Lancaster-Oslo/Bergen (LOB) corpus. The compilation of the corpus was followed by a series of analyses, in particular tagging for word-classes (see Garside, Leech and Sampson (eds.) 1987, Johansson and Hofland 1989). The tagging was done with the Lancaster software package called Claws (Constituent Likelihood Automatic Word-tagging System), which has been revised and improved in later versions so as to reach a success rate without manual intervention in the high 90s per cent.

International cooperation in English corpus linguistics had already started in 1977 with the birth of ICAME (with Geoffrey Leech as one of the five charter members). The International Computer Archive of Modern English, or acronymically ICAME, was set up with the primary purposes of:

(1) collecting and distributing information on English language material available for computer processing;
(2) collecting and distributing information on linguistic research completed or in progress on the material;
(3) compiling an archive of corpuses to be located at the University of Bergen, from where copies of the material could be obtained at cost.

One of the activities of this loosely organized but effectively run association of corpus users has been to arrange an annual conference on English language research on computerized corpora, the University of Toronto in Canada being the venue of the latest (16th) conference. The base of ICAME can be said to be located in Bergen where the Norwegian Computing Centre for the Humanities publishes *ICAME Journal* and distributes copies of various corpora and software packages. Five corpora are now available on one CD-ROM: the Brown and LOB corpora, the London-Lund Corpus of Spoken English, the Kolhapur Corpus of Indian English, and the Helsinki Historical English Corpus.

Returning now from Scandinavia across the North Sea to Britain and developments at Lancaster, we can record that the next step was the creation of an interdisciplinary research unit, UCREL (Unit for Computer Research on the English Language[4]), which was set up in 1984 with Geoffrey Leech and Roger Garside as directors. The tasks included, among other things, further work on the grammatical analysis of the LOB corpus, which resulted in an improved version of the tagger (Claws2), the development of a syntactic parser using probabilistic models and a spelling checker.

In 1987 a second corpus was completed: the Lancaster-IBM Spoken English Corpus (SEC), compiled by Gerry Knowles in a joint venture between Lancaster University and IBM (UK). It is a corpus of modern spoken English (monologues) which is available, also through ICAME, both on audio-tape and in transcriptions with prosodic analysis.

The latest — but certainly not the last — milestone on the Lancaster inroads into corpus-compilation is the British National Corpus Project (BNC), created as a resource for research on the

British variety of the English language, which is, in the words of Lord Pym, 'one of our most valuable national assets'.[5] The British National Corpus, compiled between 1990–1994 and released in May 1995, is unique in several respects, in that:

- it is a very large corpus totalling 100 million words (90 million of written and 10 million of spoken material), and covering a comprehensive range of text varieties within each of these);
- it is a collaborative national project involving six partners: the British Library, three publishers (Longman Group Ltd, Oxford University Press, Chambers-Harrap) and two academic institutions (Oxford University Computing Service and Lancaster University);
- it is available to both industrial and academic users;
- it is marked up according to the guidelines of the Text Encoding Initiative; and
- it is grammatically tagged.

The role in this national collaborative project played by the Lancaster team with Geoffrey Leech and Roger Garside as directors has been a major one: to undertake the corpus processing, the annotation (grammatical tagging) of the corpus and the development of a suite of corpus search and retrieval tools, so as to enable various kinds of linguistic information to be extracted. In this process, Claws4 — a much-enhanced version of the original automatic grammatical tagger — has been adapted to run on both spoken and written material, including impromptu dialogue.

1.3 Looking round the corner

After this look in the rear-view mirror it is tempting to look ahead and speculate about the future of computerized corpus linguistics, especially with regard to English language corpora. What kind of developments are we likely to see as we are approaching the turn of the century? Many of the areas where developments seem particularly promising are treated, or indicated, in the papers of this congratulatory volume. In those cases I will refer to them by the names of the authors (who, of course, are in no way responsible for any of the following speculations).

Since this is an Olympic anniversary year, it may be timely to adopt de Coubertin's epigrammatic style in predicting that computers will be faster, smaller, cheaper; and corpora will be larger, better, commoner.

1.4 Corpora will be larger

The one-million word corpus, which was long a standard size, has already been replaced by much larger corpora (witness, for example, the British National Corpus), dynamic monitor corpora, on-line textual databases, etc., and this trend is bound to continue. Chomsky's fear that any natural corpus will be skewed is certainly less well founded today than thirty years ago. (Coincidentally, as I am writing this, there is an Internet flash on my computer screen announcing the Third Workshop at MIT (!) on Very Large Corpora which 'will offer a general forum for new research in corpus-based and statistical natural language processing. Areas of interest include (but are not limited to): sense disambiguation, part-of-speech tagging, robust parsing, term and name identification, alignment of parallel text, machine translation, lexicography, spelling correction, morphological analysis and anaphora resolution'.)

There are also constantly growing numbers of other machine-readable text collections now available on CD-ROM: broadsheets (such as *The Times*), periodicals (such as *The Economist*), parliamentary records (*Hansard*), etc. They are unannotated, i.e. they consist of raw text. Corpora planned for linguistic uses, such as LOB and the BNC, are increasingly annotated in some way, usually by word-class tagging. Annotation is useful in providing linguistic information about the structure of texts, and will be further used as test beds for linguistic theory, and for improving lexical and grammatical descriptions (see Sampson, chapter 2) and methods of computer content analysis (see Thomas and Wilson, chapter 7). Previous laborious manual analysis is being replaced by sophisticated techniques for automatic word-class tagging as well as syntactic and semantic parsing with astonishingly high success rates (see Briscoe and Carroll, chapter 9; Garside, chapter 11; Fligelstone, Rayson and Smith, chapter 12).

Lexicography is the applied field that, so far, has benefited most spectacularly from corpus use, and it is now customary for the major publishers to support and actively engage in the compilation of corpora and, of course, to make extensive use of them in making dictionaries aimed at a wide range of users (see Summers, chapter 16). The dictionary, traditionally based on the word, which has been a sacred unit in lexicography, is being supplemented by results from studies on collocation and phraseology. While inherent lexicological problems do not run away, even with fast machines, the question of loanwords adoption in a global language like English (see Quirk and Stein, chapter 3) is likely to be easier to handle by dating, style and geographical labelling, etc. based on increased corpus coverage recording current usage in international varieties.

1.5 Corpora will be better

Not only are corpora going to be larger and often tagged, but they will also cover a greater range of language uses and users. In addition to 'general-purpose corpora' such as LOB we are likely to see a variety of 'domain-specific corpora' designed for more specialized functions (see further Leech 1991: 11).

Greater care will be taken to provide information which characterizes individual texts, including setting, time, audience, topics, text difficulty and participant details (gender, age, first language, occupation, education, social group, dialect). Such information will be helpful for research on varieties, text typology, stylistics (see Greenbaum, Nelson and Weitzman, chapter 6; Short, Semino and Culpeper, chapter 8), for studies on discourse, syntax and semantics (see Johansson and Oksefjell, chapter 5), and for testing language proficiency (see Alderson, chapter 15).

While the vast majority of language use takes place in the spoken medium, conversation — the quintessence of spoken language — is either missing or seriously underrepresented in most existing corpora. There seems to be no short-cut to reduce this imbalance in data quantity: 'Even at that time [1961] I was assured that an automatic transcription of speech was "just around the corner". It still is.' (Sinclair 1991: 16). What we may hope for is to get some established convention of transcription to represent prosody (see Knowles, chapter 4), and to benefit from technical innovations, such as linking transcription and sound. Further progress will be made in corpus-based research in information technology, including speech synthesis and speech and handwriting recognition (see Atwell, chapter 10).

1.6 Corpora will be commoner

Judging by the increasing number of requests (for example on Internet discussion groups: 'Does anybody out there know about ...?') for information about how to locate, access and make use of corpora suitable for a particular research topic, it is a safe bet that corpora will be more common in a wide range of languages and research areas. During the last thirty-year period it is in English that development in corpus research has been most spectacular, but we are likely to see a similar spread of corpus work also to other languages, which should give a welcome boost to language studies generally — as has been the case for English studies.

Corpora of foreign and native learner language, including bilingual and multilingual corpora, child and teenage language corpora, etc., will improve our understanding of the language learning process and result in better methodologies and teaching materials. In spite of ambitious claims about the use of computers in language teaching, this is an area which has been largely unaffected by the corpus revolution: 'There is obviously a kind of school English which does not seem to exist outside the foreign language classroom' (Mindt, chapter 14). An important contribution to the use of corpora in language learning will be 'to make it possible for learners not only to have access to real rather than contrived language data, but also to explore language data on their own and to generate hypotheses and rules about the language' (Alderson, chapter 15). Work on parallel text corpora is already a burgeoning field, and will become useful in research on automatic translation and contrastive linguistics (see McEnery, chapter 13).

1.7 A new philosophical approach

While we can confidently maintain that corpus linguistics has made impressive progress during its 30-year history, it is only fair to add that, among linguists at large, corpus linguistics is not universally acclaimed for its contributions to linguistic theory. For example, in a review of a recent corpus-oriented book, Donald C. Freeman points to the lack of 'any ground-breaking theoretical discoveries or falsifications of major theoretical claims made by chalk-and-blackboard linguistics. [...] What seems most problematic in these "corpus-driven" studies is their tendency to equate statistical and theoretical importance.'[6]

With scholars like Geoff Leech and his colleagues having made Lancaster a world centre for imaginative corpus linguistics, the time has indeed come for making bolder theoretical and methodological claims. Geoff's adult view of computerized corpus linguistics is far more ambitious than it was thirty years ago when, as indicated at the outset, it was said to be a matter of 'detailed quantitative analyses'. Today the field represents to him a new philosophical approach to the study of language. Computerized corpus linguistics (Leech 1992a: 106):

> ... defines not just a newly emerging methodology for studying language, but a new research enterprise, and in fact a new philosophical approach to the subject. The computer, as a uniquely powerful technological tool, has made this new kind of linguistics possible. So technology here (as for centuries in natural science) has taken a more important role than that of supporting and facilitating research: I see it as an essential means to a new kind of knowledge, and as an 'open sesame' to a new way of thinking about language.

This introduction to his Festschrift is my humble tribute to Geoffrey Leech: a respected linguist, a valued colleague, co-author and friend, and a keen pianist. From experience of research administration many of us have learned that some people finish research projects late, others not at all — their projects just evaporate, leaving no visible or electronic results. Discussing this problem, a colleague of ours said very emphatically (and the fact that it was actually uttered under the arches of Winchester Cathedral should make the statement no less credible): 'But Geoff delivers the goods'.

It is a safe prediction that his thinking about language will not stop because he happens to be getting into his sixties, but that he will open sesames well into the next century. Geoff will deliver.

Notes

1 *Newsview* (May 1993).

2 *Cambridge International Dictionary of English* (C.U.P., 1995), P. 143. Cf.: 'Only a backroom boffin out of touch with the classroom could hold this pious belief' (*Picture Post*, 30 August 1952).

3 *ICAME News* 10 (5), 1985.

4 In 1995 the name was changed to 'University Centre for Computer Corpus Research on Language' (the acronym UCREL remains unchanged). This change reflects the increasing amount of corpus-based research on languages other than English.

5 *Parliamentary Debates (Hansard) House of Lords 1994–95*, 1st February 1995, col. 1493.

6 Donald C. Freeman in a review for the Internet LINGUIST Bulletin Board, March 1995, of Mona Baker, Gill Francis and Elena Tognini-Bonelli (eds) 1995 *Text and technology: in honour of John Sinclair*. John Benjamins, Amsterdam and New York.

2 From central embedding to corpus linguistics

GEOFFREY SAMPSON

It is not easy nowadays to recall how idiosyncratic, in the years immediately after the LOB Corpus was completed in 1978, was Geoffrey Leech's assumption that a good way to discover how the English language works is to look at real-life examples.

In those years I was a colleague of Geoffrey's at Lancaster University, but I knew little about LOB and was not actively conscious of my lack. I had learned my linguistics as a graduate student in the USA in the late 1960s, and at that period the concept of testing grammatical theories against objective evidence played little part in the life of the discipline. I had less excuse than some for overlooking the possibility of empirical work in linguistics: I was aware of the earlier Brown Corpus, indeed I had once been a house guest of its creator W. Nelson Francis; but such was the mood of the times that the sober virtues of corpus research had little power to counteract the abstract intellectual fascination of generative grammar, based on the 'evidence' of native speakers' intuitions. For me and for many others, the excitement of linguistics lay in discovering universal constraints on the structural diversity of languages, which were held to reflect the structure of innate language-processing machinery built into our minds as part of the human genetic endowment.

In due course I had ceased to believe in Noam Chomsky's argument inferring innate cognitive mechanisms from universal features of language; the argument eventually seemed not merely fallacious but backwards, in the sense that some of the universal properties to which Chomsky's argument appealed in fact constituted evidence for a very different, *tabula rasa* account of human cognition (Sampson 1980, 1989a). But this did not affect the idea that the properties of a language were to be discovered by consulting one's properties of a language were to be discovered by consulting one's intuition. Objective data were not really relevant: either they corroborated the speaker's intuitions, in which case they offered a slow and cumbersome way of getting at facts which intuition revealed more immediately, or they contradicted intuition in which case the objective data were suspect, as possibly resulting from contamination by 'performance' considerations. In principle, I had argued (Sampson 1975: ch. 4), this could not be the whole story; but for practical purposes I went along with the idea that users of a language know what is grammatical and what is not.

One structural feature of language seen as important, in the context of universal constraints and innate processing mechanisms, related to the phenomenon of 'central embedding'. It was in connexion with central embedding that I finally realized how crucial it is to make linguistic theories answerable, not just in principle but in practice, to objective evidence. In the following pages I shall describe how central embedding converted me into a corpus linguist.

Central embedding refers to grammatical structures in which a constituent occurs medially within a larger instance of the same kind of tagma; an invented example is [*The book* [*the man left*] *is on the table*], where a relative clause occurs medially within a main clause, as indicated by the square brackets. A single level of central embedding like this is normal enough, but linguists agreed that multiple central embedding — cases where X occurs medially within X which occurs medially within X, for two or more levels — is in some sense not a natural linguistic phenomenon. Theorists differed about the precise nature of the structural configuration they regarded as unnatural. De Roeck *et al.* (1982) distinguished four variant hypotheses about the unnaturalness of multiple central embedding. For Variant 1, the unnatural structures are any trees in which a node has a daughter node which is not the first or last daughter and which is nonterminal, and where that node in turn has a nonterminal medial daughter, irrespective of the labels of the nodes; that is, the unnaturalness depends purely on the shape of the tree rather than on the identity of the higher and lower categories. De Roeck *et al.* showed that several writers advocated the very strong hypothesis that multiple central embedding in this general sense is unnatural. For other linguists, the tree structure had to meet additional conditions before it was seen as unnatural. Variant 2 is a weaker hypothesis which rules out only cases where the logical category is the same, e.g. S within S within S, or NP within NP within NP. Variant 3 is a weaker hypothesis still, which treats structures as unnatural when the concentric logical categories not only are the same but occur within one another by virtue of the same surface grammatical construction, e.g. relative clause within relative clause within S; and Variant 4 weakens Variant 3 further by specifying that the structure is unnatural only when the hierarchy of tagmas incorporated into one another by the same construction are not interrupted by an instance of the same category introduced by a different construction (e.g. relative clause within nominal clause within relative clause within S would violate Variant 3 but not Variant 4).

These variant concepts notwithstanding, there was general agreement that multiple central embedding in some sense of the concept does not happen in human languages; theorists debated why that should be. For generative grammarians, who laid weight on the idea that grammatical rules are recursive, there was a difficulty in accounting for rules which could apparently apply once but could not reapply to their own outputs: they solved the problem by arguing that multiple central embeddings are perfectly grammatical in themselves, but are rendered 'unacceptable' by falling foul of psychological language-processing mechanisms which are independent of the rules of grammar but which, together with the latter, jointly determine what utterances people can produce and understand (Miller and Chomsky 1963: 471). The relational-network theorist Peter Reich urged that this did not adequately explain the fact that the limitation to a single level of central embedding is as clearcut and rigid a rule as languages possess: 'The first thing to note about [multiple central embeddings] is that they don't exist. ... the number of attested examples of MCEs in English can be counted on the thumbs of one hand' (Reich and Dell 1977). (The thumb was needed because Reich and Dell were aware of a single reported instance of multiple central embedding during the many years that linguists had been interested in the topic — but then, what linguistic rules are so rigid as never to be broken even on just one occasion?) Reich argued that generative grammar ought to make way for a finite-state theory of language within which the permissibility of one and only one level of central embedding is inherent in the model (Reich 1969).

Even William Labov, normally an energetic champion of empirical methods when that was a deeply unfashionable position to take (he was scathing about Chomsky's confusion of his own intuitions with objective evidence, e.g. Labov 1975: 101) felt that empirical observation of naturally-produced language was irrelevant to the multiple central embedding issue. Labov believed that multiple central embeddings are grammatical in every sense, but he saw them as a paradigm case of constructions that are so specific and so complex that instances would be vanishingly rare for purely statistical reasons: 'no such sentences had ever been observed in actual use; all we have are our intuitive reactions that they seem grammatical … We cannot wait for such embedded sentences to be uttered' (Labov 1973: 101).

Thus, linguists of widely diverse theoretical persuasions all agreed: if you wanted to understand the status of multiple central embedding in human language, one thing that was not worth doing was looking out for examples. You would not find any.

Doubt about this was first sown in my mind during a sabbatical I spent in Switzerland in 1980-81. Giving a seminar to the research group I was working with, I included a discussion of multiple central embedding in which I retailed what I took to be the standard, uncontroversial position that speakers and writers do not produce multiple central embeddings and, if they did, hearers or readers could not easily interpret them. In the question period Anne De Roeck asked 'But don't you find that sentences that people you know produce are easier to understand?' Well, perhaps, I responded, but this did not refute the theory because … — and I got quite a long way through my answer before the expression on Anne's face alerted me to the fact that the point of her question had been its grammar rather than its semantics. So evidently, if multiple central embeddings were indeed 'unacceptable', this did not mean that if produced they will necessarily draw attention to themselves by being impenetrable to the hearer. Perhaps, then, it was worth checking whether they were so completely lacking from natural language production as the doctrine alleged. I began to monitor my reading, and quite soon encountered a series of examples which our research group assembled into the De Roeck *et al.* paper already cited. Many of the examples violated even the weakest Variant 4 of the orthodoxy (all violated at least Variant 2); some of them involved more than two layers of central embedding.

A sceptic might have felt that there was something not fully convincing about that initial collection. More than half of them came from a single book — it is dangerous to rest conclusions about language in general on the linguistic behaviour of one individual, perhaps idiosyncratic, writer; and most of the remainder were taken from a very serious German-language newspaper: German is a language with rigid and unusually complex word-order rules, and when used in highly formal written registers is arguably a more artificial category of linguistic behaviour than most. But, on returning from Switzerland to Lancaster, I went on looking for multiple central embeddings, and I began to find examples in very diverse linguistic contexts.

Thus, one could hardly find a newspaper more different in style from the *Neue Zürcher Zeitung* (from which the De Roeck *et al.* examples came) than the British *News of the World*: this is a mass-market Sunday paper beloved for its titillating exposures of the seamier side of life, and those responsible for its contents would, I believe, feel that they were failing if they allowed a highbrow or intellectual flavour to creep into its pages. But the LOB Corpus contains an extract from a story 'Let's give the Welfare State a shot in the arm', by Kenneth Barrett, which appeared in the 5.2.1961 edition of that paper, and which includes the following sentence:

> [And yet a widow, [whose pension, [for which her husband paid], is wiped out because she works for a living wage], will now have to pay 12s. 6d. for each lens in her spectacles, and 17s. 8d. for the frames].

This is a case of *wh*- relative clause within *wh*- relative clause within S, violating Variant 4.

Even if popular writing for adults contains these constructions, it may be thought that writing for children will not. At this time my own children were aged seven and five, and their favourite books by a large margin for paternal bedtime reading were the series of boating adventure stories by Arthur Ransome. The following sentence occurs in Ransome's *Swallowdale*:[1]

> [But Captain Flint laid to his oars and set so fast a stroke that John, [who, [whatever else he did], was not going to let himself get out of time], had enough to do without worrying about what was still to come].

S within S within S: violates Variant 2. (Indeed, the clause beginning *whatever* is quite similar in structure to a relative clause; if the two kinds of clause were regarded as varieties of a single construction, the sentence would violate Variant 4. But probably almost any grammarian would treat the two clause-types as separate.) For what it is worth, my daughters showed no observable sign of difficulty in understanding this sentence, though similar experiences in the past resigned them to their father's temporary unwillingness to proceed with the story while he scrutinized it.

Still, while published writing addressed to unsophisticated readers apparently does contain multiple central embeddings, one could nevertheless argue that they are not likely to be found in writing produced by people unskilled with language. But the following sentence occurred in an essay-assignment written in February 1983 by S.S., a first-year Lancaster University undergraduate student of (at best) moderate ability:

> All in all it would seem [that, [although it can not really be proved [that the language influences the script in the beginning at its invention], simply because we seldom have any information about this time in a scripts history], the spoken language does effect the ready formed script and adapts it to suit its needs].

Subordinate clause within subordinate clause within subordinate clause: violates Version 2. (Here I assume that when a nominal clause is introduced by *that*, this word is part of the clause it introduces; this is the consensus view among linguists, but even if it were rejected the example would still be a case of S within S within S — the outer S would then be the main clause, i.e. the first opening square bracket would be repositioned at the beginning of the quotation.) The various solecisms in the passage (*can not* for *cannot*, *scripts* for *script's*, *effect* for *affect*, *ready* for *already*) were characteristic of the student's writing.

Conversely, a true believer in the unnaturalness of multiple central embeddings might suggest that while laymen may sometimes produce them, professional linguists, who may be expected to be unusually sensitive to grammatically objectionable structures, would avoid them. (For the idea that professional linguists may be in some sense more competent in their mother tongue than native speakers who are not linguists, see e.g. Snow and Meijer 1977.) However, in a review of a book edited by W. S.-Y. Wang, the eminent linguist E. G. Pulleyblank (1982) wrote:[2]

> [The only thing [that the words [that can lose -d] have in common] is, apparently, that they are all quite common words].

That relative clause within *that* relative clause within S: violates Variant 4.

Again, a defender of the orthodox line might suppose that, while the pressures of journalism, academic publication, and the like allow a certain number of 'unnatural' constructions to slip through, at least when a short text is composed and inscribed with special care there should be no multiple central embeddings. What would be the clearest possible test of this? A ceremonial inscription ornamentally incised on marble seems hard to beat. Visiting Pisa for the 1983 Inaugural Meeting of the European Chapter of the Association for Computational Linguistics, I noticed a tablet fixed to one wall of the remains of the Roman baths. Apart from the conventional heading 'D O M' (*Deo Optimo Maximo*), and a statement at the foot of the names of the six persons referred to, the inscription on the tablet consists wholly of the following single sentence, in a language where word order is much freer than in German or even English, so that undesired structural configurations could easily be avoided. I quote the inscription using upper and lower case to stand for the large and small capitals of the original, and replace its archaic Roman numerals with modern equivalents:

> [{Sex uiri, [qui {Parthenonem, [ubi {parentibus orbæ uirgines} aluntur, et educantur], [{qui} {uulgo} {charitatis Domus} appelatur]}, moderantur, eiusque rem administrant]}, quum ad suum ius ditionemque pertineat hic locus, in quo Sudatorium Thermarum Pisanarum tot Seculis, tot casibus mansit inuictum, et officii sui minime negligentes, et Magni Ducis iussis obtemperantes, et antiquitatis reuerentia moti reliquias tam uetusti, tam insignis ædificii omni ope, et cura tuendas, et conseruendas censuerunt An: Sal: MDCXCIII].

> [Since this place, where the sudatorium of the Pisan Baths has remained unconquered by so many centuries and so many happenings, comes under their jurisdiction, {the six men [who govern and administer {the Parthenon, [where {orphaned girls} are brought up and educated], [{which} is known by {the common people} as {the House of Charity}]}]}, being diligent in the performance of their duty, obedient to the commands of the Grand Duke, and moved by reverence for antiquity, ordered every effort to be used carefully to protect and to conserve the remains of this building of such age and distinction, in the Year of Grace 1693].

Here, curly brackets delimit NPs, and square brackets delimit clauses. Thus we have four NPs within NPs within NP, a quadruple violation of either Variant 2 or Variant 4 (depending on the definition of identity of grammatical constructions); at the same time, with respect to clauses, we have two relative clauses within relative clause within sentence, a double violation of Variant 4. (The fact that one of the innermost relative clauses, together with the relative clause containing it, are both compound might be thought to make the constructions even more similar and accordingly more 'unnatural' than they would otherwise be.) The central embeddings occur at the beginning of the original text, making it wholly implausible that they were produced through careless oversight even if such carelessness were likely in inscriptions of this sort.

At this period I did not record any examples with more than two levels of central embedding, so that a defender of the orthodox view might conceivably try to rescue it by arguing that the boundary between permissible and impermissible degrees of central embedding lies not between one and two levels but between two and three levels. This would be a gross weakening of the standard claim, which asserts not only that there is a fixed boundary but that it occurs between one and two levels (cf. Reich 1969, and his quotation from Marks 1968). If such a strategy were adopted, then at least the first and probably also the second of the following new examples would be relevant:

> [Laughland's assertion that [the presence of [Delors — [14 years] old when [the war] began —] in the Compagnons de France, the Vichy youth movement,] meant that he supported fascism] is ridiculous.[3]

The phrases *14 years* and *the war* are both cases of NP within NP within NP within NP, a double violation of the two-level limit (incidentally, two paragraphs later the same letter contains a case of S within S within S).

> [Your report today [that any Tory constituency party [failing [to deselect its MP], should he not vote in accordance with a prime ministerial diktat,] might itself be disbanded], shows with certainty that Lord Hailsham's prediction of an 'elective dictatorship' is now with us].[4]

Infinitival clause within present-participle clause within *that* nominal clause within S: again a violation of the two-level limit, except that if the *should* clause were alternatively regarded as a subordinate to *deselect* rather than to *failing* then the structure would violate only the one-level limit.

All in all, it seemed clear that no matter what kind of language one looks at, multiple central embeddings do occur. The examples here include no case from speech; that is regrettable but not surprising, first because spoken language is structurally so much less ramified than writing that *any* kind of multiple embedding, central or not, is relatively unusual there, and equally importantly because it is difficult to monitor such cases in speech (when I happen on a written multiple central embedding, I always have to re-read it slowly and carefully to check that it is indeed one, and with speech this is not possible). Nevertheless, De Roeck *et al.* did record one case from spoken English, which happened to have been transcribed into print because it was uttered by a prime minister in the House of Commons; and the example requiring the single thumb in Reich & Dell (1977) occurred in extempore spoken English. Here is a third case I recently encountered, from the late Richard Feynman's Nobel Prize address given in Stockholm on 11.12.1965:[5]

> [The odds [that your theory will be in fact right, and that the general thing [that everybody's working on] will be wrong,] is low].

That relative clause within *that* nominal clause within S, violates Variant 2. While this speech was obviously not a case of extempore chat, the quotation does contain several features characteristic of spoken rather than written language (*everybody's* for *everybody is*; colloquial use of *thing*; failure of agreement between *odds* and *is*). In any case, Reich and Dell's footnote 2 makes it clear that their belief in the unnaturalness of multiple centre embedding applies to writing as well as to speech.

Incidentally, the difficulty of identifying multiple central embeddings on first reading offers a further argument against the claim that they are 'unnatural'. During fluent reading for normal purposes I register no reaction more specific than 'clumsy structure here', and passages which provoke this reaction often turn out to include only structures that linguists do not normally claim to be 'unnatural' or ungrammatical, e.g. non-central embeddings. If the orthodox view of multiple central embedding were correct, one would surely predict that these structures should 'feel' much more different from other structures than they do.

The examples listed earlier were not the only cases of multiple central embedding I encountered in the months after I returned from Switzerland; they are ones I copied down because they seemed particularly noteworthy for one reason or another. More recently I tried to achieve a very rough estimate of how frequent these structures are, by systematically taking a note of each case I encountered over a period. This project was triggered by the experience of spotting two cases in quick succession; but the following list includes only the second of these, which I read on 4 October 1993, because having decided to make a collection I did not manage to locate the earlier case in the pile of newsprint waiting to go to the dustbin. Thus the list represents the multiple central embeddings noticed during a random period starting with one such observation and continuing for a calendar month (I made the decision to stop collecting on 4 November 1993 — both start and stop decisions were made in the middle of the day rather than on rising or retiring, though there may have been a few hours' overlap). In view of my failure to register Anne De Roeck's trick question, discussed above, there could have been further cases in my reading during this month which escaped my attention.

> A greater issue of principle there could not be than the transfer of self-government away from the British electorate to the European Community; [but, [though Tony Wedgwood Benn thought that '[if only Harold would look and sound a bit more convincing (on that subject)], we might have a good chance'], Wilson not only did not do so but his tactics on taking office steered his party, his government, Parliament and the electorate into a referendum of which the result is only now in course of being reversed].[6]

Adverbial clause within adverbial clause within S: violates Variant 4.

> Harris and I would go down in the morning, and take the boat up to Chertsey, [and George, [who would not be able to get away from the City till the afternoon (George goes to sleep at a bank from ten to four each day, except Saturdays, when they wake him up [and put him outside] at two)], would meet us there].[7]

Reduced relative clause within relative clause within S (the relative clause beginning *when they wake* … would make a fourth level, but this clause is right-embedded in the *who* clause): violates at least Variant 2 and perhaps Variant 4, depending on the definition of similarity between grammatical constructions.

> [When the pain, [which nobody [who has not experienced it] can imagine], finally arrives], they can be taken aback by its severity.[8]

Wh- relative clause within *wh-* relative clause within adverbial clause: violates Variant 4.

> [That the perimeters of [what men can wear and [what they cannot], what is acceptable and what is not,] have become so narrow] goes to show how intolerant our society has become.[9]

Reduced antecedentless relative clause within compound antecedentless relative clause within nominal clause: violates at least Variant 2 and perhaps Variant 4, depending on the definition of similarity between grammatical constructions.

> [For the remainder of his long and industrious life (apart from during the second world war [when he worked in the Ministry of Information — [where he was banished to Belfast for being 'lazy and unenthusiastic'] — and the Auxiliary Fire Service]) Quennell made his living as an author, a biographer, an essayist, a book-reviewer, and as an editor of literary and historical journals].[10]

Adverbial relative clause within adverbial relative clause within S: violates Variant 4.

> [In the 18th century, [when, [as Linda Colley shows in her book *Britons*], the British national identity was forged in war and conflict with France], our kings were Germans].[11]

As clause within adverbial relative clause within S: violates Variant 2.

> [The cases of Dr Starkie, the pathologist whose procedures in the diagnosis of bone cancer is now being questioned, and Dr Ashok Kumar, [whose nurse, having been taught by him, used the wrong spatula, [which must have been provided by the practice], to obtain cells for cervical smears], are very different].[12]

Wh- relative clause within *wh-* relative clause within S: violates Variant 4 (and the *having been* clause constitutes a separate violation of Variant 2).

To assess what rate of occurrence of multiple central embeddings these examples imply requires an estimate of my overall rate of reading, which is very difficult to achieve with any accuracy. On the basis of word-counts of typical publications read, I believe my average daily intake is perhaps 50,000 and certainly not more than 100,000 written words, so that the seven multiple central embeddings quoted above would imply a frequency of perhaps one in a quarter-million words (more, if we suppose that I missed some), and at least one in a half-million words. Some time soon, it should be possible for language-analysis software automatically to locate each instance of a specified construction in a machine readable corpus, and we shall be able to give relatively exact figures on the frequency of the construction. For a construction as complex as multiple central embedding we are not yet at that point; but on these figures there is no reason to suppose that the single example quoted earlier from the LOB Corpus is the only example contained in it.

The conclusion is unavoidable. Multiple central embedding is a phenomenon which the discipline of linguistics was united in describing as absent from the real-life use of language; theorists differed only in the explanations they gave for this interesting absence. Yet, if one checks, it is not absent. I do not go so far as to deny that there is any tendency to avoid multiple central embedding; I am not sure whether there is such a tendency or not. Independently of the issue of central embedding, we have known since Yngve (1960) that the English language has a strong propensity to exploit right-branching and to avoid left-branching grammatical structures — this propensity alone would to some extent reduce the incidence of central embedding. Whether, as for instance John Lyons continues to believe (Lyons 1991: 116), multiple central embeddings are significantly less frequent than they would be in any case as a by-product of the more general preference of the language for right branching is a question whose answer seems to me far from obvious. But it is clearly a question that must be answered empirically, not by consulting speakers' 'intuitions'.

Hence, as I picked up the threads of my working life at Lancaster after the Swiss sabbatical, I knew it was time for a change of intellectual direction. If intuition could get the facts of language as wrong as this, there seemed little purpose in continuing to pursue abstract philosophical arguments for or against the existence of innate knowledge of language. There had to be some way of engaging with the concrete empirical realities of language, without getting so bogged down in innumerable details that no analytical conclusions could ever be drawn.

And once I perceived this need, I did not have to look far to satisfy it. There along the corridor was Geoffrey Leech, looking out for collaborators to help him work on grammatical analysis routines for the LOB Corpus. It was the best career move I have ever made.

Notes

1 Arthur Ransome 1931 *Swallowdale*. Jonathan Cape, London, pp. 113–14.

2 *Journal of Chinese Linguistics* 10: 410.

3 Charles Grant, letter to the editor, *The Spectator*, 12.11.1994, p. 35.

4 Vice-Admiral Sir Louis Le Bailly, letter to the editor, *The Times*, 25.11.1994, p. 21.

5 Quoted from J. Gleick, *Genius*, Abacus Books, 1994, p. 382.

6 J. Enoch Powell, review of P. Ziegler, *Wilson*, p. 35 of *The Times* of 4.10.1993, read 4.10.1993.

The brackets surrounding *on that subject* were square in the original, and are replaced by round brackets here to avoid confusion with the square brackets of the grammatical annotation.

7 Jerome K. Jerome, *Three Men in a Boat*, 1889, p. 17 of Penguin edition, 1957, read 7.10.1993.

8 Leader, p. 17 of *The Times* of 16.10.1993, read 16.10.1993.

9 Iain R. Webb, 'Begging to differ', p. 70 of the *Times Magazine* of 9.10.1993, read 21.10.1993.

10 Obituary of Sir Peter Quennell, *The Times* of 29.10.1993, read 29.10.1993.

11 Timothy Garton Ash, 'Time for fraternisation', p. 9 of the *Spectator* of 30.10.1993, read 29.10.1993.

12 Thomas Stuttaford, 'Patients before colleagues', *The Times* of 10.9.1993, read 31.10.1993; the agreement failure (*procedures … is*) occurs in the source.

3 Sipping a cocktail of corpora

RANDOLPH QUIRK and GABRIELE STEIN

In his long-admired *Linguistic Guide to English Poetry*,[1] written when he was little more than half way to the three-score years that the present volume celebrates, Geoffrey Leech examined the values of 'obtrusive' language (p. 73) but also its downside. Indeed, the pejorative implication of the word *obtrusive* itself suggests how easy it is for the excitingly striking to pall and become just tritely habitual.

The occasional sonorous alliteration can make a piece of rhetoric stirring and memorable. A novel can be attractively reviewed under a heading with intertextual reference ('The Gripes of Roth', for example). Serious discursive prose can be enlivened by the occasional, startlingly short verbless sentence. The advent of large corpora and the electronic means (as well as the human enthusiasm) for scrutinizing various kinds of recurrence can only be promising for the evolution of a more informed stylistics.

The point at which repetition of the same feature starts striking one as unwelcome (as 'poverty of linguistic resource', in Leech's words, p. 79) varies from feature to feature. Alliteration is an early offender. Punny intertextuality has a fairly low threshold, too. Recurrent use of the 'same word', as we all learn in school composition classes, is dangerously obtrusive within twenty or thirty lines of text. But which the words are that so obtrude is another matter, and we shall return to this below: clearly the repetition of *and*, *with*, *come*, *give*, *soon* matters less than the repetition of *egregious*, *reciprocate*, *cyberspace*, or the preposition *modulo*. By contrast, units of syntax such as sentence patterns have a much wider textual span before recurrence will be noticed, let alone objected to.

We mentioned earlier the phenomenon of the short verbless sentence. This seems to be a feature regularly used as an enlivening device in the elegant prose of *The Economist* journal. Having noticed this, but with enjoyment of the feature still unadulterated, we decided to check on the frequency that apparently sustained effectiveness without danger of over-kill. In a whole year's issue of *The Economist* (approximately half a million words) we found about 300 instances, or roughly one per 1700 words of text. For example, in issues numbered 7889 and 7890 of November 1994:

> Fine words. Not so. Not so. Not this time. Not this time. Why? Perhaps so. Fair enough. Why not? Really? Quite so. True. Not quite. And not quietly. Hardly. Fat chance. Quite possibly not. Maybe.

The examples are given here in the order of occurrence in the two issues. The pairs of instances were separated by four pages (*Not so*) and six pages (*Not this time*), yet we doubt whether even this degree of saturation undermined the effectiveness of the stylistic ploy.

Lexical items are rather more likely to assume unwelcome obtrusiveness: not only the quite obvious cases of individual words but, more interestingly, *categories* of lexical items. We have mentioned the editorial style of *The Economist*: let us now look at what this journal's reviewer thought to say about the six novels shortlisted for the 1994 Booker award.[2] Linguistic aspects of style were striking enough to be noted in no fewer than four of them. In one it was the clever representation of deviant grammar and idiom: 'the mistakes made by foreigners who are almost fluent in colloquial English'. But for the other three, the obtrusiveness was lexical — and in all cases categorial. James Kelman's 'crude, limited vocabulary is at first startling, then mesmerizing, then numbing and, finally, bor-rrring.' In George Mackay Brown's novel, it is the category of dialectal vocabulary that claimed the reviewer's attention: 'strange words' like 'blyde, ruckle, noust, thirled, bissom, selkie, bothy.' And Aboulrazak Gurnah's *Paradise* 'also has lots of odd words: vibarua, kanzus, maandazi, bismillah, kifa urongo, malai, waungwana.'

The categories of words obtrusive enough to blow this reviewer off-course from assessing content, plot, characterization, commitment, and other literary parameters seem to be chiefly those that worry lexicographers most. Is this word or that word one that should be put in an English dictionary? Analogously, which should the translator into (say) German actually translate, and which leave as in the original? Around the very large core of indisputably 'English' words there is always also a very large penumbra of questionable items, especially perhaps words 'that may not be completely naturalized yet, or may even be stuck in immigration,' as William Kretzchmar nicely puts it.[3] Here again is an area that the era of large corpora opens up to more definitive examination than ever before.

R. E. Allen's splendid 1990 edition of the *Concise Oxford Dictionary*, 'probably' — it is modestly confessed — 'the best-known household dictionary' (p. vii), has the very proper aim of embracing expressions 'that are well attested in current English', and it marks as *lit.* or *obs.* or *offens.* or *math.* or *hort.* or *NZ* or *Ind.* (etc.) items that are deemed by contrast to be restricted in currency. But no such restricted marking appears with many entries that surely are current in only a minority of 'households': for example, *burrka, dojo, hajj, hajji, nacho, tzatziki*: not forgetting, of course, *glasnost* and *perestroika.* Some of these are indeed proudly mentioned in Mr Allen's preface as illustrations of his thoroughness in updating the book, but no explicit measures (such as corpus occurrence) are offered to show how the criterion 'well attested in current English' is established.

Trying to be up-to-date on marginal items is, in fact, a risky business for lexicographers. It is a fair bet that even a medium-sized corpus of the late 1980s would contain both *glasnost* and *perestroika*, extended beyond their original reference to developments in the Soviet Union. *The Economist* in 1988:[4]

> Stockbrokers, merchant banks and Euromarket firms are hiring management consultants as fast as they lay off idle traders ... This perestroika should be good for the City's long-term health and reputation.

It is an equally fair bet, however, that a similar-sized corpus of English from 1994 would not contain either word. Yet just how risky is the lexicographers' task when they try to offset the risk was shown by the Merriam-Webster team's handling of the exhibitionist sense of *streak(er).* The major Third Edition of 1961 was too early for it but when the supplementary *6000 Words* of 1976 was being prepared, it was deemed too late, and the sense was excluded as being among those that 'enjoy a brief vogue, when they are on practically every tongue, then disappear' (p. 17a). The editors were not to know that within a few weeks of the supplement's publication, *streak(er)* was back on 'practically every tongue' in consequence of a dramatically public re-appearance of the phenomenon itself at the Montreal Olympics.

At any rate, given an inclusionary policy as liberal as Allen's, we may feel reasonably safe in regarding items that do not win a place in his *COD* as *not* 'well attested in current English'. By this measure, recent Indian writing in English seems to be notably rich in exotica, and we have looked through three-quarters of a million words from Indian writers with this in mind. The material in fact primarily comprises two novels, Upamanyu Chatterjee's *English, August*[5] and Vikram Seth's *A Suitable Boy*.[6] In both, exotic words are certainly an obtrusive feature, and Chatterjee is sufficiently conscious of this to supply a glossary of seventy-three items he feels may be beyond his readers' experience. Yet the density of exotica in his book is such that at least as many again occur without benefit of glossing (thus he glosses *lakh* but not the analogous 'crores and crores' of p. 137), and several of these are not in Allen's *COD* either: for example, *chhole* (as on p. 180), *ding(o)* (as on p. 213), *kaka (kaku)* (as on p. 151 and p. 147), *masala* (as on p. 132), *rotis* (as on p. 180), *tikka* (as on p. 164), *wah-wah* (as on p. 139).

Vikram Seth's foreword admits that his vast novel will 'strain your purse and sprain your wrists', but he strains his readers lexically as well, with a continual torrent of what we are calling 'exotic' words — and no concessionary glossary at all. The first couple of dozen pages are not atypical in confronting the reader with a different non-*COD* item on average every 400 words of text. Referring to dress: *achkan, choli, juti, patola, salwar-kameez*; along with the '*COD*' items *sari* and *turban*. Referring to eatables: *barfi, gajak, gulab-jamun, kachauri, laddu, puri*; along with *COD* items *paan* and *samosa*. Referring to people: *abba, bao, bhabhi, bhai, daadi, -ji, khatri, kuchuk*; along with the *COD* items *ayah, pandit* (*COD pundit*), *sahib* (though the *COD* definition does not quite account for Seth's usage), *wallah* (though ditto). Referring to flora and fauna: *harsingar, zamindar*; along with the *COD* items *bulbul* and *krait*. And finally, items with cultural reference: *ghazal, jaymala, namasté, pitthu, shehnai*; along with the *COD* items *inshallah, purdah, raga* (if this is the same as Seth's *raag*).

One unfamiliar word per 400 words of text — so unfamiliar as to be inaccessible even with the help of the average reader's dictionary — is not presumably beyond the threshold of unwelcome obtrusiveness, if we may judge from the book's public success. But for the next reviser of the *COD*, the exotic words presented by Seth offer additional problems. In the first place, there are two kinds of exotica: the foreign words already illustrated; and words that are apparently English but used in a non-English way. This applies to Chatterjee also, who has a verb *bunk* apparently meaning 'dodge', *call for* 'invite to', *reach* 'arrive' ('we'll reach at 7' p. 142), *stooge* (something) 'scrounge'. Several of his nouns are equally unfamiliar: *beat* as in '(she) would be out on a beat', p. 203; *bogey* (of train) pp. 135, 143, etc.; *hooligan* pp. 22, 23, etc. 'chap', with no pejorative implication; *tubelight* p. 162. Note also 'There's nothing such as absolute honesty', p. 138 (= there's no such thing); '(I'll) take your leave' pp. 89, 203, 248 (= take leave of you). With these and many other such examples, it is not easy to know whether we have authorial idiolect, authorial characterization of a character's idiolect, or what the author regards as normal among Indian speakers of English.

Where, in the narrative mode, Chatterjee and Seth use the same expressions, we can of course safely assume general 'Indian English': *fair* 'light-skinned', *stay* 'live', *thrice*. For example, '(his) long, fair appraising face', Seth p. 911, 'fair and black-haired' Seth p. 64; cf Chatterjee p. 38. But several factors make the status of oddities in Seth's English especially problematical. His characters are highly sophisticated, multi-lingual, much given to linguistic debate, interlinguistic and interliterary allusion, elaborate pastiche, and witty linguistic satire (for example, in criticism of other people's command of English, Hindi, Bengali). While many turns of language seem to carry authorial sanction (*convince* NP *to* V 'persuade' p. 1333; *do* as in 'He did namasté or adaab as was appropriate' p. 1097; *drowse off* 'dose off', p. 607; *fire up* NP 'verbally attack', p. 1256; 'shoes with a *glacial* shine' p. 621; *lock-up* 'police-cell', p. 1326 ff; *parcher-woman*, p. 567; *pugmarks*, p. 678; *take* NP's *name* 'use, utter', p. 1316, 1321; *telegram* as verb, p. 604; interrogative *which* 'what' p. 1405f; along with words for animals and birds not in *COD* such as *brain fever, coppersmith, jungle cat, jungle fowl*), many seem to be satirized as malapropisms ('without intimating him', p. 294; '"His mammary berry shurp", said Sanaki ... in English', p. 771; 'he became lustrious and debauching', p. 181; 'several peels of musammis', p. 239, for 'several pieces of musammi peel'; 'No fears!', p. 497; 'impassionate love', p.181; 'the heat is very delapidating', p. 48; 'illiquid', p.260; 'elders ... treated their youngers like children', p. 324; 'it runs off my back like duck's water', p. 416). But what about *tight* in 'tight slap(s)', p. 1127, 1429, *abscondence*, p. 1020, (etc.)?

Very many expressions in fact can by no means be placed with confidence in either category — not least because of a further complication. Seth's novel is temporally located in 1951, long before the author's birth, and it is clear that he has carried out a good deal of research to make his political, social, and cultural allusions contemporaneously valid. This extends to satirizing those who still call Kanpur 'Cawnpore', p. 980. It is likely therefore that he has made pervasive efforts to make the language true to his fictive era, and that the use of *ayah* and *sahib* ('Doctor Sahib', p. 22, 'the Minister Sahib', p. 4) as well as reference to the *tonga-wallahs* passim can say little about courtesies or modes of transport in India today. So also the English-based items such as (a liveried) *bearer*, p. 602, *covenanted*, p. 72, *floor-desk*, p. 660, *saloons* on the railway: these may well be intended to catch the flavour of the Raj (as also *kafir*, p. 1145, in the sense of 'non-Muslim') and the early years of Independence. As we note the Westminster model in a state parliament with its 'short-order starred questions', p. 267, and presided over by 'The Hon'ble the Speaker', p. 300, we may wonder how the corpus-analysts and the lexicographers are to disentangle this diachronic strand in the whole complex linguistic web.

Stepping back from corpora of the present to look at such a penumbra existing in earlier decades may improve our sense of perspective. To this end, we have examined a quarter-million word corpus of prose by Rudyard Kipling, all of it written about a hundred years ago. There is much of interest to reflect upon, by no means all of it lexical. The tolerance of syntactical complexity (certainly by editors, presumably also by the reading public) suggests a very different level of sophistication than we dare expect today. Consider the following passage, reporting from South Africa on the Boer War:

> They, being children of nature and buck-hunters to boot, allowed their quarry to pass, and after twenty rounds at four hundred yards — the Boer in a hurry is not a good shot — dropped him with a broken arm. Setton was not pleased; but the five Australians who, without orders, so soon as they saw what he would be at, had galloped parallel with him behind the kopjes, were immensely gratified. They dismounted, lay down, and slew the Boer on the tired horse as he returned to join his fellow-plunderers, of whom they shot two and wounded one.

That was part of a much longer narrative in the *Daily Express* published on the three successive days, June 19-21, 1900. The language is very different, obviously, from the way an incident in the Bosnian conflict would be described in the *Daily Express* (or any other London newspaper) of 1995. What sub-editor would allow the expectation that readers would be comfortable with the second of the above sentences, in which a subject ('the five Australians') is separated from its verb by a 21-word sequence comprising three embedded clauses?

But as with the Chatterjee and Seth material, there is special interest in Kipling's lexicon as we try to determine what constitutes a 'word' in the English language, especially a word (to quote Allen's *COD* again) 'well attested in current English'. How might we objectify the concept of 'marginality' in the lexicon? May it be that marginality is critically related to what Christian Kay[7] calls 'the survival rates of words'?

In the Kipling passage quoted above, there occurs the item *kopje*, presumed to have been familiar to readers of the *Daily Express* in 1900 (and still in the *COD* of 1990). But Andrew Rutherford, the latest editor of Kipling, could make no such presumption in respect of even the well-educated literary readers of the World's Classics (*War Stories and Poems*, Oxford 1990, p. 345). The item is glossed in his explanatory notes and he helps likewise with a good number of other words that were doubtless familiarly topical for the original readers through the wars fought by Lord Roberts and others in South Africa a century ago: *aasvogel, burgher, donga, kloof, kop, kraal, kranz, Mauser, meer-cat, mesa, rooinek, schel, sjambok, Vlei, vrouw* (*ibid*. pp 343–57).

So too with the far more numerous words from India that peppered Kipling's writing. The difference between the assumptions that could be made, indeed, as late as the mid-1930s and those that can be made today can be seen by comparing the only two editions of the *Shorter Oxford English Dictionary*. The first[8] by W. Little *et al* (1933) defines *competition-wallah* with reference to 'members of the I.C.S.' — an unexplained abbreviation that must surely have been opaque outside government circles and Oxbridge hopefuls yet surviving in updated reprints as recent as 1973. In the *New SOED* of 1993[9] the item is of course retained, as is proper in a historical dictionary, but is labelled as '*Anglo-Ind. colloq.*' and defined as 'an Indian Civil Servant appointed by competitive examination'. The cultural and linguistic distance is appropriately signalled.

Such distance is indicated with exemplary sensitivity in Rutherford's editing of Kipling. The following are among the Indian words he feels it necessary to cover in his explanatory notes (*ibid* pp 329ff, and *Plain Tales from the Hills*, Oxford 1987, pp 253ff):

ahir, ayah, baba, babu, babul, batta, bhai, bhiski, bhusa, buckshish, boh, budmash, bukh, bund, bunnia, burra, bustee, chandoo-khana, changar, chaprassi, charpoy, chop ('seal'), *chumar, dacoit(y), dah, dak-bungalow, daur, deodar, dhak, dhobi, djinn, doab, doolie, duffadar, ekka, ghat, ghazi, gram, goldmohur, gunny, hoondi, huqa, hya, jadoo, jarnwar, jemadar, jezail, jhampan, jhil, jildi, jingall, kazi, khalsa, khana, khatri, khitmutgar, khud, lakh, lotah, mantra, mullah, naik, nullah, pahari, puckrow, puggree, pukka, purdanashin, rissala, rissaldar, sag* ('dog'), *sais, serai, shikar, shroff, solar-topee, subadar, tattoo* ('pony'), *terai, tetur, tonga, tulwar, tussur, two-anna* ('cheap'), *zenana*

Although these items do not occur on average more frequently than once per 400 words of text, there are occasions when the frequency rises to ten or a dozen times per 400 words. Given that these expressions of Indian origin are by no means the only kind of lexical exoticism in the Kipling texts, they go well beyond the threshold of tolerable obtrusiveness for most of us today, whatever their impression on contemporary readers whose closer acquaintance with them Kipling clearly felt able to assume. At any rate, while several items in the above Kipling list occur in Chatterjee and Seth (as we have seen) as well as in the work of numerous other contemporary Indians writing in English, Rutherford's glossing decisions on the whole surely chime with most readers' feeling that they are not 'English' words. But corpus linguists might contemplate the challenge of how to objectify the intuitions of a Rutherford, explicate the sensibilities of an *Economist* fiction reviewer, set out principles to guide a translator — and give credible advice to the editor of a 'household dictionary' on admissible words and meanings.

Notes

1 Leech, G N 1969 *Linguistic Guide to English Poetry*. Longman, London.

2 *The Economist*, 8 October, 1994 p. 129.

3 *RASK* **1**: 91, Odense 1995.

4 25 June 1988, and noted by John Ayto in his *Register of New Words*, Longman, 1989.

5 Upamanyu Chatterjee 1988 *English, August.* Faber and Faber, London.

6 Vikram Seth 1993 *A Suitable Boy.* Phoenix, London.

7 Christian Kay 1994 in A Fenton and D A MacDonald (eds.) *Studies in Scots and Gaelic.* Canongate Academic, p. 42.

8 W. Little *et al* 1933 (marginally revised by C. T. Onions, 1936).

9 Lesley Brown (ed.).

4 Corpora, databases and the organization of linguistic data

GERRY KNOWLES

4.1 Introduction

A criticism sometimes made of corpus linguistics is that it is atheoretical. Corpus linguists, according to this view, are mesmerized by the sheer quantity of data that they manage to collect, but do not actually use it to add to our understanding of language. This is not the place to argue that such a view is an ill-judged one. What is interesting about it is that it is clearly a defensive position. This raises the question what there is to be defensive about, and who or what is threatened by corpus linguistics.

An important consequence of handling large amounts of data is that it enforces rigour and discipline in data organization. Computer processing techniques cannot handle vagueness, ambivalence and common sense logical leaps. Linguists have in the past generally constructed theories on the assumption that the problems they tackle are problems *sui generis*; that is, they have no connection with problems in other fields such as history or psychology. This assumption is now increasingly being challenged. Some linguistic problems, for example, are recognized as probabilistic in nature, and these are handled by general statistical methods. Similarly, linguistic problems of data organization can be handled by general principles of relational logic, as implemented for example in the SQL programming language. That is to say, linguistic data can be organized using the data structures, data types, and data links of an SQL-based database management system such as Microsoft Access or FoxPro.

In this paper I shall argue that much of what in the past has been called linguistic theory has in fact been a discussion of the organization of linguistic data. There is a basic relational model of organization of linguistic data. There is a basic relational model of language which has evolved over many centuries, and which is now generally assumed by linguists. Different approaches to linguistics have amplified or clarified various parts of the basic model. I shall also argue that corpora, far from standing apart from theoretical issues, are an integral component of a theoretical model of language.

4.2 Traditional linguistics

Some of the unquestioned assumptions of contemporary linguistic thinking conform to a long tradition that goes back to the ancient world. Some of the basic ideas were absorbed in the English grammatical tradition that grew up from the sixteenth century and still underpin such metalinguistics as finds its way into the popular discussion of language. A more complex set of data relations is implicit in the model of language traditionally used for the teaching of Latin.

4.2.1 The English grammatical tradition

A common sense view of language is that it is made up of words. The simplest language model is therefore a list of words, or a dictionary. Early dictionaries, such as Cawdrey (1604),[1] were designed to explain the meaning of hard words. Even these were formally organized as a flatfile, each entry being a record with two fields: one is the spelling used as an identifier, and this is paired with a statement of the meaning. Later dictionaries, such as Samuel Johnson's dictionary of 1755,[2] attempted a more systematic listing of the entire lexicon, and expanded the number of fields, adding a representation of the pronunciation and a grammatical tag.

In order to use a dictionary, one has to go beyond the flatfile, and establish formal links with a text. In principle there is a one-to-one relationship between spellings and the forms in written texts, and between pronunciations and the forms heard in speech. In practice, in both cases additional fields sometimes have to be calculated, e.g. to derive plural forms from a singular headword. Secondly, for each occurrence in a text, there is in principle a match with one of the meanings given in the dictionary. The unmatched field is the grammatical tag, and this will be discussed further below.

A grammar contains generalizations about sets of lexical items. A typical orthography section deals with letters and spelling, and perhaps pronunciation and syllables. The morphology — sometimes called 'etymology' or 'accidence' — establishes formal relationships among words, and may deal with the calculation of related words from headwords. The division of the lexicon into 'parts of speech' establishes broad classes about which useful generalizations can be made, and these take up the bulk of a typical traditional grammar. Parts of speech also link the grammar to the dictionary. If a word is tagged as an article in Johnson's dictionary, one can find out what an article is by referring to the corresponding section of a contemporary grammar, such as Lowth (1762).[3]

Lowth is often dismissed as a prescriptive grammarian on account of reactionary remarks which he made in his preface, but these remarks read remarkably like advertizing copy and in any case have nothing to do with the logical organization of the grammar itself. After a short orthography section, he organizes the rest of the grammar according to parts of speech. He begins with a tagset (pp 7–8) listing for each tag a numerical identifier, a label, and a brief description, e.g. no 3 is a pronoun, standing instead of the noun. The numbers are used to tag a short text (p. 9) and the labels are explained in a brief introduction (pp 9–15). The bulk of the grammar is then devoted to a study of each word class first in isolation and in numerical order (pp 15–95), and then according to its role in sentence structure, following as far as practicable the same order (pp 95–186).

The words of a text are related to the dictionary on the one hand, and, assuming they are tagged or 'parsed', to the grammar on the other. The dictionary and the grammar are also related to each other. The dictionary lists the word-types which recur in texts, and to that extent contains generalizations about texts. The grammar in turn contains generalizations about dictionary items. In practice, dictionaries and grammars are incomplete and imperfect, but in principle they provide a structure within which information about the formal structure of language can be organized logically and economically.

Elaborations of the basic dictionary and grammar have produced more specialized works which we would now class as belonging to linguistics. Grammars from Jonson (1640)[4] onwards developed a phonological theory from the study of letters and sounds, and a more detailed study of the formation of sounds by John Wallis (1653)[5] was followed by William Holder's phonetics manual in 1669.[6] In the next century Sheridan (1762)[7] drew on the tradition of phonetics and phonology, and in lexicography the representation of pronunciation advanced from Johnson's marking of stress to the quasi-phonemic notation of Walker's pronouncing dictionary (1791).[8] According to the theory which Walker took for granted, a word consists of letters, and a letter has a name and one or more sounds, e.g. the letter ay has three different sounds in *mad*, *made* and *mare*. This theory has since been modified but not fundamentally changed, so that a modern phoneme symbol can have only one sound in this sense, and even in generative phonology, an abstract symbol can be mapped on to only one sound in any particular case.

Early grammarians such as Jonson (1640) rather naïvely transferred to English grammatical concepts from Lily and Ramus which had been designed for Latin. But this is not a fair criticism of the best practitioners from Wallis (1653) on. Lowth (1762) was quite aware of the morphological differences between English and Latin (p. 25) and even of the problematical status of the word in a genitive phrase such as *the King of Great Britain's soldiers* (p. 27). Lowth does not simply follow Latin, but uses his knowledge of Latin to find corresponding patterns in English. He recognizes the connection between the *of*-construction and the genitive (p. 26), and the use of auxiliaries as markers of tense and mood (p. 57); he also recognizes patterns which have no counterpart in Latin, such as the use of *do* to 'mark the Action itself, of the Time of it, with greater force and distinction' (pp 57–8). He uses paradigms where appropriate for pronouns (p. 33) and verbs (pp 48–55), but these are redesigned for English. He also uses the now familiar table giving the present, past and participle forms of strong and irregular verbs (pp 71–85).

4.2.2 Latin grammar

Much effort in traditional European linguistics was devoted to the codification of Latin, and it resulted in England in such monuments of scholarship as Lily's grammar[9] (actually a compilation of the work of William Lily and John Colet) in the sixteenth century, and Kennedy's *Shorter Latin Primer* in the nineteenth. In this tradition, the word and its morphology play the central role in the model of language. The approach to learning the language starts off with a number of word models or *paradigms*, which are called *declensions* in the case of nouns, and *conjugations* in the case of verbs. This approach to grammar has been called word-and-paradigm grammar or WP (Hockett 1954; Robins 1959).

Generations of Latin learners have started with paradigms which were assimilated by the now highly unfashionable process of rote learning: *mensa, mensa, mensam, mensae, mensae, mensa; amo, amas, amat, amamus, amatis, amant.* It is easy to criticize this approach — especially when the paradigm includes the appropriate form to use when talking to a table — but it is more useful to explore the model of language which this whole approach takes for granted. Someone who is 'good at Latin' is able to use the paradigms to make sense of a simple sentence such as *nauta laudat reginam* 'the sailor praises the queen', and then go on to read a text by looking words up in a dictionary and referring to a grammar where necessary. Of course, the vast majority of learners probably see little or no connection between paradigms, sentences and texts. The point is that WP presupposes a network of formal relationships which are not made explicit, which the successful learner is intuitively able to reconstruct, but which elude the unsuccessful learner. This section will follow the information trail to show how links are made between related pieces of information and how the learner is able to interpret new sentences using this model.

The words of the text are classed as either *declinable* or *indeclinable*. Words of the latter type can be looked up directly, but those of the former type must first be analysed by formally relating them to the paradigms: thus *nauta* corresponds to the first form of *mensa*, *laudat* to the third form of *amo*, and *reginam* to the third form of *mensa*. Declinable words consist of two parts, the *stem* and the *ending,* and the paradigm is a model for a set of words which pattern in the same way. The Latin noun, for example, as presented in table 4.1, has endings for six categories or *cases*, each of which is given a label such as *nominative* or *accusative,* and for singular and plural number. The identifier for any individual form has to include both case and number, e.g. 'genitive plural'. One of these identifiers, actually the nominative singular, is used as a general identifier or headword, and corresponds to the dictionary headword used to look it up. All this information can be presented explicitly in the form of a table (see Table 4.1).

Table 4.1

Case	Number	Form	Stem	Ending	Headword
Nominative	S	mensa	mens-	-a	mensa
Vocative	S	mensa	mens-	-a	mensa
Accusative	S	mensam	mens-	-am	mensa
Genitive	S	mensae	mens-	-ae	mensa
Dative	S	mensae	mens-	-ae	mensa
Ablative	S	mensa	mens-	-a	mensa
Nominative	P	mensae	mens-	-ae	mensa
Vocative	P	mensae	mens-	-ae	mensa
Accusative	P	mensas	mens-	-as	mensa
Genitive	P	mensarum	mens-	-arum	mensa
Dative	P	mensis	mens-	-is	mensa
Ablative	P	mensis	mens-	-is	mensa

The stem and the ending can be calculated from the form, and the headword is copied from the form of the first record. This information is consequently not normally listed separately in grammar books, but it is essential for the user to know how to make the calculations. Verb paradigms also have complex identifiers using two fields, person and number, as shown in Table 4.2. Again the form of the first record is taken as the headword for the whole paradigm, but in this case there is also the infinitive, which is an identifier for a whole set of related paradigms, and may be used for looking verbs up in dictionaries.

Table 4.2

Person	Number	Form	Stem	Ending	Headword	Infinitive
1	S	amo	am-	-o	amo	amare
2	S	amas	am-	-as	amo	amare
3	S	amat	am-	-at	amo	amare
1	P	amamus	am-	-amus	amo	amare
2	P	amatis	am-	-atis	amo	amare
3	P	amant	am-	-ant	amo	amare

The paradigms are linked through their headwords (or infinitive) to the dictionary. A typical dictionary entry includes the headword, grammatical tag, and meaning, e.g. **mensa** noun, 'table'; **amare** verb, 'love'. The grammatical tag refers back to the grammar, and contains the information where to look for the paradigm. Note that a Latin dictionary does not need to specify pronunciation. This is because a one-to-one relationship is assumed between letter and phoneme — assisted by adopting a suitably classical pronunciation of <c> and <gn>, and by editing away the problem of <u> and <v> — and because letters and phonemes are assumed to capture all the necessary details of speech.

So far, the procedure only gives access to the actual forms that occur in the paradigms. It is clearly necessary to generalize the procedure so that new words can be looked up. Given the form *laudat*, we have to match its ending with the ending of a form somewhere in a paradigm, in this case *amat*. We now have to detach the ending from the stem, and from the stem calculate the headword to look up in the dictionary, in this case *laudo* or *laudare*. By repeating the procedure for each word of a sentence or text, and copying the relevant information, we can construct a new table giving for each word its form, a grammatical tag or 'parse', and a meaning. For example an analysis of *nauta laudat reginam* is presented in Table 4.3.

Table 4.3

Form	Parse			Meaning
nauta	Nominative	S	noun	sailor
laudat	3	S	verb	praises
reginam	Accusative	S	noun	queen

As the student learns more Latin, the verb tables become more complicated, additional fields being added for tense, voice and mood. Verbs follow different conjugations, and the endings are different for *moneo* 'I warn', *rego* 'I rule' and *audio* 'I hear'. Similarly, nouns belong to different declensions. Drawing together the information from declensions or conjugations, and leaving out all predictable or redundant information, it is possible to represent the morphological system at an abstract level. Table 4.4, for example, gives the overall picture of declensions.

Table 4.4

Case	Number	D1	D2	D3	D4	D5
Nominative	S	-a	-us	?	-us	-es
Vocative	S	-a	-e	?	-us	-es
Accusative	S	-am	-um	-em	-um	-em
Genitive	S	-ae	-i	-is	-us	-ei
Dative	S	-ae	-o	-i	-ui	-ei
Ablative	S	-a	-o	-e	-u	-e
Nominative	P	-a	-i	-es	-us	-es
Vocative	P	-a	-i	-es	-us	-es
Accusative	P	-am	-os	-es	-us	-es
Genitive	P	-ae	-orum	-um	-uum	-erum
Dative	P	-ae	-is	-ibus	-ibus	-ebus
Ablative	P	-a	-is	-ibus	-ibus	-ebus

Table 4.4 ignores some detail, e.g. in the second declension *filius* 'son' has the vocative *fili.* The use of ? for some forms of the third declension indicates that these are unpredictable and must be recovered from the dictionary. What is interesting about this table is that it distils a vast amount of variable data and requires the minimum of storage space. A scholar who has access to such a table is able to automate the recognition and generation of word forms.

Now I am not suggesting that typical learners of Latin have constructed a relational database inside their heads and established all the links. Most learners probably set up a few links and for the rest remain totally confused. However, the database does model the kind of intuitive understanding of morphological relationships which is developed by someone who is said to be 'good at Latin'. Once such a model is set up, it can be easily modified for languages with a similar structure, and this is probably the grain of truth behind the assertion that learning Latin helps with the learning of other languages.

The well-known weakness of the model is in syntax. There are known rules for voice in subordinate clauses, sequences of tenses, and indirect speech. There are also labels for certain constructions, e.g. the first two words of *Quibus dictis caesar in foro occisus est* 'Which things having been said, Caesar was struck down in the forum' constitute a so-called 'ablative absolute'. But these are the few islands of clarity, and there is no overall organization. Nor is there anything that can be called a theory of meaning. There is no formal procedure for generating a meaning from the information in table 4.3, and this is left to an intuitive leap of common sense.

In practice syntactic analysis is carried out using intuitive probabilistic methods based on the primary assumption that sentences are syntactically well formed. Take a sentence like *agricolae in foro erant* 'the farmers were in the forum'. *Erant* can only mean 'they were' and is unambiguously tagged as third person plural. *Foro* could be dative or ablative, but after the preposition *in* it is ablative (with a probability approaching unity). *Agricolae* has four possible tags — genitive or dative singular, nominative or vocative plural — but only the nominative plural tag completes the sentence. Semantic probabilities are also used. For example, *agricolae in foro fabas venumdabant* probably means 'the farmers were selling beans in the forum' but it could also just mean 'they were selling beans to the farmer in the forum'. Probabilistic methods are also used to identify groups of words as constituents. For example, in *medicus dives domi erat* 'the rich doctor was at home' the most likely interpretation is that *medicus* and *dives* together form the subject (and in modern terminology a noun phrase). On the other hand, in *medicus dives erat* 'the doctor was rich' it is more likely that the adjective *dives* is being used predicatively.

4.3 Structural Linguistics

The kind of structural linguistics associated with Bloomfield (1933) and Hockett (1958) achieved a vast improvement in the handling of spoken data, concentrating on the relationship between units of grammar — in this case the morpheme rather than the word — and units of sound. With the benefit of hindsight, and after the battle has been won, we can now take a more relaxed attitude towards some of the points regarded by structuralists as incontrovertible, such as the primacy of speech over writing. In order to avoid any confusion between sounds and letters, phonetic transcription was regarded in principle as a response to the sound alone, taking no account of meaning or other language levels. In other words the links between related items of data were deliberately broken. At this point, too, linguistic theory enters the world of virtual reality: linguists still talk about grammars, and dictionaries and texts, but these are no longer physical objects that one can pick up and read. Even the phoneme inventory has an uncertain location, on the printed page or perhaps inside someone's head.

As phonology has developed it has extended the traditional linguistic model. Much effort, for instance, has been devoted to the optimal representation of lexical items, which relates to the dictionary, and more theoretical phonology has explored the generalizations to be made about lexical items, which is the traditional concern of grammar. What is new is the attempt to explore spoken language on its own terms, instead of treating sounds as attributes of letters. This is also the area of weakness, where the data links are broken.

The problem started with Sweet's distinction (1910) between broad and narrow transcription, later reinterpreted as phonemic and phonetic transcription. The narrow transcription was a representation of the raw speech data, and was the closest approximation to the primary data that could be achieved at that time. The broad transcription was in principle intended to handle phonetic contrast, but it was also used in practice for logically unrelated functions, such as lexical representation, and — in Britain at least — to mark the phonetic details of Received Pronunciation. Narrow transcription has since fossilized, and is used to mark the kind of phonetic detail that was known about in the early part of the century, such as dental articulation or velarization, but does not provide symbols for objects found in spectrograms, such as release bursts and formant transitions. Broad transcription has also fossilized in 'practical' phonology as exemplified in pronouncing dictionaries and books on the pronunciation of English. 'Theoretical' phonologists, on the other hand, have developed much more interesting lexical representations which account in a systematic way for a variety of patterns ranging from morphology to historical change and sociolinguistic variation.

One of the problems of phonology since Sweet's time is that phonologists have developed theoretical fragments which obviously capture some important generalizations about the language, but it is left unclear what it is that they relate to. It may not be self-evident, for example, that phonemes and syllable structure rules make generalizations about the form of lexical entries, and consequently belong to the grammar. In practice, it is assumed that phonemes are objects to be found in the phonetic data, and that they are revealed by phonemic transcription. Another branch of phonology, incidentally, deals with the processes that operate on lexical items when they come together in texts: when phonetic data is annotated in the light of these processes it becomes clear that much of the phonemic segmentation of a text is actually arbitrary. Although according to established custom it seems perfectly sensible to make a phonemic transcription of a spoken text, such a procedure is actually based on a logical contradiction, and confuses abstract lexical information with physical phonetic information. So-called 'distinctive features', on the other hand, capture generalizations about recurring patterns to be observed in the phonetic data. In practice, features are treated as the attributes of phonemes, or even lexical representations at a highly abstract level. This leads to another kind of logical contradiction, e.g. when /d/ is defined as 'voiced alveolar stop' or some equivalent specification, when at the phonetic level it need not be voiced, need not be alveolar and need not be a stop.

4.4 Transformational-generative Linguistics

The very different concerns adopted by linguists following the publication of Chomsky's *Syntactic Structures* in 1957 have at first sight nothing to do with databases. However, the theory made use of logical data structures, and if these are valid it must be possible to make data relationships explicit.

Chomsky's original phrase structure rules (1957:26–7) were of two kinds:

$$NP \rightarrow T + N$$
$$N \rightarrow \text{man, ball, etc.}$$

In the second type, N is a terminal symbol, and {man, ball} are lexical items. Such a rule presupposes a dictionary which includes entries as given in table 4.5. Whereas in traditional linguistics, the word *man* is tagged as a noun in the dictionary, and then the user has to look up *noun* in the grammar, this rule establishes a formal link the other way, from the grammar to the dictionary, albeit an imaginary one.

Table 4.5

LEX_ITEM	FORM	CLASS
1	ball	N
2	hit	V
3	man	N
4	the	T
5	took	V

The other rule identifies the constituency of structures, and corresponds to a record in a table as illustrated in table 4.6. These rules establish formal relationships among objects which are already in the grammar, e.g. 'noun phrase' is more general and abstract than 'article' or 'noun', and 'sentence' is more general and abstract than 'noun phrase' or 'verb phrase'. The place to find instances of noun phrases, verb phrases and sentences is not in the dictionary or the grammar, but in a text, again albeit an imaginary one.

Table 4.6

STRUCTURE	CONSTITUENTS
Sentence	NP + VP
VP	Verb + NP
NP	T + N

What is perhaps not so clear is how table 4.6 can be used to make formal logical links from a text — say, Chomsky's invented sentence *The man hit the ball* — to the dictionary and the syntactic analysis. First, the text can be represented as a table (see table 4.7) in which each word has an identifier (WORD_ID) and a number which points to the corresponding entry in the dictionary.

Table 4.7

WORD_ID	LEX_ITEM
1	4
2	3
3	2
4	4
5	1

By linking in to the dictionary, the form and class of each word can be recovered, e.g. word 1 recovers lexical item 4, the determiner *the*. Constituents that extend over more than one table can be kept in a further table recording the beginning and end of constituents:

Table 4.8

Constituent	Begins	Ends
S	1	5
NP	1	2
NP	4	5
VP	3	5

By linking this table to the text, *the ball*, for example can be identified as an NP. By linking through to the lexicon it is possible to recover the structure of this NP as T + N. By linking NP and T + N to the rules table, it is possible to confirm that this is a legal structure. Given this set of tables, and linking them together in different ways, it would be possible to generate random but grammatically well-formed strings, and even to design a simple parser.

From a general linguistic point of view, the interesting complication of Chomsky's model is that it introduced transformations, which could add or delete items, and change the order of items. This is not a problem from a database viewpoint. Records can be inserted into tables or deselected from them, and their order can be changed by exchanging word_id numbers.

In the later version of generative theory (Chomsky 1965), syntax was regarded as the central component of a language model, and phonology and semantics were relegated to an 'interpretative' role. Chomsky and Halle's *Sound Pattern of English* (1968) — 'SPE' — developed a model in which surface level phenomena could be predicted from abstract representations, and phonology consisted in the formulation of the mapping rules. The lexical representations were sufficiently abstract to account for regular morphological patterns, e.g. given a rule that changes /k/ to /s/ in the right places, *criticism* can be explicitly connected to *critic* (p. 54). To anyone familiar with historical methods, this approach looks remarkably similar to the method of internal reconstruction, and the operation of the rules close to the recapitulation of history. Chomsky and Halle's own rules generated a variety of American English, but other varieties could be generated by minor modifications. What is interesting is that it is possible to design a single level of annotation that has all these properties. In addition, lexical representations were found to encode prosodic information. The rules were able to predict stress levels represented as integers [1..7], which related in an admittedly vague way to observable prosodic patterns.

SPE phonology has since been elaborated in a number of ways. Natural phonology sought to clarify the relationship between abstract and surface representations. Metrical phonology presented the stress interface in the form of trees and grids rather than integers. Lexical phonology clarified the question of whether derivations belonged to the text or the dictionary, and distinguished lexical and post-lexical rules. Nespor and Vogel investigated the domains within which phonological rules operate, a concern which can be traced through generative phonology back at least to Trager and Smith (1957:37–39). Autosegmental phonology tackled the problem of alignment of segmental and prosodic phenomena.

4.5 Corpus Linguistics

The use of corpora brings back into linguistics the text about which dictionaries and grammars make generalizations. One consequence of this is that concepts dealt with in linguistic theory are forced out of the imaginary world back into the real world. The text, instead of being something the linguist has invented, or something which might possibly be said or written at some time, is a record of an actual event, and it can be printed out, picked up and examined. Corpus procedures, such as tagging, draw on real resources, including a real dictionary containing real generalizations about the behaviour of individual lexical items.

Typical modern corpora consist of contemporary written texts. Spoken texts, as in the BNC, are transcribed orthographically, and then treated as written texts. The text may then be enriched with further annotations, such as grammatical tags and a parse. For the user the texts are to be interpreted just like any other texts, and the annotations have the effect of making conscious the kind of information which is intuitively known anyway. In these circumstances, corpora may appear to be self-sufficient, and it may seem unnecessary to raise the question about the relationship between corpora and linguistic theories.

As soon as we move away from contemporary written texts,

however, this question becomes important. For a historical corpus (Knowles, in preparation), much of the information taken for granted in the case of a modern corpus — e.g. the identification of words in different spellings — has to be made explicit. Whereas a traditional scholar will intuitively class the form *yeare* as a variant of the word spelt *year*, this information can now be held in a database table. A spoken corpus, if the phonetic data it contains are to be exploited, involves the formal linking of several different kinds of information (Knowles 1994). Such corpora cannot be treated simply as textfiles, or sets of textfiles, and must be regarded as networks of explicitly related data. Contemporary written texts constitute the very special case in which these networks can be taken for granted. These networks presuppose some kind of linguistic theory.

At the present time, however, these objects are not formally linked. It is not possible, for example, to cross reference automatically from a tag in LOB to the corresponding section of CGEL. Compilers of corpora do not see it as any part of their task to relate to a particular dictionary or grammatical description. Grammarians and lexicographers are more concerned with the language as a whole than with specific texts. This is also true of pronouncing dictionaries. The new computer-readable *English Pronouncing Dictionary* simply gives standard pronunciations for words, and in this respect it belongs to a tradition unchanged since Walker (1791).[10] Computational linguists, meanwhile, set up their own grammars and dictionaries, and these have little connection with the kind of grammars and dictionaries that are published as books.

Of course, there is no guarantee that the data networks which result from the analysis of corpora ever will link up in this way. There are many different kinds of information to be stored in as many different tables, and tables can be related to each other in several different ways. There is no obvious reason why some of the information should be listed in one object called a dictionary, and all the rest in a second object called a grammar. These are the solutions for paper-and-pencil technology, and are not necessarily relevant in computer-based technology.

4.6 Conclusion

Any linguistic theory — whatever one understands by linguistic theory — has to account formally for the relationships which exist among many different kinds of data. These relationships are essentially similar to those handled by a modern relational database, and it is consequently reasonable to consider how theoretical linguistic relationships might be handled in database terms. In this paper I have taken for granted that language is manifest in the form of texts, that linguists have traditionally stored generalizations about texts in dictionaries, and generalizations about dictionary items in grammars. A brief survey of different approaches to linguistics over the last few centuries suggests that, looked at in this way, these superficially very different approaches in fact share a number of remarkable similarities.

Word-and-Paradigm grammar assumes that morphology is central to linguistic structure. Traditional English grammarians took the dictionary to be central, and this remains the popular view of language. For structural linguists, phonology was central, and proceeded from a narrow transcription of real or imagined speech events. Generative linguists assumed a central position for syntax. What all these views have in common is that they are self-evidently eccentric. When language is actually used, it is used for communicative purposes in social situations. The only aspect of language structure that is normally manifest in acts of communication is the text. It is precisely the normal manifestation of language that has been consistently backgrounded by mainstream theoretical linguists.

At this point let us return to the question raised in the introduction, whether corpus linguistics is atheoretical. It is difficult to see how the corpus linguist can add any consistent annotation to a text without implementing some kind of theory. Perhaps lurking behind the question are two assumptions. The first is that linguistic categories and concepts are to be more highly valued the more abstract they are, and that what corpus linguists do at the concrete end should not be dignified with the title of theory at all.

The reality is that by starting with real texts, corpus linguistics has the potential to develop a new kind of linguistics with a much better theoretical foundation than has hitherto been the case. The study of English morphology, for example, is conventionally based on predictions of what might happen if someone were to read aloud orthographic forms such as *cats*, *dogs* and *horses*. This approach confuses the structure of the spoken and written languages. A study based on real written texts would account for the orthographic forms (Peters, in press), and a study based on spoken texts would account for the spoken forms; a unified approach might then relate the two to each other. Conventional phonology relates abstract representations to idealized phonetic forms and leaves to the phonetician the task of relating these forms to real events which can be observed in speech data. In other words the theory does not have access to the primary data which it attempts to explain. A theoretically well-founded phonology would surely start with the observable speech events themselves.

The second lurking assumption is that linguistic theory proper is restricted to a particular set of formal relationships. These just happen to be remarkably similar to the set developed in medieval Europe for the study of Latin. There are in fact many more generalizations to be made about texts. There are generalizations to be made about the people who generate texts, the writers or speakers, and at the level of register about the relationship between the producers and receivers of texts. Texts exist not for the sake of the form, but in order to communicate meaning. The meaning of a text, like the form, can be handled at different degrees of abstraction, at the level of semantics, pragmatics (Thomas 1995) and discourse (Fairclough 1993). From the point of view of the corpus linguist, it makes no sense to classify some text annotations as theoretical and others as not. Far from being atheoretical, corpus linguistics potentially undermines a number of conventional assumptions about the nature of linguistic theory itself.

Another objection raised against the corpus approach is that corpus linguists collect a restricted sample of an arbitrary subset of the language and then pontificate about the language as a whole. If only they could be persuaded to invent their own data, then they would not have any such problem!

Notes

1 Cawdrey, R 1604 *A table alphebeticall … of hard vsuall English words.*

2 Johnson, S 1755 *An English Dictionary.*

3 Lowth R 1967 [1762] *A short introduction to English grammar* Scolar Press, Menston.

4 Jonson B 1972 [1640] *An English grammar* Scolar Press, Menston.

5 Wallis, J 1969 [1653] *Grammatica Linguæ Anglicanæ*. Scolar Press, Menston.

6 Holder, W. (1967) [1669] *Elements of English speech*. Scolar Press Reprint 49, Menston.

7 Sheridan, T. 1968 [1762] *Course of lectures on elocution*. Scolar Press, Menston.

8 Walker, J 1791 *A critical pronouncing dictionary of the English language*.

9 Lily, W., Colet, J. 1549 *A short introduction of grammar*. Scolar Press reprint 262.

10 Walker J 1791 *A critical pronouncing dictionary of the English language*.

PART 2

Corpus-based language studies

5 Towards a unified account of the syntax and semantics of *GET*

STIG JOHANSSON and SIGNE OKSEFJELL

5.1 Background

GET is one of the most common and most flexible verbs in English. In the comprehensive grammar of Quirk *et al* (1985) it is separately dealt with or referred to in as many as seven chapters, and it is indeed taken as an example of multiple class membership (p. 720). Yet there is no attempt in the grammar to show the connections between the various uses of the verb. The present paper searches for such a unified account.[1]

5.2 Material

The material for the paper was taken from the Brown Corpus (Francis and Kučera 1979), the Lancaster-Oslo/Bergen (LOB) Corpus (Johansson *et al* 1978), and the London-Lund Corpus (Svartvik 1990), representing printed American English, printed British English, and spoken British English, respectively.

5.3 Overall distribution

The overall distribution of *GET* in the three corpora is summarized in Table 5.1. We see that this verb is far more common in the spoken corpus than in the written corpora, particularly taking into account the fact that the spoken corpus is only half the size of the million-word written corpora. The difference is found with all the major forms of the verb, though it is especially large with the form *got*. Perhaps the verb, though it is especially large with the form *got*. Perhaps somewhat surprisingly, the distribution was very similar in the Brown and LOB corpora; the only notable differences were the occurrence of *gotten* and the somewhat higher frequency of *got* in the American material.

Some differences were found in the distribution of the verb in the text categories of the written corpora, with overrepresentation in the fiction categories and underrepresentation in the categories of informative prose; the opposite poles were popular fiction vs. learned and scientific English. On the other hand, the distribution was quite even in the text categories of the London-Lund Corpus. For details on these matters, see Oksefjell (1994).

We may conclude (1) that the verb *GET* is highly characteristic of spoken English, (2) that it is fairly evenly represented in different types of spoken English, (3) that it is found in writing particularly in fiction of a less formal character, and (4) that the distribution is much the same in printed British and American English.

Table 5.1 The distribution of forms of *GET* in three corpora: the Brown Corpus, the LOB Corpus, and the London-Lund Corpus (LLC)

[*Got* represents both the past tense and the past-participle form.]

Forms	BROWN	LOB	LLC
get	749	739	1,362
gets	66	58	116
getting	165	178	296
got	482	428	1,853
gotta	5	2	4
gotten	16	0	2
Total	1,483	1,405	3,633

The sharp contrast in frequency between speech and writing must be seen against the background that *GET* has greatly expanded its areas of use over the centuries; speech is at the forefront of linguistic change. The contrast is probably strengthened by the common prescriptive reaction against the verb (in particular, against the use of *HAVE GOT* in place of *HAVE*). It is worth noting that *GET* is less common in the Kolhapur Corpus of Indian English (cf. Shastri *et al* 1986) than in its British and American English counterparts: 1,163 examples vs. 1,405 for the LOB Corpus and 1,483 for the Brown Corpus. It is tempting to speculate that the reason may be that printed Indian English is more formal and tends to retain the style of a previous age.

5.4 The uses of *GET*

A detailed study was carried out of the uses of *GET* in the first three text categories of the LOB Corpus (representing journalistic writing) and the first three text categories of the London-Lund Corpus (representing spontaneous conversation). The material selected amounts to about 176,000 words from each corpus. The categories were chosen as they are fairly uniform and represent typical uses of speech vs. writing.

The material was classified according to the scheme of Quirk *et al* (1985). Examples:[2]

A. Monotransitive:

> I ^got this *:c\ard* from 'Africa# LLC 1.9: 1399
> ... anyone foolish enough to trust him as a guide in the current theatrical scene would get a quite lunatic idea of what was going on in it. LOB A19: 20

B. Transitive with obligatory adverbial (SVOA):

> they were ^given a w\eek . {^by the !\Allies#}# to get the "^whole army 'back to :G\ermany# LLC 2.3: 255–256
> ... it took my son and I all day on Monday to get the place in order again. LOB A43: 43

C. Complex transitive:

> I'm ^going to _buy a _new !k\/it to'morrow# . for [r@] ((to)) ^get it 'ready for :Chr\istmas# LLC 1.7: 1164–1165
> We really ought to get this thing straight. LOB B22: 87

D. *GET* + O + *to*-infinitive:

> ... to ^get them to give me a sub:stantial sum of money/ to enable me to :f\inish it# LLC 2.1: 96
> In this, the manager of a firm putting out a new toothpaste (Eric Barker) gets a couple of dentists to endorse it. LOB C16: 20

E. *GET* + O + V-*ed*:

> ... I'd ^got the [pri] 'paper :f\olded# LLC 1.14: 357
> Publicity is the first necessity if we are to get the extraordinary measures implemented ... LOB A13: 52

F. Intransitive with an obligatory adverbial (SVA):

> ... by the !time they 'got to the s/ummer# there was ^no 'more !w\ork to 'do# LLC 1.4: 679–680
> In the front room of Anglesey-road is a congregation who never actually got to church, but who are gathered with devotion around Brendan Behan and a brandy bottle. LOB C06: 9

G. Copular verb:

> ... do you feel that it was perfectly satisfactory just [@] letting you practise on the students and just get better . LLC 3.6: 1033
> Under automation work was getting more monotonous and that was bringing mental and bodily illness. LOB A27: 14

H. The *GET*-passive:

> I ^think he got :paid for ['dhi:] — ((sort of)) :odd w\/eek# LLC 2.7: 302
> ... my point is that all Waterloo pupils are getting blamed. LOB B23: 68

I. Monotransitive *HAVE got*:

> ... we've ^got a . a whole !list of :\/interview'ees ... LLC 3.1: 557
> It was the directors of newly-constructed British Lion, who have got faith in fresh faces, talent ... LOB C17: 81

J. The modal idiom *HAVE got to*:

> in ^some re'spects you've :got to 'make a diag:n\osis# LLC 2.9: 1215
> Well, you've got to have something different. LOB C04: 66

K. Phrasal verb (transitive or intransitive):

> I'd just ring 'up and /ask# ^how she's !getting /on and# LLC 1.12: 1104–1105
> He never got up much speed, and made few turns. LOB C10: 66

L. Prepositional verb:

> I'm ^going to get to get /\into th/is# LLC 1.12: 130

M. Phrasal-prepositional verb:

> and and Harrod gets on with him quite well ... LLC 1.9: 776
> ... given a free hand, he could get away with a bit-by-bit encroachment on western rights ... LOB B21: 90

The following uses were less commonly found in the material:

N. Ditransitive:

> OK and just I'll get you some LLC 2.11: 826

O. *GET* + O + V-*ing*:

> ^this got them g\oing# LLC 1.3: 696

P. *GET* + V-*ing*:

> if ^{you'll t\ell me} what I could ":st\/art on# and get *^g\/oing 'on# LLC 3.1: 503–504

Q. *GET* + *to*-infinitive:

> ^when we 'got to kn/ow each 'other# LLC 1.14: 997

In addition, there were a number of idioms: *GET rid of*, *GET hold of*, *GET in touch with*, etc. In the spoken material there were also a number of examples which could not be classified because of lacking context (due to interruptions, hesitations, and the like).

Table 5.2 gives a survey of the material from the two corpora; the less common uses are grouped together under 'minor patterns'. All the main uses were found in both corpora. All of them were much more frequent in the spoken corpus, most notably the *HAVE + got* construction.

Table 5.2 The uses of *GET* in the LOB Corpus (categories A, B, and C) and the London-Lund Corpus (LLC, categories 1, 2, and 3)

[The uses are ordered according to their frequency in LOB.]

Use	LOB		LLC	
	Freq	%	Freq	%
monotransitive	83	36.5	434	26.9
SVA	35	15.4	145	9.0
copular	20	8.8	91	5.6
phrasal verb	18	7.9	60	3.7
minor patterns	12	5.3	64	4.0
HAVE + got + O	11	4.8	457	28.3
HAVE + got + to-inf	11	4.8	101	6.4
GET-passive	9	4.0	43	2.7
phr.-prep. verb	7	3.1	46	2.8
GET + O + *to*-inf	7	3.1	20	1.2
complex transitive	6	2.6	20	1.2
GET + O + V-*ed*	3	1.3	32	2.0
SVOA	3	1.3	40	2.5
prepositional verb	2	0.9	38	2.4
unclassifiable	0	0.0	24	1.5
Total	227	100	1,615	100

In the search for a unified account of *GET* in the rest of this paper, we will only consider the material provided by the London-Lund Corpus, as the verb is particularly characteristic of spoken English and as the spoken corpus provides ample material for the various uses.

5.5 Towards a unified account

GET has a special relationship to two of the three English verbs which are singled out as **primary verbs** by Quirk *et al* (1985). The primary verbs have a central place in English because of their role in building basic grammatical structures, such as interrogative and negative clauses, the passive, and the progressive and perfective aspect. Moreover, they are the most frequent verbs in English.

In English conversation *GET* is next to the primary verbs in frequency. Although it lacks the 'NICE' properties of auxiliaries in English (cf Huddleston 1976: 333), some of its uses are clearly auxiliary-like, especially its uses as a passive auxiliary and as a modal idiom. In addition, it partakes in many other grammatical patterns. Yet it is normally assigned a marginal role in English grammar, compared with the primary verbs. We shall now attempt to define the role of this important verb by relating its uses to those of the primary verbs *HAVE* and *BE*.

5.5.1 GET vs. HAVE

In the first five uses listed in section 5.4 (A–E) *GET* is closely related to *HAVE*; the same applies to the special uses of *HAVE got* (I–J). At the outset, *GET* and *HAVE* appear to be clearly different. *GET* is an action verb, *HAVE* a state verb. The notions of change and causation are at the heart of *GET*, but are missing in the basic uses of *HAVE*. The relationship between the two verbs is, however, far more complicated.

5.5.1.1 Monotransitive verbs

GET was first recorded as a monotransitive verb in the sense 'to obtain possession of (property, etc.) as the result of effort and contrivance' (*OED*):

> ORMIN 10219 Forr whase itt iss thatt grediz iss To winnenn erþlic ahhte, Azz alls he mare & mare gett Azz lisste himm affterr mare. (c 1200)

In present-day English monotransitive *GET* normally means 'receive' or 'obtain' and combines with a recipient or an agent subject:

> he ^got that j/ob# -- be^cause there was a m/an# -- who was the "!head of the 'Celtic Mus/eum# LLC 1.14: 951–953
> well he ^said I !g\/ot them# . ^I !got the 'lot with!\out 'your h/elp# LLC 1.14: 516–517

The relationship between *GET* and *HAVE* can be expressed as follows: if you get something, the result is that you have it; 'to get' means 'to come to have/possess'.

The difference between the two verbs is not clear-cut, however. *HAVE* can be used in action propositions. Compare (the examples have been taken from Swan 1980: 266):

> Could I have a glass of beer? (= 'Please give me one.')
> Could I get a glass of beer? (= 'Can I go to the fridge and help myself?')

Although both are action propositions, there is a difference in that *GET* retains the original meaning of effort on the part of the subject referent. Note also:

> she'd ^had a !l\etter ^{n\o} she'd had a :ph\one call 'from h/im# ^Fr\/iday night# for about "^two h/ours# and had a "^l\etter 'from him# on ^S\aturday# LLC 2.12: 36–40
> and then - she ^suddenly . 'had a :l\egacy# . got a ^l\etter {^through the p\ost#}# LLC 1.11: 577–578

Here *had a letter* and *got a letter* are both used in the sense of 'receive'. Note also *had a legacy* in the second example.

5.5.1.2 Monotransitive HAVE got

Just as *HAVE* may acquire the meaning of 'receive', *GET* may lose the meaning of change and become identical to *HAVE*. This is true of the phrase *HAVE got*, where *got* is 'felt as a meaningless, empty addition' (Visser 1973: 2202). The development is not unnatural; 'to have got' entails 'to have'.

Monotransitive *HAVE got* is the most frequent use of *GET* in the spoken corpus material (cf table 5.2). What factors might affect the choice of *HAVE got* vs. *HAVE* (apart from text type and formality)? One possible factor is tense. The past tense rarely occurs in the *HAVE got* construction; only 25 out of 457 instances recorded in the first three text categories of the London-Lund Corpus contained a past tense form. Another relevant factor is the type of clause; see table 5.3. We see that *HAVE got* is close to *HAVE* in overall frequency, but that it clearly exceeds the other forms in negative and interrogative clauses. *DO + HAVE* is a minority pattern in all the clause types, but there is reason to believe that frequencies would be higher in American English.

Table 5.3 The frequencies of monotransitive *HAVE*, *HAVE got*, and *DO + HAVE* in text category 2 of the London-Lund Corpus.

['Negative' includes negative interrogative clauses.]

Context	HAVE	HAVE got	DO + HAVE
positive	207	136	3
negative	1	27	17
interrogative	6	16	5
Total	214	179	25

Occasionally *got* alone acquires the meaning of *HAVE*:

one of ^[dhi: @:] . sort of . :teen'age !N\outs# - [@m] got ^hold of a !fN\ick-'knife# and . ^Ella !wh\ipped it 'off him# and ^went 'down at :dead of n/ight and ^chucked it 'in the !Th\ames# (- - laughs) (- coughs) ^still got a 'lot of :hot/ pr/operty# be^hind her !((t\ele'vi-sion))# ^hasn't she# LLC 2.13: 371–378

The question tag *hasn't she* underlines the fact that *got* is equivalent to *HAVE got* here. Eleven instances of this 'reduced' construction were recorded from a total of 457 occurrences of *HAVE got* in categories 1, 2, and 3 of the London-Lund Corpus.

5.5.1.3 The modal idiom HAVE got to

In the same way as monotransitive *HAVE got* has become equivalent to *HAVE*, *HAVE got to* has acquired the meaning of necessity and obligation of *HAVE to*. Table 5.4 gives the distribution of *HAVE*, *HAVE got to*, and *DO + HAVE to* in category 2 of the London-Lund Corpus. We note that the relative frequency of *HAVE got* vs. *HAVE to* is much smaller than the proportion of monotransitive *HAVE got* vs. *HAVE*. Only *HAVE to* allows a combination with a modal auxiliary. Negative and interrogative clauses are infrequent, but they all have *DO + HAVE to*. No occurrences of negative *HAVE got to* were found in the material (but two instances of this kind were found in the total material of text categories 1, 2, and 3).

Table 5.4 The frequencies of *HAVE to*, *HAVE got to*, and *DO + HAVE to* in text category 2 of the London-Lund Corpus

'Negative' includes negative interrogative clauses.

Context	HAVE to	HAVE got to	DO + HAVE to
positive	86	38	1
negative	0	0	10
interrogative	0	0	6
modal	28	0	0
Total	114	38	17

Like monotransitive *HAVE got*, the modal idiom has a reduced variant, usually represented as *gotta* (see table 5.1). Although the form was rarely instanced in our material, we have reason to expect it to be more widespread in casual spoken English (particularly American English).

5.5.1.4 Causative verbs

The original monotransitive use of *GET* could be paraphrased as 'cause oneself to have', with a ditransitive pattern. Compare:

> I often advise these women to get themselves an interesting job. LOB F17: 112

The meaning of *GET* is causative in a number of the patterns exemplified in section 5.4: B, C, D, E, N, and O.

Causative *GET* and *HAVE* overlap in constructions with a direct object followed by an infinitive or a past-participle form. Compare:

> I "^might get 'Victor :Gr\/ayling# to do *^something on the !last [tsh] on the ^last !V\i*king 'bit# LLC 1.9: 888–889
> ^how 'na:\ive 'they 'are# ^r\/eally# ^how !easily 'taken /in# ... I ^m/ean . to ^have a 'student 'come to you and [s] - ((oh)) ^I !read a b\ook# LLC 1.6: 354–359

> ^we can g\et# . "^one of the 'obsolete 'buildings in the c\ollege# . de^stroyed# LLC 3.4: 241–243
> he ^b\orrowed them from [dhi:] . ^oh you know "'ch\ose them# from the ^P\/orn# +and ^had them _all carried !\over# LLC 1.8: 143–145

GET and *HAVE* appear to be much the same in force, except that *GET* makes the causative intent more explicit.

Also instanced in the material was causative *GET* + O + V-*ing*. Compare:

> ^this got them g\oing# LLC 1.3: 696
> ^you can !have !two r\eels w/orking# ... and ^switch from 'one to the /other# LLC 1.7: 1246–1249

Here there is a clear difference, in agreement with the basic uses of *GET* and *HAVE*.

5.5.2 GET vs. BE

The relationship between *GET* and *BE* is parallel to that between *GET* and *HAVE*. While *BE* is a state verb, *GET* is an action verb denoting a change of state or location. The relevant uses are F–H and P in section 5.4.

5.5.2.1 Intransitive verbs

Both *GET* and *BE* are used as intransitive verbs with an obligatory adverbial (see the examples of *GET* in section 5.4, F). The contrast between *BE* and *GET* is 'location' vs. 'change of location': *she is there* vs. *she got there*.

5.5.2.2 Copular verbs

Both *GET* and *BE* occur with adjective phrases (see the examples of *GET* in section 5.4, G). The contrast is 'state' vs. 'change of state': *she is better* vs. *she got better*. Copular *BE* can, however, be used dynamically, as in:

> I ^f/elt 'cold# but I was* sur^prised to 'hear :you say it was **!r/aining# LLC 1.7: 520–521
> ^this sort of re!m\inded 'me# that ^when my 'mother was 'forty# my ^father pro'duced a :b\ottle# - of ^p/\ort# that ^was [@m] !bottled the 'same y/\ear {as ^sh\e 'was}# LLC 2.13: 501–505

It is clear that *was surprised* means 'became surprised' and *was forty* 'reached forty'.

A major difference between copular *GET* and *BE* is that only *BE* combines with noun phrases (*he was a general* vs. **he got a general*), presumably to prevent confusion with monotransitive *GET*. But note the type illustrated in:

> you could ^be a you could ^get to be a "!g\eneral# to ^be an ar/istocrat# ... but ^what you could "!n\ot 'get to 'be# was what ^really !c/ounted in the 'German 'army# was to be the ^general's _Chief of !St\aff# LLC 2.3.: 180–186

The construction *GET to be* unambiguously provides a dynamic reading.

5.5.2.3 Passive auxiliaries

There is not a sharp borderline between the use of *BE* and *GET* as copular verbs and as passive auxiliaries. It is therefore no surprise that we find basically the same relationship between the verbs in both construction types. *GET* and *BE* both occur in dynamic passive constructions, expressing a change of state as the result of some action (see the examples of *GET*-passives in section 5.4, H). In addition, *BE* is used with statal passives. Compare:

> They got married yesterday.
> They were married yesterday.
> They were married for ten years.

Though both *BE* and *GET* are found with dynamic constructions, there is a great difference in frequency. The proportion of *GET*-passives to *BE*-passives in text categories 1, 2, and 3 of the London-Lund Corpus is approximately 1:30. It is possible, however, that frequencies are higher in other types of spoken English than those represented in the London-Lund Corpus.

An additional difference is that agent phrases are very rare with *GET*-passives. In text category 2 of the London-Lund Corpus there were 27 *BE*-passives with an expressed agent phrase (out of a total of about 400 occurrences). None of the 14 *GET*-passives in the same material contained an expressed agent phrase. *By*-phrases do, however, occur, though very rarely.

The differing behaviour with respect to agent phrases may reflect a slight difference in meaning between *GET*-passives and dynamic *BE*-passives. *BE* focuses more on the action, *GET* more on the result of the action; hence, we would expect agent phrases more frequently with the *BE*-passive.

The very low frequency of agent phrases with *GET*-passives may also be connected with the type of subject. It has been reported that 'While the subjects of *BE*-passives divide roughly equally between human and non-human ones, the *GET*-passive shows a lopsided 9:1 preference for human subjects' (Givón 1993: 69). Givón relates this to the 'agentive nature of the patient-subject of the *GET*-passive' (p. 68). See further section 5.5.3 below.

5.5.2.4 Ing-constructions

GET is sometimes followed by *ing*-constructions, chiefly in some lexicalized expressions like *get cracking*, *get going*, *get moving*. The following example is more unusual:

> !one lot might 'want to do the 'medieval ro:m\/ances# and ^then they can 'get r\eading them# LLC 1.9: 1144–1145

Though *GET* + V-*ing* cannot normally be substituted for the progressive aspect, the contrast with respect to the progressive is much the same as the one we have observed before: change of state vs. state (or rather in this case: inchoative action vs. action in progress). And again we find that *GET*-constructions involve an agentive subject, exercising intent and control.

5.5.3 Inchoative vs. causative constructions

It is a characteristic feature of English that a large number of verbs have both transitive and intransitive uses. One important type is the group of so-called ergative verbs, which are either found with an agentive subject and a patient object, or with a patient subject. Examples:

She broke the glass.	The glass broke.
The sun ripened the fruit.	The fruit ripened.

GET is 'double-faced' in the same way as verbs like *BREAK* and *RIPEN*.

Compare:

She got the glass broken.	The glass got broken.
The sun got the fruit ripe.	The fruit got ripe.

If we go back and examine the uses in sections 5.5.1 and 5.5.2, we find that it is possible to set up many pairs like:

She got it there.	It got there.
She got it ready.	It got ready.

She got it folded.	It got folded.
She got it going.	It got going.

Compare also:

She got him a book.	He got a book.

GET makes it possible to express a change without an expressed initiator (the inchoative use) or a change caused by some agent (the causative use).

The relationship between the causative and inchoative uses is even closer than shown above. In many cases the inchoative constructions permit an expansion by a reflexive pronoun, transforming the constructions to the corresponding causative type:

I got (myself) into hospital.
She got (herself) ready.
He got (himself) killed.

Note also:

She got (herself) a new car.

Instances of this kind do not occur very often. There were fewer than 10 examples in the whole of the Brown Corpus and some 15–20 examples each in the LOB Corpus and the London-Lund Corpus.

Where the reflexive pronoun is used, the subject is clearly at the same time agent and patient (or recipient). But it seems to be characteristic of *GET* that, even where there is no reflexive pronoun, we may find an agentive meaning. See sections 5.5.1.1 and 5.5.2.3–4.

5.5.4 Prototypical GET

We are now ready to summarize the characteristic features uniting the uses of *GET*.[3] Following the approach of Aijmer (1985, 1987), we will attempt to connect the uses of *GET* both synchronically and diachronically using the notion of a syntactic-semantic prototype. According to Aijmer (1987: 22), 'the prototype can be regarded as a schema consisting of a set of grammatical and semantic properties.'

In the search for the prototypical features of *GET*, it is

instructive to examine the earliest recorded uses of the verb: the monotransitive use (in the sense 'obtain as the result of effort'), the ditransitive use, the intransitive use with an obligatory adverbial, and the transitive use with an obligatory adverbial; see section 5.4 (A, B, F, and N). Early examples (see also 5.5.1.1):

> *Cursor M.* 3502 (Gött.) Ay was he bone, To gete [*Cott.* fete] his fadir venisun. (*OED*, c. 1300)
>
> *Cursor M.* 7902 In batail sua he suld be sette, that he awai suld neuer gette. (*OED*, c. 1300)
>
> *Will. Palerne* 2895 The grettest of the grim bestes he gat to prison sone. (*OED*, c. 1350)

The four initial *GET* constructions share the following features:

+ agentive S
+ change
+ cause

In addition, the monotransitive pattern contains a patient O (object), and the subject is simultaneously an agent and a recipient. The ditransitive pattern contains the same semantic roles, except that the recipient role is realized by an indirect object. The intransitive pattern with an obligatory adverbial has a locative A (adverbial) rather than a patient O. Finally, the transitive pattern with an obligatory adverbial has both a patient O and a locative A.

In the course of the centuries there have been some changes in the original patterns, and new patterns have developed. In the process some of the original features have been lost or weakened. The three original features have been preserved in the following patterns (cf section 5.4 and the discussion in section 5.5.1–3): B, C, D, E, N, and O. Some of the patterns are no longer necessarily marked by a causative feature and an agentive subject, or there are vestiges only of these features: A, F, G, H, P. The inchoative feature is preserved in all these patterns, however. The inchoative feature only is preserved in one pattern: Q.

One of the uses of *GET* lacks all of the three prototypical features: monotransitive *HAVE got.* This then represents a new prototype. Arguably, the modal idiom *HAVE got to* is closer to the original prototype in that obligation and necessity are connected with agency and causation.

To sum up, we might say that there is some unity in the uses of *GET*. Despite the variety in syntax and semantic content, there appears to be a prototype to which all constructions conform more or less closely; that is, all constructions except the derived prototype *HAVE got*.[4]

5.6 A comparison with *KEEP*

Like *GET*, *KEEP* is a very common and very flexible verb. It is closely related to *GET* as well as to *HAVE* and *BE*. Compare:

I have a new PC.
I got it last month.
I will keep it for a long time.

I have it in my office.
I got it into my office.
I will keep it in my office.

I had it working last week.
I got it working last week.
I will keep it working.

She was quiet.
She got quiet.
She kept quiet.

It was moving.
Get moving.
Keep moving.

The relationship between the four verbs can be summarized as follows:

	BE/HAVE	GET	KEEP
state	+	–	+
change	–	+	–
continuity	–	–	+

This representation is too simple, however. We have seen above that both *BE* and *HAVE* may be used dynamically. Similarly, both verbs are compatible with the meaning of continuity:

I will have/keep the PC in my office until it breaks down.
She was/kept quiet during the whole meeting.

The special advantage of *GET* and *KEEP* is that they more clearly single out the meanings of change and continuity, respectively.

There is a close parallel between *BE*, *HAVE*, *GET*, *KEEP* and some important verbs in German and Norwegian:[5]

German:	HABEN	–	BEKOMMEN	–	BEHALTEN
Norwegian:	HA	–	FÅ	–	BEHOLDE
English:	HAVE	–	GET	–	KEEP
German:	SEIN	–	WERDEN	–	BLEIBEN
Norwegian:	VÆRE	–	BLI	–	FORBLI
English	BE	–	GET	–	KEEP

Though these verbs are by no means parallel in all their uses, the basic contrasts are the same. The fundamental difference is that, while German and Norwegian use different verbs, the English verbs *GET* and *KEEP* appear in both series.[6]

5.7 Conclusion

The uses of *GET* are not as multifarious as one might expect from accounts in grammars and dictionaries. With the exception of the frequent *HAVE got* construction, the main uses can be connected to one general prototype (see section 5.5.4).

GET is not only one of the most frequent verbs in English; it is basic in the sense that it contrasts with the primary verbs *HAVE* and *BE*, both of which play a central role in English grammar. *GET* is clearly not grammaticalized in the same sense as *HAVE* and *BE*; for example, it lacks the 'NICE' properties of the English auxiliaries. Yet, if the focus is shifted from form to meaning, it is hard to escape the conclusion that it deserves a place at the centre of grammar.

Notes

1 A fuller account is given in Oksefjell (1994).

2 The examples have been taken from the WordCruncher version of the corpora contained in the ICAME Collection of English Language Corpora. References to the London-Lund Corpus give the text category, text number, and tone unit number; the LOB Corpus references specify the text category, text number, and sentence number. Grammatical tags have been omitted in the examples from the LOB Corpus.

3 Phrasal and prepositional uses are ignored here.

4 The description of prototypical *GET* is worked out somewhat differently and in greater detail in Oksefjell (1994).

5 As regards the German verbs, see the detailed account in Fabricius-Hansen (1975).

6 Needless to say, there are other English verbs which partake in similar contrasts (e.g. *BECOME*). These are ignored here, as the main focus is on the verb *GET*.

6 Complement clauses in English

SIDNEY GREENBAUM, GERALD NELSON and MICHAEL WEITZMAN

Many modern grammars of English find it useful to set up a three-way distinction between sentence, clause, and phrase though these terms are used variously. In this paper, as in Quirk *et al* 1985, clauses are constructions that can be analyzed as exhibiting grammatical relations or constituent elements such as subject, verb, and direct object, but are either contained within a larger construction, or minimally are co-extensive with an independent sentence.[1] We recognize nonfinite and verbless constructions as clauses. For example, *playing music* is a clause in *They enjoy playing music*, since we can analyze the construction as consisting of a verb *playing* and the direct object *music*.[2] In this respect, we differ from another grammatical tradition that insists that a clause must have a finite verb.

In this paper we focus on clauses that complement verbs and adjectives. These clauses are complements in that their form is determined by the lexical verb or the adjective. The choice of the complement *that*-clause in *I believe that it is too late* depends on the lexical verb *believe*, which would not allow (say) a *whether*-clause as its complement. Similarly, the *that*-clause is a complement of the adjective *aware* in *I am aware that it is too late*. Complement clauses may have a range of functions within the host clause in which they are embedded, including that of subject: the *that* clause in *That it is too late must depress you* is a complement of the verb *depress* while the same clause in *That it is too late must be obvious to everybody* is a complement of the adjective *obvious*.[3] We have also included in our discussion of complement clauses those that are complements of prepositional verbs and phrasal-prepositional verbs, since we take these combinations to be multi-word verbs. On the other hand, we have excluded appositive clauses, which have been analyzed as complements of nouns: their status is less clear, since they are often considered to be modifiers of nouns (cf. Quirk *et al* 1985, 16.84 and 17.26f). More relevantly, they are embedded within noun phrases and are generally less integral to the structure of their host clause.

For our data we have drawn on the material in the Leverhulme Corpus, a subset of the British component (ICE–GB) of the International Corpus of English (ICE).[4] The Leverhulme Corpus consists of 42 texts each containing about 2,000 words. Thirty texts were selected from samples of spoken English: 20 texts of spontaneous natural conversations, five unscripted monologues (lectures and talks), and five broadcast discussions. The remaining twelve texts came from written English and were divided equally into personal letters, academic writing and non-academic writing. We have annotated the Leverhulme Corpus for clause relationships manually.

Complement clauses are subordinate clauses that are embedded in their host clauses. We have excluded other types of subordinate clauses: relative clauses, appositive clauses, comparative clauses, and adverbial clauses. These are either embedded in phrases (restrictive relative clauses, appositive clauses and comparative clauses) or are loosely linked in varying extent to their host clauses (nonrestrictive relative clauses and adverbials).

Table 6.1 displays the frequencies — expressed per 1,000 words — for all types of subordinate clauses in the Leverhulme Corpus. As in the other tables in this paper, Table 6.1 gives the total frequencies, the frequencies for the two modes of writing and speech, and the frequencies for the three text types within each mode. The most conspicuous result is the relatively low frequency for subordination in conversation, which accounts for the total differences between the written and spoken material. Since there is variation within the two modes (most obviously between conversations and the other spoken categories), the distinction between speech and writing as such is not a factor that accounts for the differences in frequency of subordination. Presumably it is the lack of premeditation in casual conversation that tends to reduce the use of subordination in that type of language. For detailed analysis of subordination across genres in the Leverhulme Corpus, see Greenbaum and Nelson (1995).

Table 6.1 Subordinate clauses per 1,000 words

Category	Number of words	Number of subordinate clauses	Subordinate clauses per 1,000 words
Non-academic writing	8,508	568	66.8
Academic writing	8,588	481	56.0
Letters	8,190	571	69.7
WRITTEN	25,286	1,620	63.6
Monologues	11,198	790	70.5
Broadcast discussions	11,161	828	74.2
Conversations	41,406	2,054	49.6
SPOKEN	63,765	3,672	57.6
Total	89,051	5,292	59.3

In Table 6.2a we compare the frequencies of complement clauses, our main concern in this paper, with those for the other types of subordinate clauses in terms of percentages. We count separately those clauses that are coordinated; for example, the two *that*-clauses in [1], where the second clause is a zero *that*-clause:

[1] When the PCB has been etched and trimmed, ensure that all mounting holes are in line and a PP3 battery slips easily between the two protrusions each side of the square cutout, as filing a completed board is awkward and may damage components. [W2B–032–64]

Table 6.2a Types of subordinate clauses

Category	Complements	Adverbials	Restrictive relatives	Other	Total
Non-academic writing	25.9% (147)	33.6% (191)	29.2% (166)	11.3% (64)	100% (568)
Academic writing	27.4% (132)	32.4% (156)	32.8% (158)	7.3% (35)	100% (481)
Letters	46.0% (263)	27.5% (157)	18.6% (106)	7.9% (45)	100% (571)
WRITTEN	33.4% (542)	31.1% (504)	26.5% (430)	8.9% (144)	100% (1,620)
Monologues	30.4% (240)	26.1% (206)	31.8% (251)	11.8% (93)	100% (790)
Broadcast discussions	48.7% (403)	20.8% (172)	21.8% (181)	8.7% (72)	100% (828)
Conversations	45.8% (941)	26.0% (535)	18.5% (380)	9.6% (198)	100% (2,054)
SPOKEN	43.1% (1,584)	24.9% (913)	22.1% (812)	9.9% (363)	100% (3,672)
Total	40.2% (2,126)	26.8% (1,417)	23.5% (1,242)	9.6% (507)	100% (5,292)

Complement clauses are compared chiefly with adverbial clauses and restrictive relative clauses; the other types of subordinate clauses occur infrequently and are therefore combined as 'other'. We expect complement clauses to be the most frequent of the subordinate clauses, since complements belong to the essential core of the host clause (cf. Quirk *et al* 1985: 2.16), whereas the other subordinate clauses qualify the core in some way. Overall our expectation is borne out: complement clauses account for the highest percentage of subordinate clauses (40.2%), the nearest competitors being adverbial clauses (26.8%) and restrictive relative clauses (23.5%). Complement clauses also have the highest percentage in the totals for the two modes, but more clearly in speech (43.1% compared with 24.9% for adverbials) than in writing (33.4%, adverbials 31.1%). The proximity in percentages for writing is accounted for by the higher percentages of adverbial and restrictive relative clauses in the two categories of informational writing (academic and non-academic). As in writing, so in speech there is variation, since the monologues exhibit similar percentages for complement clauses and relative clauses. In absolute frequencies — as we can see from Table 6.2b — the conversations contain far fewer instances of other types of subordinate clauses than any of the other categories: 26.9 per thousand words. Perhaps the qualifications carried by the other subordinate clauses are not needed to the same extent in conversations, where immediate interactive clarification is possible.

Table 6.2b Complement clauses and other subordinate clauses per 1,000 words

Category	No of words	Complement clauses	Other sub-ordinate clauses	Total
Non-academic writing	8,508	17.3 (147	49.5 (421)	66.8 (568)
Academic writing	8,588	15.4 (132)	40.6 (349)	56.0 (481)
Letters	8,190	32.1 (263)	37.6 (308)	69.7 (571)
WRITTEN	25,286	21.4 (542)	42.6 (1,078)	64.1 (1,620)
Monologues	11,198	21.4 (240)	49.1 (550)	70.5 (790)
Broadcast discussions	11,161	36.1 (403)	38.1 (425)	74.2 (828)
Conversations	41,406	22.7 (941)	26.9 (1,113)	49.6 (2,054)
SPOKEN	63,765	24.8 (1,584)	32.7 (2,088)	57.6 (3,672)
Total	89,051	23.9 (2,126)	35.5 (3,166)	59.4 (5,292)

In Table 6.3 we look exclusively at complement clauses, and we separate them into finite and nonfinite types. The table shows a clear distinction between speech and writing ($P < 0.001$).

Table 6.3 Finite and nonfinite complement clauses

Category	Finite	Nonfinite	Total
Non-academic writing	44.9% (66)	55.1% (81)	100% (147)
Academic writing	34.1% (45)	65.9% (87)	100% (132)
Letters	44.9% (118)	55.1% (145)	100% (263)
WRITTEN	42.3% (229)	57.7% (313)	100% (542)
Monologues	68.7% (165)	31.2% (75)	100% (240)
Broadcast discussions	68.7% (277)	31.3% (126)	100% (403)
Conversations	71.5% (673)	28.5% (268)	100% (941)
SPOKEN	70.4% (1,115)	29.6% (469)	100% (1,584)
Total	63.2% (1,344)	36.8% (782)	100% (2,126)

The relative proportions of finite and nonfinite complement clauses are reversed in the two modes. There is no significant variation among the spoken categories, and among the written categories, letters and non-academic writing display the same percentages. The apparent differences among the three categories of writing, and among the three categories of speech, were not found to be significant (P = 0.09 and 0.49 respectively). Nonfinite clauses involve a greater degree of compression, so that it is reasonable to expect them to occur more frequently in writing, which tends to be more compact. Similar differences for nonfinite clauses in general are recorded by Beaman (1984: 64f.) and by Chafe (1982: 40f), though Chafe includes preposed participles in his counts. They based their counts on a different selection of data from each other and from us: Beaman contrasts narrative speech with narrative writing, whereas Chafe contrasts informal conversations with formal academic papers. Chafe's sets of samples parallel our categories of conversations and academic writing. Beaman draws on more limited and more artificial uses of language, since the narratives were elicited after the subjects viewed the same film.

Taking our investigation a step further, we now examine finite and nonfinite complement clauses in turn. We begin by distinguishing between the different types of finite clause. The four named types are exemplified below: *that*-clauses [2], zero *that*-clauses [3], nominal relative clauses [4], and *wh*-clauses [5].

[2] Archaeological and philological evidence in fact confirms *that early Rome was the product of a union of Latin and Sabine communes.* [W2A–001–9]

[3] I knew *it was not the answer.* [W2B–012–112]

[4] But he was just painting *what he wanted to paint* and the quality was variable [S1A–015–85]

[5] Uh an American lady that I gave a lecture uhm on architecture to fairly recently said she was able to take her sons around London telling them *which was Doric Ionic and Corinthian* [S2A–024–34]

Table 6.4a displays the frequencies per thousand words for each type of finite clause, and their distribution across the text categories.[5] Finite complement clauses as a whole are much less frequent in the two categories of informational writing, a difference that may be largely attributed to the low number of zero that-clauses and nominal relative clauses (cf. Quirk, *et al* 1985: 15.8f). Nominal relative clauses are generally fewer in written English than in spoken English, a point made by Beaman (1984: 63) for written and spoken narratives (0 versus 2.2, compared with our 0.7 versus 2.7). There are relatively few *wh*-interrogative clauses in our data, and a roughly similar frequency in the spoken and written components. In contrast, Beaman found no *wh*-clauses in writing as compared with a frequency of 2.1 per thousand words in speech, but their absence in her written material may be ascribed to the dependence of the written narrative on a film, since the narration of events would not call for indirect speech. Zero *that*-clauses are *that*-clauses in which the subordinator *that* has been omitted — an option available when the clauses are not functioning as subject (cf. Quirk *et al* 1985: 15.4). *That*-clauses constitute the most frequent type of finite complement clause. Chafe (1982: 44) found a difference in his data between informal conversations and expository prose (6.0 and 10.4 *that*-clauses per thousand words respectively), whilst Beaman (1984: 62) found the reverse proportions in her narrative texts (6.6 for spoken and 3.8 for written). Like Beaman, Biber (1988: 231) reports a greater frequency for *that*-clauses in spoken genres. Our data tend to support Chafe's view, though the findings are not strongly significant (P = 0.004). As Table 6.4b shows, the stylistic option of omitting *that* is adopted in the majority of instances in the two informal categories, letters and conversations, and generally rejected in the two formal written categories.[6] There seems to be a tendency towards a greater use of *that*-clauses in writing than in speech (P = 0.006).

Table 6.4a Types of finite complement clauses per 1,000 words

Category	No. of words	*That*	Zero *that*	Nominal relative	*wh-*	Other	Total
Non-academic writing	8,508	4.7 (40)	0.8 (7)	0.6 (5)	1.2 (10)	0.5 (4)	7.7 (66)
Academic writing	8,588	3.8 (33)	0.3 (3)	0.3 (2)	0.7 (6)	0.1vå1)	5.2 (45)
Letters	8,190	2.1 (17)	7.2 (59)	1.2 (10)	2.2 (18)	1.7 (14)	14.4 (118)
WRITTEN	25,286	3.5 (90)	2.7 (69)	0.7 (17)	1.3 (34)	0.7 (19)	9.0 (229)
Monologues	11,198	5.7 (64)	2.6 (29)	3.3 (37)	1.9 (21)	1.2 (14)	14.7 (165)
Broadcast discussions	11,161	10.2 (114)	7.5 (84)	2.9 (33)	1.3 (15)	2.8 (31)	24.8 (277)
Conversations	41,406	2.8 (117)	6.1 (254)	2.4 (101)	0.9 (37)	4.0 (164)	16.2 (673)
SPOKEN	63,765	4.6 (295)	5.7 (367)	2.7 (171)	1.1 (73)	3.3 (209)	17.5 (1,115)
Total	89,051	4.3 (385)	4.9 (436)	2.1 (188)	1.2 (107)	2.6 (228)	15.1 (1,344)

Table 6.4b *That*-clauses and zero *that*-clauses

Category	That	Zero that	Total
Non-academic writing	85.1% (40)	14.9% (7)	100% (47)
Academic writing	91.7% (33)	8.3% (3)	100% (36)
Letters	22.4% (17)	77.3% (59)	100% (76)
WRITTEN	56.6% (90)	43.4% (69)	100% (159)
Monologues	68.8% (64)	31.2% (29)	100% (93)
Broadcast discussions	57.6% (114)	42.4% (84)	100% (198)
Conversations	31.5% (117)	68.5% (254)	100% (371)
SPOKEN	44.6% (295)	55.4% (367)	100% (662)
Total	46.9% (385)	53.1% (436)	100% (821)

The distribution of nonfinite clause types is shown in Table 6.5: *to*-infinitive clauses [6], bare infinitive clauses [7], *for to* infinitive clauses [8], *-ing* clauses [9], and *-ed* clauses [10].

[6] I would much prefer *to tell you one-to-one.* [W1B-008–58]

[7] There were to be problems later when John Dickens could no longer afford to pay the tuition fees of his daughter but on this occasion her prospects seemed bright indeed; bright compared with those of her brother who was one of the family assembled to see *Princess Augusta congratulate Fanny on her achievement* [...] [W2B–006–55]

[8] It's also important *for management to provide an environment in which people and ideas can develop* [S2A–037–59]

[9] This can make *entering data* very laborious. [W2A–016–68]

[10] So uhm the ideal of selling songs appeals from that point of view to to actually hear *them done well* [S1A–033–68]

Table 6.5 Types of nonfinite complement clauses per 1,000 words

Category	No. of words	*To* infinitive	Bare infinitive	*For to* infinitive	*-ing*	*-ed*	Total
Non-academic writing	8,508	6.0 (51)	0.3 (3)	0.5 (4)	2.5 (21)	0.2 (2)	9.5 (81)
Academic writing	8,588	8.3 (71)	- (0)	- (0)	1.6 (14)	0.2 (2)	10.1 (87)
Letters	8,190	12.9 (106)	1.6 (13)	0.2 (2)	2.7 (22)	0.2 (2)	17.7 (145)
WRITTEN	25,286	9.0 (228)	0.6 (16)	0.2 (6)	2.2 (57)	0.2 (6)	12.4 (313)
Monologues	11,198	5.1 (57)	0.3 (4)	0.1 (1)	0.9 (10)	0.3 (3)	6.7 (75)
Broadcast discussions	11,161	7.5 (84)	0.8 (9)	0.6 (7)	1.9 (21)	0.4 (5)	11.3 (126)
Conversations	41,406	4.5 (188)	0.3 (14)	0.1 (5)	1.2 (52)	0.2 (9)	6.5 (268)
SPOKEN	63,765	5.1 (329)	0.4 (27)	0.4 (13)	1.3 (83)	0.3 (17)	7.3 (469)
Total	89,051	6.2 (557)	0.5 (43)	0.4 (19)	1.6 (140)	0.2 (23)	8.8 (782)

There is no significant difference in their distribution between speech and writing. Within the spoken component, there is again no significant variation; in the written component the prevalence of zeros and low figures precludes the application of significance tests. *To*–infinitive clauses are more frequent in writing than in speech, a result in agreement with what Beaman (1984: 64) found. The difference between the two modes is less striking in our data (9.0 in writing and 5.1 in speech) than in the data adduced by Beaman (7.6 versus 2.5). However, there is considerable variation within the modes, particularly in writing. Formality is not a factor in our data, since the informal category of letters has by far the most *to*-infinitive clauses. The other nonfinite clauses do not yield significant differences in our data either between speech and writing. Within the two modes, the prevalence of low figures impeded the application of significance tests.[7]

Table 6.6a Syntactic functions of complement clauses per 1,000 words

Category	No. of words	Subject as complement	Verb complements	Adjective complements	Total
Non-academic writing	8,508	4.1 (35)	10.1 (86)	1.9 (16)	16.1 (137)
Academic writing	8,588	3.4 (29)	7.7 (66)	3.0 (26)	14.1 (121)
Letters	8,190	2.4 (20)	23.3 (191)	3.2 (26)	28.9 (237)
WRITTEN	25,286	3.3 (84)	13.6 (343)	2.7 (68)	19.6 (495)
Monologues	11,198	2.8 (32)	15.6 (175)	2.1 (24)	20.6 (231)
Broadcast discussions	11,161	4.6 (52)	27.9 (312)	2.1 (24)	34.8 (388)
Conversations	41,406	1.8 (76)	19.6 (812)	1.1 (44)	22.5 (932)
SPOKEN	63,765	2.5 (160)	20.4 (1,299)	1.4 (92)	24.3 (1,551)
Total	89,051	2.7 (244)	18.4 (1,642)	1.8 (160)	23.0 (2,046)

We now turn to the syntactic functions of complement clauses in general terms. Table 6.6a distinguishes their function as subject from their other functions as complement of verb and adjective. In this table and in those that follow, we are counting functions and so we treat coordinated clauses as having a single function. For example, the coordinated clauses in [1] — repeated below for convenience — constitute one direct object.

[1] When the PCB has been etched and trimmed, ensure *that all mounting holes are in line and a PP3 battery slips easily between the two protrusions each side of the square cutout*, as filing a completed board is awkward and may damage components. [W2B-032-64]

The highest proportion of subject clauses occurs in the formal categories of informational writing, whereas the lowest occurs in the informal categories of letters and conversations.

In Table 6.6b we look exclusively at the subject clauses, distinguishing those in subject position [11]–[12] from those that are extraposed when their position is occupied by anticipatory *it* [13]–[14]:

[11] Using only the guide described above may lead to a 'techno-centric' system. [W2A–016–48]

[12] Uh then *what I had in mind* was that at the end of the sentence grammar which is a necessary condition of the text grammar of course one would then be able to uh take up the knowledge system that had been developed [...] [S1A–024–110]

[13] It is indeed tempting *to say that at this time the Italians had become a nation.* [W2A–001–16]

[14] But it's unlikely *that enough oil-booms can be placed around the islands to protect them*, and so it is possible *that those turtles which escape the slick will find themselves with nowhere to breed*. [W2B–029–88]

Extraposition is shown to be the norm. It is especially the preferred choice in writing, where postponement of the subject occurs in 81% of the possible instances. The preference is much less conspicuous in speech, and indeed monologues are exceptional in that non-extraposed subjects occur slightly more frequently.

Table 6.6b Subject clauses

Category	Subject	Extraposed subject	Total
Non-academic writing	20% (7)	80% (28)	100% (35)
Academic writing	10.3% (3)	89.7% (26)	100% (29)
Letters	30% (6)	70% (14)	100% (20)
WRITTEN	19% (16)	81% (68)	100% (84)
Monologues	53.1% (17)	46.9% (15)	100% (32)
Broadcast discussions	38.5% (20)	61.5% (32)	100% (52)
Conversations	48.7% (37)	51.3% (39)	100% (76)
SPOKEN	46.2% (74)	53.8% (86)	100% (160)
Total	36.9% (90)	63.1% (154)	100% (244)

Finally, in Table 6.6c we examine the different functions of verb complement clauses. As we might expect, direct objects are by far the most common. Their frequency is further boosted if we merge the columns of direct object, extraposed object and transitive complement,[8] and possibly also prepositional object. We were surprised to observe the much lower frequency of direct objects in informational writing and in the monologues. Writing and speech contrast prominently in their use of subject complement clauses, the written categories having far fewer.

Table 6.6c Verb complements per 1,000 words

Category	No. of words	Direct object	Extraposed object	Subject complement	Transitive complement	Prepositional object	Object complement	Total
Non-academic writing	8,508	5.4 (46)	– (0)	1.1 (9)	3.1 (26)	0.5 (1)	0.1 (1)	10.1 (86)
Academic writing	8,588	5.0 (43)	– (0)	0.9 (8)	1.6 (14)	0.1 (1)	– (0)	7.7 (66)
Letters	8,190	17.6 (144)	0.1 (1)	1.5 (12)	3.4 (28)	0.7 (6)	– (0)	23.3 (191)
WRITTEN	25,286	9.2 (233)	0.1 (1)	1.2 (29)	2.7 (68)	0.4 (11)	0.1 (1)	13.6 (343)
Monologues	11,198	8.7 (97)	0.1 (1)	3.7 (42)	2.6 (29)	0.3 (4)	0.2 (2)	15.6 (175)
Broadcast discussions	11,161	20.5 (229)	0.2 (2)	3.9 (44)	3.0 (34)	0.2 (2)	0.1 (1)	27.9 (312)
Conversations	41,406	14.6 (607)	0.2 (9)	2.9 (120)	1.3 (55)	0.5 (20)	0.1 (1)	19.6 (812)
SPOKEN	63,765	14.6 (933)	0.2 (12)	3.2 (206)	1.8 (118)	0.4 (26)	0.1 (4)	20.4 (1,299)
Total	89,051	13.1 (1,166)	0.1 (13)	2.6 (235)	2.1 (186)	0.4 (37)	0.1 (5)	18.4 (1,642)

We have observed a number of interesting points about complement clauses in our data. Complement clauses constitute the highest percentage of subordinate clauses, especially in dialogues. *That*-clauses are preferred over zero *that*-clauses in the formal categories in both speech and writing, and there is a preference in favour of extraposed subject clauses in both modes, though the preference is more prominent in writing. In accordance with our expectations, most verb complement clauses are direct objects. The most conspicuous result relates to the overall relative proportions of finite and nonfinite complement clauses. Our investigation has shown a clear distinction between speech and writing along this measure, and within the two modes there is no significant variation. In speech, the majority of complement clauses are finite, while in writing nonfinite complement clauses are the most frequent type.

Notes

1 Some theories dispense with the term *clause*, using *sentence* for a clause that is contained within a sentence, though they tend to retain traditional terms such as *relative clause*. Clauses, both nonfinite and finite, have been considered by some linguists to be a type of phrase (cf. Huddleston 1984: 117). Matthews (1981: 160) notes that present usage of the term is 'confused' and discusses its uses by linguists (pp 165f.).

2 Subjective and objective are employed in analyzing some noun phrases with genitives or *of* phrases, as in *the reviewers' criticism of the musical*, but these express semantic relationships that are analogous to those found in their paraphrases by clauses. Similar paraphrases are invoked for compounds such as *earthquake* and *book review*.

3 *Complement* is here used in a wider sense than in Quirk *et al* (1985, cf. 2.17f), since it embraces subjects, objects and obligatory adverbials as well as subject complements and object complements. In regarding the subject as a complement, we agree with (for example) Huddleston 1984: 180f and Noonan 1985: 42f.

4 The research for this paper is indebted to a grant from the Leverhulme Trust. The compilation of ICE–GB was supported in part by grant R000 23 2077 from the Economic and Social Research Council. For the source of the texts in the Leverhulme Corpus, see

Greenbaum and Nelson (1995).

5 The 'other' column in Table 4a is made up largely of reported clauses in direct speech, that is, clauses which are complements of reporting verbs.

6 In our data there is only one instance of a *that*-clause functioning as subject. It occurs in non-academic writing and its exclusion from Table 4b would not materially affect the relative proportions of *that* and zero *that*-clauses.

7 Chafe (1982: 44) provides a count of complement *to*-infinitive clauses, but they also include appositive clauses. Nevertheless, the ratio (8.8 in writing and 2.9 in speech) is close to that reported by Beaman. Both Chafe and Beaman refer to *-ing* participle clauses, but their criteria do not coincide with ours, since they included modifiers. As a result, they record far more instances than we do: Chafe (1982: 41) reports 20.7 in writing and 7.1 in speech, while Beaman (1984: 65) reports 22.8 in writing and 15.0 in speech.

8 Transitive complements are nonfinite clauses where the status of a noun phrase following the transitive verb is indeterminate, functioning as either object of the transitive verb or as subject of the nonfinite clause:

Well they don't like *you taking interior shots* [...] [SIA-009-12]

[...] I'll write to them and ask *them to send you an appointment* {SIA-051-349]

7 Methodologies for studying a corpus of doctor-patient interaction

JENNY THOMAS AND ANDREW WILSON

7.1 Introduction

There are many different ways of analyzing textual data. In this paper, we propose to compare three of the most commonly used approaches to the analysis of data in social scientific research: manual discourse analysis, analysis of questionnaires and computer content analysis. We will demonstrate that computer content analysis, despite the several criticisms which have been levelled against it, not only overcomes the shortcomings of straight quantitative analysis, but also has the potential to provide results which are in some respects comparable to manual discourse analysis (but with considerably less manual effort) and which in other respects usefully complement it. There are, of course, aspects of language — for example pragmatic strategies such as indirectness, conversational tactics such as blocking behaviours, discoursal features such as topic control and interruptions — which computer content analysis either cannot identify at all, or can identify only with difficulty. Even so, we believe that the practical advantages of automated analysis make the use of this method worthwhile.

Neither content analysis nor discourse analysis is new in the study of health worker-patient communication. Computer content analysis has been employed in the past in health communication research (e.g. Kelly and Sime 1990), as has discourse analysis (see, for example, Labov and Fanshel 1977, Grainger 1989, Robins and Wolf 1988, ten Have 1991). However, the merits of the two approaches have not been systematically compared. The fortuitous coincidence of two projects running at Lancaster University — an ESRC project[1] on the effectiveness of communication in a cancer support service the effectiveness of communication in a cancer support service (Thomas 1994a and b) and two SERC/EPSRC/DTI[2] projects on the automatic content analysis of spoken discourse (Wilson and Rayson 1993) — has enabled us to re-analyze some of the data which were manually analyzed in the ESRC project using the automatic content analyzer which we developed in the SERC/DTI and EPSRC/DTI projects. We therefore set out to compare the results offered by the two approaches.

7.2 Background to cancer research project

The overall aim of the study (which ran from October 1989 until March 1993) was to assess the effectiveness of communication between cancer patients and a range of health service carers (hospital doctors, general practitioners, support nurses, therapists, etc) in two adjoining District Health Authorities in the North West of England; the two areas have a similar demography and each has a consultant specializing in cancer.[3] The first District Health Authority (DHA-A) has a very elaborate and comprehensive psychosocial cancer support service and a staff committed to an holistic approach to the treatment of cancer (see McIllmurray 1993), while the neighbouring district (DHA-B) was without these services at the time the research was carried out. Some of the specific questions addressed in the project were:

- How well do patients and their relatives understand the diagnosis and treatment?
- Where does their information come from?
- Can patients and their families obtain the information they want, as and when they want it and can accept it?
- To what extent do the services provided improve/optimize communication and understanding?
- Are patients satisfied with the communication between themselves and their carers?

The study included both qualitative and quantitative research methods. The qualitative research took three forms: a preliminary ethnographic study of the cancer services in the two areas, long-term case studies of the interaction between cancer patients and their carers, and research interviews. Over a two and a half year period, a total of

75 case studies were conducted in the two DHAs. 415 recordings[4] were made, of which 279 were clinic consultations — i.e. consultations between the consultant oncologist and the patient, typically in the presence of a relative and sometimes (in DHA-A only) a cancer support nurse.

The quantitative research took the form of 270 questionnaires administered to different groups[5] of patients in the two DHAs (for more details see Thomas 1994a, 1994b, 1994c), including 50 patients attending the out-patient clinics of each of the two doctors. The questionnaires were complicated and touched upon extremely sensitive issues. For these reasons the questionnaire was always administered by a researcher — it was never left to the patient to fill it in for himself or herself.[6] In some questions patients were offered a choice, in others the response was left entirely open. Some questions were purely factual — relating to demographic issues or to specific aspects of the patient's illness/treatment — whilst other questions sought the patients' views on various issues.

7.3 The data

In total the qualitative research yielded approximately two million words; at the time of writing just over half of the recordings (1.25 million words) have been transcribed verbatim. Because the transcribed data required reformatting (see section 7.4 below), for this preliminary experiment we used only 10% of the transcribed corpus, taking data only from the oncology out-patient clinic sessions (i.e. interactions between patients, their relatives and a consultant oncologist), selected roughly equally from both districts.

7.4 Problems in combining methodologies

The only real difficulty which we encountered in combining methodologies was that of data format. Our content analysis software requires running text with standard punctuation. The original CancerCare data, however, were transcribed in stave format without punctuation, for ease of use in conversation analysis. They thus required considerable manual preprocessing for input into the content analyzer. If this method is to be adopted more widely, stave transcription will have to be discarded in favour of a SGML-based markup such as that being used in the British National Corpus (Crowdy 1995: 230-31). This form of annotation retains all the information encoded in stave transcription, but at the same time results in a punctuated, running text. It should, in principle, be **much** easier to design software which will convert SGML text to staves than vice versa.

7.5 Automatic content analysis

ACAMRIT (Automatic Content Analysis of Market Research Interview Transcripts) is a suite of programs for the computer-assisted analysis of English texts. The programs are intended primarily for the analysis of spoken discourse, but their application to written language has also been piloted (Wilson and Leech 1993).

As its name suggests, the central function of ACAMRIT is content analysis. However, ACAMRIT also includes a number of other modules which set it apart from other content analysis packages such as Textpack and even the more sophisticated programs such as the General Inquirer (Stone *et al.* 1966): these modules provide wider functionality for ACAMRIT and enable it to be used as a computational aid to discourse analysis in the paradigm of Fairclough (1993) and others, as well as for basic content analysis. In the following, we shall describe the various modules in the ACAMRIT program suite.

The input data which ACAMRIT accepts are machine-readable English texts in plain ASCII format, transcribed according to standard orthography. Although the system will operate on a raw unannotated ASCII text, the full range of features for comparative analysis can only be made use of if any desired subclassifications in the input data (e.g. gender, age) are marked up using Standard Generalized Markup Language (SGML). This can be done in full at the transcription stage, or the transcribers may employ a specially-designed shorthand markup which is converted by a special program (TOSGML) into full SGML markup.

The text is first run through the stochastic part-of-speech tagger Claws (Garside, Leech and Sampson 1987 and Garside, this volume), which assigns a grammatical word-class (such as singular common noun, comparative adjective, past tense form of lexical verb) to each lexical item and syntactic idiom in the text. Claws operates on the basis of a probability model based on previously analyzed and corrected data, and has a success rate of approximately 95–96%.

The part-of-speech tagged data are then passed to ACAMRIT's central program, the semantic tagger SEMTAG, whose role is to assign a semantic field category to every word and multi-word unit in the text.

The categories which are used in this analysis belong to the thesaural tradition in lexicography and are broadly based on the categories in the *Longman Lexicon of Contemporary English* (McArthur 1981); they represent both abstract and concrete lexical fields such as 'Colour', 'Power', 'Education', 'Happiness and Sadness' and so on. The categories are assigned on the basis of pattern matching between the text and two computer dictionaries developed for use with the program: a lexicon of single word forms and an idiom list of multi-word units. (The latter is comprised of phrasal verbs, multi-word proper nouns, genuine 'idioms', and other multi-word units which are felt to constitute phraseological units for the purpose of semantic analysis.) Some fixed patterns with many possible instantiations are instead tagged by automatic rules: for example, the pattern '*X*km', where '*X*' is a number, is automatically assigned the category of linear measurement. There are also a number of words and multi-word units which cannot easily be classified into just one category: for instance, *sportswear* belongs almost equally in the categories 'Sport' and 'Clothing'. In these cases, we assign what are known as 'slash tags', where a word is classified in both categories and the tags representing the categories are separated by the slash character. The 'slash tag' can then be treated as a unitary category, or one of the two categories can be selected at a later stage in the analysis as the category which is to be counted in that instance.

The lexical resources for SEMTAG are constantly updated as new material is analyzed. To reduce the amount of manual work in this stage — at least as far as the single-word lexicon is concerned — it is possible to include any word-form in the lexicon and analyze all textual variants of it by means of a two-way lemmatization program (LEMMINGS) based on the work of Beale (1989). LEMMINGS reduces both text words and lexicon words to the base form (e.g. *examines*, *examined*, *examining*, would be reduced to the base form *examine*) and pattern matching for semantic category assignment then takes place on the basis of these base forms.

At present, SEMTAG can assign the correct category to approximately 80–90% of the words and multi-word units in a text. This rate of disambiguation is founded upon four main methods:

(1) the use of the part-of-speech categories assigned by Claws;

(2) the intuitive frequency-ordering of the possible semantic categories for each word/multi-word unit in the lexical resources (e.g. on the basis of frequency-ordering the word *clinical* would be assigned first to the semantic category 'Medicine', second to the semantic category 'Unfriendly');

(3) a module (AUXRULE) which disambiguates the auxiliary and main verb senses of *be*, *do* and *have* with a high degree of accuracy on the basis of their close collocation, or lack of collocation, with specific participial forms: e.g. *We haven't proven that it's recurred* (auxiliary *have*) vs. *... you do have a form of skin cancer, Mrs X* (main verb *have*);

(4) the preference of 'domain' senses over others (e.g. the noun *condition* most frequently has the sense of 'Physical property', but if we specify to the program that our text falls into the medical domain then it will automatically prefer the sense of 'Illness' over the other possible semantic categories of 'Physical property', 'Necessity' and 'Health').[7]

At this stage the semantically-annotated text may optionally be further analyzed. Traditional criticisms of content analysis as a methodology (e.g. Billig 1988 and some of the respondents in Barcus 1969) have focused particularly on the lack of any contextualization of the concept frequency analyses. For example, a high frequency of the concept 'Bad' in a text may tell us that there is a strong emphasis on negative evaluation, but it cannot tell us much more and thus is perhaps not such a useful observation: the question naturally arises, what or whom does the speaker/writer consider to be bad? ACAMRIT attempts to resolve this problem through the identification of key syntactico-semantic links (see Wilson 1993). The data are first run through a probabilistic noun phrase parser (NPEXT), developed on the EC-funded ET10-63 project (Garside, McEnery and Rayson 1993), which marks the maximal extent of each noun phrase in the text and thus enables links to be made to the entire relevant noun phrase (e.g. *Lancaster District Health Authority*) rather than to just a part of it. A program called MATRIX then makes use of characteristic part-of-speech sequence patterns derived from previously analyzed data to:

(1) link adjectives with the nouns which they modify (e.g. in the question 'What were your original symptoms?' *original* is linked to *symptoms*, so that an analyst wanting to investigate the contextual meaning and use of *original* can do so);

(2) link negative articles and particles with the items that they negate (e.g. in the statements 'We haven't decided yet' and 'It isn't inevitable' *n't* and *decided* and *n't* and *inevitable* are linked, so that the collocations are allocated to the semantic categories X6– ('Decision-minus') and A7– ('Probability-minus') respectively, rather than having the two negative particles assigned independently (and unhelpfully) to the category 'Negative'. The treatment of negation includes so-called 'transferred negation', which is especially important in colloquial spoken English (see Wilson 1991) (e.g. *I don't think, Mrs X, that we've met before* [= *I think we have not met before*] is tagged as 'not met' rather than 'not think');

(3) link modifying adverbs with the adjectives that they modify. As we shall show in section 7.6.1 below, there are occasions when it is useful to compare the use of boosters in different sets of data or across different text types, but more often the analyst wants to know exactly what is being modified (e.g. in the question 'Did all that come as a very great surprise to you?' *very* is linked to *great*).

It is envisaged that these key links will be extended in the future to include other important relations for discourse analysis, e.g. agency. The key links module has two important roles to play in the overall text analysis: first, it enables the relational aspects of concepts such as evaluation, agency, etc. to be handled in a quantitative manner, and second, it enables negated concepts to be mapped into the appropriate negative categories in the statistical analysis (for example, the collocation *not good* would be classified with *bad* rather than as two words in the independent categories 'Negative' and 'Good').

As described above, the SEMTAG module classifies words in texts according to a thesaural classification of the English lexis (what is known in the field as 'conceptual analysis'). However, many social scientists prefer to carry out 'content analysis' which, strictly speaking, involves the classification of words according to the operationalization of a theory or research hypothesis rather than on general semantic grounds.[8] Previously, the performance of such content analyses has required a different dictionary for each theory or hypothesis. In contrast, ACAMRIT includes a module (MAPPING) which enables word + sense combinations to be mapped automatically into research-specific **content** categories (which are developed quite separately from semantic categories), thus obviating the need for separate dictionaries. Note that we are not here referring to the domain-specific semantic reclassification of particular lexical items (for example, in the CancerCare data recategorization was required in the case of the expression *waterworks*, which is never used in its normal sense of 'a public utility' (SEMCAT 01.2/H1c), but as a euphemism used by one of the doctors to refer to the urinary system (SEMCAT B1). Similarly *lump* (originally categorized only as O4.4 — 'Shape') required an additional tag to re-allocate it to the same category as *tumour* (B2–) when the data fall into the domain of 'cancer'). However, as we shall show in section 7.6.1 below, an important issue arose in relation to a number of categories: we found that Dr B used vastly more highly technical terms than Dr A. In any future research on the CancerCare data this is an issue we shall want to explore and (regardless of a word's semantic category) we shall give some domain-specific items the **content tag** 'Technical' (*urino-genital system*) or 'Informal' (*waterworks*) and perhaps also introduce content tags such as 'Specific' (*tumour*, *cancer*) versus 'General' (*lump*, *disease/illness*).[9] To accomplish this the researcher simply needs to produce a set of rules for mapping the **semantic field categories** (and individual words in the case of exceptions) onto **content categories**. The flexibility of ACAMRIT means that texts can be examined from both general semantic and research-theoretical perspectives.

The final module of the ACAMRIT system is the concordance and statistics package X-SEMSTAT (for X-Windows) or SEMSTAT (for ordinary text-based terminals). This module provides a rich range of information and data retrieval options for the analyst. Making use of the SGML markup, it is possible to split the data into categories according to any encoded variables (for example, age, sex, social class) and make comparisons on the basis of these. (In addition, in the case of the CancerCare corpus, we were able to explore differences between the language use of the two doctors, between the doctors and the health visitors, cancer support nurses and between patients and any of their carers. It would also be possible to examine the effect of type of cancer, 'stage' of cancer, type of treatment, etc.). The program (X-)SEMSTAT provides three main forms of information:

7.5.1 Basic text information

Overall word counts, type/token ratios, and mean lengths of turns are provided for the entire text and for the various subclassifications which have been defined.

7.5.2 Frequency counts

Frequency listings, both raw and percentage, can be called up for the word forms themselves and/or for any level of linguistic annotation (parts of speech, semantic field categories, content categories), in any combination. The results of the various linkings of adjectives, negatives, modifiers and nouns can also be displayed in this format. Frequency listings can be sorted alphabetically, on frequency, or on any of the annotation types. This sorting can be in either ascending or descending order. It is also possible to produce a reverse index of the words in the text. Where subclassifications of the text have been defined, the frequencies of items in each class are presented in parallel columns and χ^2-tests are automatically performed to test whether the difference between classes on a given item is statistically significant. Alternatively, the results of analyses of other texts or of a normative corpus can also be loaded into the system (for comparative purposes the χ^2 is also calculated for these data).

7.5.3 Concordances

By selecting items from the frequency listings, concordances of those items can be called up. The user has full control over the amount of context shown and what linguistic annotations (if any) are displayed in the concordance. Information about the subclassification from which each example is taken can also be displayed if desired.

7.6 Data analysis

The greatest difference in the questionnaire responses of cancer patients attending oncology outpatient clinics in DHA-A and DHA-B related to the third section of the questionnaire, in which we investigated the emotional support available to patients in the two district health authorities. In tables 7.1 and 7.2 we reproduce the relevant questions and a summary of the questionnaire responses reported in Thomas (1994b).

Question 14 *Have you had the opportunity of talking about your feelings concerning your illness to any health care workers involved in your care?*

Table 7.1 Number of patients having opportunity to talk about their feelings

	Clinic A	Clinic B
Yes	40	30
No	10	20

These results give us a χ^2 of 4.762 (1 d.f., $P < 0.03$), a highly significant difference between the two clinics.

Question 22 *In general, how much emotional support do you feel you have had from health care workers involved in your care?*

Table 7.2 Patients' perceptions of the degree of emotional support given by healthcare workers

	Clinic A	Clinic B
A lot of support	22	11
Enough support	23	26
Some support	2	6
Not enough support	1	6
Support not wanted	2	1

These results give us a χ^2 of 9.755 (4 d.f., P <0.05), again a significant difference between the two clinics.

In the mini-study which follows, we shall try to show that statistical evidence from ACAMRIT can explain the difference in satisfaction between the two groups in terms of the language used by the two doctors.

7.6.1 Frequency counts

Twenty-five ACAMRIT semantic categories show statistical differences between the language used by the two doctors. The χ^2 values ranged from 55.2 ('Discourse particles') to 3.9 ('Good'). Of the ten categories showing the highest statistical significance (see table 7.3), a startling total of eight categories[10] ('Discourse particles', first and second person pronouns, 'Totality', 'Boosters', 'Downtoners', 'Present time', 'Thought' and 'Hedges') load positively onto Factor 1 of Biber's (1988) study. Biber's factor 1 is a continuum from, at one end, a highly 'involved', 'interactive' style to an 'informative' style at the other. Biber (1988: 105) notes:

> The features with positive weights on Factor 1 are ... complex. All of them can be associated in one way or another with an involved, non-informational focus, due to a primarily interactive or affective purpose ... These features can be characterized as verbal, interactional, affective, fragmented, reduced in form, and generalized in content.

A further category 'Female person' (SEMCAT S2.1), proved on inspection to relate to the address form *Mrs*, which has an obvious relationship to the 'involved', 'interactive' style. Here we have massive evidence, in terms of linguistic features shown by ACAMRIT to be statistically significant, that Dr A was very concerned with the interpersonal aspects of the (sometimes devastating) information he had to convey to his patients. This finding is completely supported by the ethnographic studies, discourse analysis and research interviews.

Table 7.3 Ten semantic categories showing highest significance[11]

Semantic category	Example	Dr A	Dr B	χ^2
Discourse particles	*y'know*	9.24%	5.13%	55.2
Pronouns	(see table 7.4)	17.47%	12.23%	42.9
Comparison	*as*	0.23%	0.0%	11.8
Female person	*Mrs*	0.2%	0.0%	10.5
Totality [Amplifier]	*all, complete, every*	0.43%	0.1%	10.4
Boosters	*very, really, jolly*	0.98%	0.44%	9.7
Downtowners	*a bit*	0.55%	0.19%	8.5
Present time		0.58%	0.21%	8.2
Thought [Private verbs]	*think*	0.9%	0.46%	6.9
Hedges		0.9%	0.46%	6.9

In Biber's research only first and second person pronouns emerged with a high loading for 'interactiveness'. In table 7.4 below we have separated out first and second person pronouns from SEMTAG Z8 (i.e. excluding *you* occurring as a discourse particle, such as *you know*).

Table 7.4 Breakdown of semantic category 'Pronouns' (raw frequencies)[12]

	Dr A	Dr B
1st and 2nd person pronouns	374	255
3rd person pronouns	144	170

The far greater use by Dr A of first and second person pronouns is shown to be highly significant (χ^2 = 15.647 (1 d.f., P = 0.0001)).

Among the 'top ten' significant categories only for the semantic category 'Comparison' (category A6) was there no obvious reason why Dr A used so many more comparisons than Dr B.

Table 7.5 shows the remaining fifteen significant categories identified by ACAMRIT.

Table 7.5 Remaining fifteen significant categories

Semantic category	Example	Dr A	Dr B	χ^2
Start	*begin, starting*	0.23%	0.04%	6.7
Cause	*depend, reason,*	0.55%	0.23%	6.4
Groups	*group, team, organisation*	0.18%	0.02%	6.4
Being	Main verb *To be*	5.11%	3.99%	6.3
Farming/growing	*(tissue) culture*	0.0%	0.15%	6.1
Measurement	*dose, dosage*	0.0%	0.15%	6.1
Change	*switch, progress*	0.48%	0.19%	5.9
Body		1.3%	1.95%	5.7
Power	*control, fix*	0.28%	0.08%	5.5
Treatment		2.38%	1.7%	5.3
General actions		1.9%	1.3%	5.3
Modality	*ought to, should*	0.03%	0.17%	4.5
Learning	*learn, find out*	0.03%	0.17%	4.5
Family/kinship	*family, husband, relation*	0.18%	0.04%	4.4
Good	*dandy, magic, good, promising*	0.6%	0.32%	3.9

In Table 7.5 one category — 'Being' (or, more precisely, main verb as opposed to auxiliary *be*[13]) — loads positively onto Biber's factor 1, while 'Modals' (specifically non-epistemic modals) load negatively onto factor 1. In order to explain why the remaining categories were selected by ACAMRIT we had to use the concordancing facilities described in section 7.5.3 above.

Five semantic categories which were significant for Dr A ('Start', 'Cause', 'Change', 'Power' and 'Treatment') proved to relate wholly or mainly to explanations offered by the doctor to the patient of the treatment which he or she would receive. Of the nine instances of SEMCAT 'Start', all but two related to descriptions of new forms of treatment. All the instances of SEMCAT 'Cause' referred to the functions of new medication or treatment which were to be used; of the nineteen occurrences of SEMCAT 'Change', 13 related to explanations of changes/modifications in the patient's treatment, 4 to changes in the patient's emotional state and 2 to changes in the patient's disease. The 11 occurrences of the category 'Power' initially struck us as odd. However, when we checked the concordances we found that in every case reference was being made to control of symptoms or side effects. The final category 'Treatment' is self-explanatory. These statistics confirm the findings of the discourse analysis that Dr A spent far more time than Dr B explaining to patients the course their treatment would take, what side effects (both physical and emotional) they could expect, etc.

Four semantic categories ('Farming/growing', 'Measurement', 'Body' and 'Learning') emerged as significant for Dr B. At first we were utterly bewildered by the frequency of occurrence of semantic category F4 ('Farming/growing')[14]; this, it transpired, was because Dr B kept referring to *culture*, but we found that in each of the 8 occurrences the word was being used in the sense of the *tissue culture*! Dr B had almost twice as many occurrences of category B1 ('Body') as Dr A (102 occurrences versus 52). But the differences revealed by the concordancing went further than that: while Dr A's 'Body' vocabulary was largely non-technical (e.g. *vagina*) or informal (*tummy*), Dr B used a large number of highly technical terms (*low grade endometrial stromal sarcoma, epithelium*). It also included a rather entertaining example of a miscategorized body part (an idiom we had not then entered in the idiomlist): *horse's mouth*! Dr B had 9 instances of category X2.3+ ('Learning') as against 1 instance for Dr A. In every case this related to finding out the results of tests or to drugs research. These statistics confirm the findings of the discourse analysis and ethnographic studies that Dr B spent a lot of time explaining in great technical detail the progression of the patient's disease.

Two semantic categories ('Groups' and 'Family/kinship') which the discourse analysis had led us to expect to emerge as significant in the talk of Dr A did so. Dr A was always very concerned to indicate to patients the support services and cancer support groups available to them and to involve the patients' family, friends, etc. in their care and to attend to the emotional and practical needs of their significant others.

Finally, we found a small, but significant difference between the two doctors in their use of positive evaluation and optimistic language as in the following example from Dr A: *Zofran is absolutely magic for controlling sickness.*

7.7 Conclusion

Perhaps the most obvious question to put at the end of this trial study is: did ACAMRIT reveal anything which we did not know already? The answer is 'no' (but we had already spent more than five years working with the two doctors and with the data). What ACAMRIT did do was to provide ample evidence from the language produced that Dr A's language was 'interactive' (in Biber's sense of the word), interpersonally-oriented and informal; Dr B's was more 'informational' (again, in Biber's usage), disease-centred and technical. Dr A's professed holistic, patient-centred approach to the treatment of cancer was amply reflected in aspects of language use unlikely to be within his conscious control.

On the positive side, ACAMRIT was able to reveal accurately and within minutes certain important aspects of the two doctors' language use which could only have been uncovered by months of painstaking work using traditional conversation analysis or discourse analysis. On the other hand, as we noted in the introduction, some aspects of their discourse (politeness, indirectness, topic control, interruptions, etc) could not be identified using ACAMRIT.

ACAMRIT would seem to offer a very accurate quick 'way in' for any researchers confronted with large quantities of data with which they are unfamiliar. But it would be foolish to ignore the fact that two of the approaches which we have here compared, and intend in future to combine, arise from research philosophies which are diametrically opposed. For the conversational analyst it is anathema to approach the data with preconceived ideas:

> Conversational analysis, as practised by Sacks, Schegloff and Jefferson ... is a rigorously empirical approach which avoids premature theory construction ... The methods are essentially

> *inductive*; search is made for recurring patterns across many records of naturally occurring conversations, in contrast to the immediate categorization of (usually) restricted data ... There is as little appeal as possible to intuitive judgements — they may, willy nilly, guide research, but they are not explanations and they certainly do not circumscribe the data; the emphasis is on what can actually be found to occur, not on what one would guess would be odd (or acceptable) if it were to do so. Intuition, it is claimed, is simply an unreliable guide in this area, as indeed it may be in other areas of linguistics. There is also a tendency to avoid analyses based on single texts. Instead, as many instances as possible of some particular phenomena are examined across texts ...
> (Levinson 1983: 286–7)

For the content analyst, on the other hand, those who approach their data without prior hypotheses and who go on 'fishing expeditions' are objects of mockery:

> When working with text, our alchemists are rarely interested in the tedious task of thinking through a theory and attempting to make the theory operational for content-analysis purposes. Instead, they argue, why not just *try* all the existing dictionaries and statistical techniques on their data? Who knows what pleasant surprise might result?
>
> After seeing this kind of approach again and again, it can only be concluded that, despite the enthusiasm of the moment, the results are almost never worth the effort. Without theory many of the statistically significant results tend to be fortuitous. A certain number of statistically significant results can always be expected by chance, and users generally can select those they like from the thousands of numbers produced by the computer. Further, the issue in research is usually not the null hypothesis. Simply to say that the world is not random is not saying much.
> (Ogilvie, Stone and Kelly 1982/1989: 221)

The sort of analysis carried out by ACAMRIT is theory-neutral. It can be used in any way the researcher pleases: to raise hypotheses or simply to confirm them.

Notes

1 Economic and Social Research Council (ESRC) Project No. R-000-23-1739.

2 SERC (the Science and Engineering Research Council) was replaced by the EPSRC (the Engineering and Physical Sciences Research Council) in 1994. The first of our projects (GR/F 36385), was funded by SERC and the second (project number GR/H 88152 IED4/1/5803) by its successor EPSRC, both in conjunction with Reflexions Communication Research and the Department of Trade and Industry.

3 At the time the research began there were only eight such consultant oncologists in *district* (i.e. local) — as opposed to *regional* — health authorities in England and Wales.

4 At the time of writing, approximately half of the recordings have been transcribed, yielding a corpus of 1.25 million words of spoken interaction between doctor and patient (279 recordings), cancer support nurse/health visitor and patient (73 recordings in DHA-A only) or research interviewer and patient (63 recordings).

5 Other groups who were compared using the questionnaire were 'urban' vs. 'rural' patients, patients treated surgically (with and without additional radiotherapy) vs. those receiving chemotherapy alone.

6 It was therefore possible for the researcher to abandon the interview if the patient became distressed. Wherever possible the questionnaire was coded immediately by the researcher.

7 In the future we are planning to work on the disambiguation of word senses on the basis of a numerical model of the senses of surrounding words in context. Thus in the CancerCare data the word *round* (which could be a noun, verb, adjective, adverb or preposition) would, in a particular syntactic context, be assigned the Claws tag 'singular noun'. On the basis of frequency-ordering within the English language the word would be interpreted as 'a round of events, talks' and assigned first to the semantic category N5 ('Quantity'). On the basis of frequency-ordering within the domain of discourse the word would be interpreted as 'ward round' and re-assigned to the category B3 ('Medical'), a semantic classification which would be confirmed by examining the semantic categories of words in the immediate linguistic context: 'On Fridays Dr McM does

his round at ten, straight after the oncology case conferences and before the out-patient clinic', four of which (*doctor*, *oncology*, *out-patient* and *clinic*) have already been assigned the semantic tag B3 as their main or most likely meaning.

8 For this distinction see Schmidt (1986).

9 This content tag could be important for verifying patients' degree of understanding of their condition (for example, we found that some patients were unclear about the meaning of *tumour*: one patient we interviewed maintained that he did not have cancer, only a tumour). It could also be significant in assessing a patient's psychological state: (we already knew from the discourse analysis and research issues that Dr A never used the word *cancer* until the patient used it himself or herself) and for identifying patients 'in denial' (people who know, at some level, that they have cancer but who will not admit it).

10 ACAMRIT semantic categories sometimes have different labels from those used by Biber. Where appropriate, we have shown Biber's label in brackets. ACAMRIT's 'totality', for example, is equivalent to Biber's 'Amplifiers' and our 'Thought' is equivalent to Biber's 'private verbs'.

11 Note that χ^2 is calculated on the raw frequencies, but we have given the figures in percentages in these tables for ease of comparison.

12 In Table 7.4 the chi-square is calculated on the basis of the 2 x 2 table rather than in relation to the sum of the remaining variation in the frequency profile as a whole, which is the basis for caluculation elsewhere.

13 See section 7.5 for a discussion of how ACAMRIT distinguishes main and auxiliary forms of verbs.

14 This category was subsequently renamed 'farming/cultivation'.

8 Using a corpus for stylistics research: speech and thought presentation

MICK SHORT, ELENA SEMINO and
JONATHAN CULPEPER

8.1 Introduction

It is particularly appropriate that this article, which is the first report on an ongoing corpus-based research project investigating patterns of speech and thought presentation in texts,[1] should be published in a collection of papers to honour Geoff Leech. Firstly, all three authors owe a considerable debt to him for his long-term, patient and intelligent support, both as a teacher and a colleague. Secondly, the corpus approach adopted here is one with which Geoff's name has been associated from the very early days of corpus linguistics. Geoff was spending Sunday afternoons creating what became the LOB corpus long before corpus work became fashionable and began to attract significant funding support. And finally, the model of speech and thought presentation (henceforward S&TP) used in our work is based upon that first presented in Leech and Short (1981), an influential work in prose stylistics. For the last thirty years, Geoff Leech has been at the forefront of a large range of developments in linguistics, and stylistics is one of a number of areas which would have been much the poorer without his work (see, for example, Leech 1966, 1969, 1985, 1992b, and Leech and Short 1981).

We will describe the establishment and preliminary results of a pilot research project which uses a corpus-based approach to examine patterns of S&TP in contemporary prose fiction and newspaper reports. The corpus is small (40 extracts of approximately 2,000 words each, giving a total corpus of 88,631 words), and is split into four roughly equal parts. There are 10 extracts from each of the following areas: (a) 'high' literature (21,911 words), (b) popular fiction (23,301 areas: (a) 'high' literature (21,911 words), (b) popular fiction (23,301 words), (c) broadsheet newspapers (22,814 words) and (d) tabloid newspapers (20,605 words). Unlike most present linguistic corpora, then, this one has been constructed not for general research purposes, but with some very specific research aims in mind:

(i) To test out the categories (including their definitions and functions) of Leech and Short's (1981) model of S&TP. We have chosen this model not just because it is local to Lancaster, but also because of the fact that it has been used by many other scholars for both literary and non-literary analysis (e.g. McKenzie 1987, Roeh and Nir 1990, Simpson 1993). There has been a tendency (including in Leech and Short 1981) to base discussion on the invention and/or quotation of prototypical examples. We decided to investigate whether the Leech and Short model is robust and explicit enough to cope with the analysis of texts not chosen to be 'good' (i.e. untroublesome?) examples of S&TP.

(ii) To enable us to investigate the similarities and differences in the presence and patterning of the S&TP categories in literary and non-literary texts. In stylistics and literary theory there has been considerable debate over the last few years concerning whether literary texts have special linguistic properties (see Sell 1991 for a number of papers on this topic and extensive references to previous work). Given the predominance of the study of viewpoint in 20th century criticism of the novel, S&TP — one of the most prominent areas associated with viewpoint manipulation — would appear to be a good candidate for investigation with respect to the 'special language of literature' claim.

(iii) To investigate a linguistic phenomenon which is textual/discoursal rather than to restrict ourselves (as has usually been the case for corpus studies to date) to what, in textual terms, are relatively low-level grammatical and lexical phenomena. Instances of the S&TP categories, although based canonically on well-known deictic contrasts (some grammaticalized and some not), also depend for their recognition on pragmatic and contextual factors.

(iv) To open up new directions in stylistics and corpus linguistics. So far there are few scholars interested in both areas (honourable exceptions include Biber 1988, Louw 1993, Rissanen *et al* 1993 and Taavitsainen 1994).

(v) To explore the possibilities for automatic 'parsing' of texts for S&TP categories (see section 8.4 below).

The corpus approach has some significant advantages for us. It enables us to test out hypotheses in an explicit, empirical way, and to quantify the presence of categories and patterns of categories across text-types. Our results can only be preliminary, of course. This pilot project does not establish a large enough corpus to be sure that what we have found is truly representative of the text-types examined, and there are many other text-types which could be usefully explored in a larger project. But we believe that our work is important in helping to put what has traditionally been an area of armchair-based research onto a firmer empirical footing. We hope that it will also prompt interesting empirical work on informant responses to S&TP categories in texts.

A machine-readable corpus approach also forces the analyst to label every single part of a text and not to ignore examples inconvenient to the theory. It is, of course, possible to be systematic in this way without a computer, as, for example, Sinclair and Coulthard's (1975) work in discourse analysis showed, but a computerized corpus forces us to be explicit and consistent in coding all the text. The corpus approach does not produce magical findings or do away with the need for careful intuition-based thought, but it does help us to test out hypotheses. More specifically, attempts to write programs to code S&TP in texts automatically can only be checked and improved with detailed, explicit, systematic and exhaustive manual codings.

8.2 The corpus

8.2.1 Prose fiction

The ten samples of 20th century 'high' literature were all extracted from the Oxford Text Archive at Oxford University. In order to get independent judgements on what texts within the archive counted as 'high' literature, we asked a group of nine postgraduate students who were members of Lancaster University's Stylistics Research Group to make judgements on each of the prose fiction texts available in the archive. We included extracts from the ten texts which six or more of our nine informants judged to be in this category. We then selected extracts from those works by choosing independent units (e.g. chapters, sections or short stories) which had a total of around 2,000 words. The authors of the texts selected were William Golding, Graham Greene, Aldous Huxley, D. H. Lawrence, Doris Lessing, Malcolm Lowry, Somerset Maugham, Iris Murdoch, H. G. Wells and Virginia Woolf. The D. H. Lawrence selection was a short story and the rest were from novels. There were five first-person and five third-person narrations.

Eight of the popular fiction samples were extracted from the relevant category of the British National Corpus. As all of these were third-person narrations, we added two first-person narration extracts to complete the set of ten extracts. Six of the extracts were from romantic novels and four from action novels.[2]

8.2.2 Newspapers

The press data were taken from newspapers published on 4–5 and 11–12 December 1994, in order (a) to achieve some overlap in the stories covered, and (b) to enable us to compare different newspaper styles. We decided to take stories from broadsheet newspapers which were felt to be uncontroversially 'high quality' and from tabloids at the opposite end of the 'quality' spectrum, so that the 'high – low' contrast in the fictional data was matched as far as possible in the newspaper data. News stories, rather than other genres (e.g. editorials or magazine-style articles) were chosen in order to make the newspaper data as similar as possible in typological terms to the fictional narrative data. In each two-day period, articles were taken from (a) the following tabloids: The *News of the World*, *The Sun*, *The Daily Star*, *The Daily Mirror*, *The Daily Express*, and *Today*, and (b) the following broadsheets: *The Independent, The Independent on Sunday*, *The Guardian*, *The Daily Telegraph* and *The Times*.

The original intention was to take a sample of roughly 2,000 words from each of five tabloid and five broadsheet newspapers in each two-day period. But the shortness of the tabloid articles forced us to add a sixth newspaper (*Today*) to our tabloid set. Even in the broadsheets, newspapers rarely have articles of 2,000 words in length, and so the newspaper data differ from the prose fiction data in that each 2,000 word sample consists of more than one complete article. The main criterion for choosing newspaper articles for the data set was that if possible the stories covered should appear in more than three newspapers. Each article covering that story was then used. Where a newspaper did not cover enough of the chosen stories, other prominent news stories were chosen in order to complete the quota of words. Each extract was made up of complete articles.

8.3 Speech and Thought Presentation

The detailed study of S&TP started in work on the novel, where it has been treated extensively. The original realization (e.g. Bally 1912a, 1912b) that there were more categories of speech presentation than the traditional Direct Speech (DS) and Indirect Speech (IS) has enabled researchers to isolate a number of categories and associated meanings/effects derived from using them. The most recent influential work in this tradition is Fludernik (1993), the most comprehensive and scholarly treatment of the field to date. Other important works include Banfield (1982), McHale (1978) and Pascal (1977). Over the last few years, analysts working on non-literary texts have also begun to examine S&TP (see McKenzie 1987, Roeh and Nir 1990, Slembrouck 1992, Caldas-Coulthard 1994). The myriad ways in which speech and thought can be represented in texts cuts across the literary/non-literary divide. This has consequences for a wide range of issues in text linguistics, from the study of literary characterization and point of view to ideological manipulation of the sort examined in critical discourse analysis.

8.3.1 The Leech and Short model

In speech or thought report it is important to remember that two discourse situations are involved. For example, in a newspaper there is the current (written) discourse, where the report is being made, and the anterior discourse situation (usually spoken), where the language being reported was originally produced. Fictional prose depends on our assumption of this discoursal intertwining, but it should always be borne in mind that in *fiction* (where the study of S&TP began), there never was an anterior discourse situation: the novelist makes it all up.

The Leech and Short model assumes that the S&TP categories available to writers[3] are not always sharply distinguished from one another, but arranged along a pair of related *clines*, or *continua*, which are mapped out below. Although the same categories of presentation are available for both speech and thought, Leech and Short treat the two separately. This is because the effects of the categories are different depending upon whether speech or thought is being represented. Leech and Short's clines are reproduced below:

NRSA	IS	FIS	DS	FDS
NRTA	IT	FIT	DT	FDT

NRSA	=	Narrator's Representation of Speech Act
IS	=	Indirect Speech
FIS	=	Free Indirect Speech
DS	=	Direct Speech
FDS	=	Free Direct Speech
NRTA	=	Narrator's Representation of Thought Act
IT	=	Indirect Thought
FIT	=	Free Indirect Thought
DT	=	Direct Thought
FDT	=	Free Direct Thought

An important general point is that as you move leftwards on each cline you encounter presentations which are perceived by readers as more and more under the control of the narrator or reporter, whereas moving to the right produces representations which are felt to be more and more dominated by the form of the original utterance being reported.

We will now give brief definitions of the Leech and Short categories, with canonical examples drawn from our corpus. The definitions are derived from an admixture of (i) formal grammatical and deictic features and (ii) functional and pragmatic features. For ease of presentation, we will begin with the direct and indirect categories, as they are the best-known.

8.3.2 The categories

Direct Speech (DS) and Direct Thought (DT)

[1] 'We are not at liberty to change the word of God just to be politically correct', said the Rev. Tony Higton.
(*The Daily Express*, 'For God's Sake Stop Rewriting our Bible')

DS in its canonical form consists of a *reporting* clause which is deictically related to the narrator's time and place of utterance and a semi-independent *reported* clause, deictically related to the original speaker's time and place of utterance, and marked off by the use of inverted commas. Often, as in the above example, the reported clause comes before the reporting clause. Because of the deictic positioning involved in DS, it is usually assumed that in using DS the reporter claims to represent faithfully three aspects of the original utterance: (a) the propositional content of the utterance, (b) the words and structures used to encode the propositional content and (c) the speech act value of the utterance. In fact, there is something of a problem over the assumption that DS is always a verbatim report of the original speech. DS forms which do not include verbatim report have been discussed in Short (1988) (in newspaper headlines) and Tannen (1989) (in informal conversation).

With thought presentation, the deictic relations are the same as for speech presentation, but the functions and effects are not necessarily the same. In DT, for example, it is even more difficult to apply the three faithfulness criteria spelled out for DS, as we have no way of knowing the linguistic form of the original thought, if indeed it had one:

[2] 'What an extraordinary face!' thought Mary, as he approached.
(Aldous Huxley, *Point Counter Point*)

In this DT example, like the DS in [1], the reported clause comes first, and its positioning helps to emphasize the exclamatory nature of the thought, something also marked by the DT form itself and the lexical content. DT thus suggests strikingness or strength of thought, and consequently is often interpreted by readers as a representation of conscious 'thinking to yourself' thought.

Indirect Speech (IS) and Indirect Thought (IT)

With IS, there are only two faithfulness claims, relating to speech act value and propositional content, and this is reflected in the fact that the deictic properties of IS assume that the narrator/reporter is the deictic centre of the utterance. The reported clause is also subordinated to the reporting clause, and the inverted commas are removed. As a consequence, readers tend to feel much more distanced emotionally from the views of the original speaker than with DS:

[3] Michael Carttiss said he had received overwhelming backing from his constituents over his stand on Europe.
(*The Daily Mirror*, 'Tory Rebels Who Could Kill off Tax on the Old')

The effects of IT are not wildly different from IS:

[4] Jed thought he understood.
(Rupert Thomson, *The Five Gates to Hell*)

It is often the case, as in this instance, that IT is used in novels rather like a meta-summary, introducing some more expansive thought representation of that character (in this case Free Indirect Thought (FIT): see below):

[5] Jed thought he understood. It was like Vasco and the mudbanks of the river. It was where Creed came to do his thinking. Where was Vasco?
(Rupert Thomson, *The Five Gates to Hell*)

Narrator's Representation of Speech Acts (NRSA) and Narrator's Representation of Thought Acts (NRTA)

NRSA and NRTA are to the left of their IS/IT counterparts on the S&TP clines. In NRSA, the three faithfulness claims of DS are reduced to one, an indication of the speech act value of the utterance. The speech report thus has an obvious summarizing and backgrounding/distancing effect.

[6] His criticism was echoed by another former party chairman, Lord Parkinson.
(*The Daily Telegraph*, '14 Tories Ready to Defeat VAT Rise')

NRSA material is also integrated even more into the narrative report than IS. The NRSA in [6] is in effect a simple sentence in the narration which just happens to be about an act of speech rather than a physical action. NRTA is similar to NRSA in both form and function:

[7] I reflected for a minute or two.
(Somerset Maugham, *The Moon and Sixpence*)

Free Direct Speech (FDS) and Free Direct Thought (FDT)

At the opposite end of the Leech and Short speech/thought presentation continuum from NRSA/NRTA are FDS and FDT. In essence, these are examples of DS or DT with one or more of the indications of the presence of the narrator removed. Hence the reporting clause, or the inverted commas, or both, might be removed. There is a marked tendency in prose fiction for FDS to be characterized by the omission of the reporting clause, and for FDT to be marked by the omission of the inverted commas. This helps the novelist to keep speech and thought separated for the reader when they are interleaved:

[8] 'Do we mind?' Damned insolent little bounder! George was working up a righteous indignation. 'I should just think we do mind. And I'll trouble you to ...'
(Aldous Huxley, *Point Counter Point*)

Here, the first sentence is George's FDS (no reporting clause), helping to catch the suddenness of his reaction. The second sentence is also Free Direct (no reporting clause or quotation marks). The fact that the second sentence does not have inverted commas marks it off from the first sentence, forcing an FDT rather than an FDS interpretation. The third sentence is a piece of narrator comment, and then we return to FDS in the last two sentences of the extract.

The form of FDS which has quotation marks but no associated reporting clause would often be referred to by ordinary language users as Direct Speech, and Short (1988) has argued that the distinction between DS and FDS is not really a category distinction, but a variation within a larger category of Direct Speech. His argument for this view, which is linked to an examination of some newspaper headline data, is based on the fact that although stylisticians have made a distinction in *formal* terms between the Direct and Free Direct forms, there is no clear *functional* difference associated with the faithfulness criteria discussed above. In other words, although NRSA, IS and DS can be distinguished (a) formally *and* (b) in terms of an increase in the number of faithfulness claims from one to three, FDS does not appear to bring a fourth faithfulness claim with it. In order to test this proposal, we decided to keep the Direct/Free Direct difference when coding the data, so that we could then see (a) how easy or difficult it was to make the distinction in coding terms, and (b) whether a functional distinction between DS and FDS could be found. Note that the faithfulness argument does not really apply to thought presentation, and so the DT/FDT issue needs to be examined separately. FDT, like DT, often appears to represent conscious thought of the 'she said to herself' type.

Free Indirect Speech (FIS) and Free Indirect Thought (FIT)

The final category of the Leech and Short (1981) model is Free Indirect Speech/Thought. There is quite a wide variation in Free Indirect forms, but their essential characteristics are that (a) they contain a mixture of the features associated with the categories on either side of FIS/FIT on the cline (namely IS/IT and DS/DT) and (b) they are ambiguous with respect to the faithfulness claim which distinguishes the Direct and Indirect forms — in other words it is impossible to determine with certainty whether the words used in the speech/thought report belong to the original speaker/thinker or to the narrator/reporter:

[9] Neighbours said 35-year-old Dr Meenaghan, a genetic fingerprinting expert, lived alone but had regular visits from girlfriends.
A pretty young woman and her son moved in with Dr Meenaghan shortly after his wife walked out.
(*The Sun*, 'Ponytail Boffin Shot Dead by Love Rival')

In [9], the first sentence is clearly IS, committing the reporter to the truthful presentation of the content of what the neighbours said, but making no such faithfulness claims about the words they used to make their statements. On the other hand, it is impossible to determine whether the words of the second sentence belong to the reporter or one or more of the neighbours interviewed. At one extreme it could be a summary by the reporter of what he was told. At the other, he could be using the actual words of one of his interviewees. And it could equally well be a mixture of these two extremes. The reasons for this are that (a) the deixis and vocabulary can be made appropriate to either the reporting or reported situations and (b) the sentence is neither marked off by inverted commas (a DS feature) nor subordinated under a reporting clause (an IS feature).

In the following example, the subordination associated with IS occurs, but the fact that some of the reported clause comes *before* the reporting clause makes the report more free than canonical IS, and again the deixis and vocabulary can be appropriate to both the original speaker or the reporter:

[10] It was doubtful, he argued, that the 15 member states could achieve a single currency by the end of the century.
(*The Independent on Sunday*, 'Blair Puts Labour Troops on Alert for Snap Election')

In the following example, a sequence of FIT is introduced by a sentence of NRTA:

[11] As she walked down the Charing Cross Road, she put to herself a series of questions. Would she mind, for example, if the wheels of that motor-omnibus passed over her and crushed her to death. No, not in the least ...
(Virginia Woolf, *Night and Day*)

We can see that we have FIT here by 'translating' the relevant sentences into DT and IT, and noting that the FIT above has features of both of these forms (below changes from the original are emboldened):

[11′] As she walked down the Charing Cross Road, she put to herself a series of questions. Would **I** mind, for example, if the wheels of that motor-omnibus passed over **me** and crushed **me** to death. No, not in the least ...

[11″] As she walked down the Charing Cross Road, she put to herself a series of questions. **She wondered if she would mind**, for example, if the wheels of **the** motor-omnibus **she could see** passed over her and crushed her to death. **She decided that she would not mind** in the least ...

The form actually occurring in the novel has the third-person pronouns we would expect in IT, but does not exhibit the subordination typical of that form. The indirect form would also require more 'infill' of the character's assumptions to make it well-formed discoursally.

We have already seen some differences in meaning and effect for DS and FDS on the one hand and DT and FDT on the other. If we compare [10] and [11] we can also see a clear difference in effect for the two Free Indirect forms. FIS usually has a distancing effect for readers, helping us to be more critical of what is said. In the novel this distancing is often associated with irony. But the effect of the FIT in [11] is very different. We appear close up to the character, 'sitting in' on her thoughts as she thinks them. To explain this difference, it was proposed in Leech and Short that the 'norms' for speech and thought presentation were in different places on the S&TP cline:

			Norm	
			↓	
NRSA	IS	FIS	DS	FDS
NRTA	IT	FIT	DT	FDT
	↑			
	Norm			

The argument for the norms being in different places on the continuum was a *semantic* one. It is reasonable to assume that a reporter has access to the original utterance when speech report is involved, but when we 'report' the thoughts of others we can only do so by inferring what they think from some other activity — for example what they say, their facial expressions and how they act.

A computerized corpus allows us to examine what the S&TP norms are in *quantitative* terms, both generally and in relation to specific text-types. It also allows us, through a quantitative analysis of our coding decisions, to examine evidence for and against the assumption that the S&TP cline is really a cline and not a set of discrete, well-defined categories.

8.4 Tagging the corpus

The tagging system that we developed for our study is best explained with reference to an example. This is the coded version of the direct speech extract given in section 8.3.2 above.

[DS>NRS/0.8/16] 'We are not at liberty to change the word of God just to be politically correct,' [NRS>DS/0.2/5]said the Rev. Tony Higton.

First of all, codings were enclosed within square brackets, placed before the stretch of text that they refer to, and attached to the first word of the stretch, so as not to affect automatic word counts (in some word-processing packages, at least). Consider the opening tag: [DS>NRS/0.8/16]. The opening square bracket is followed by an acronym indicating the category that the following stretch of text belongs to, which in this case is Direct Speech (DS). Because we were interested in studying sequencing phenomena in S&TP, we also indicated what category immediately follows the stretch of text that is being tagged. We used the symbol > to separate the two. In our first example, Direct Speech is followed by a reporting clause, which receives the tag NRS (Narrator's Report of Speech). Clearly, NRS does not represent a separate category, but we decided to give reporting clauses a special tag in order to be able to study their patterning and position relative to the stretches of report that they relate to (the tag NRT was used for reporting clauses in thought presentation). We then inserted a slash mark /, and followed it with a number indicating how many sentences, or what proportion of a sentence, make up the stretch that is being coded. Finally, another slash mark precedes the number of words contained in the stretch. In this case, the stretch of direct speech contains sixteen words, which amount to approximately 0.8 of the 21-word sentence ending after 'Higton'. The second tag should now be clear: it says that the following stretch of text is a reporting clause, that the reporting clause is in turn followed by more direct speech, that the reporting clause represents approximately 0.2 of the sentence it occurs in, and that it consists of five words.

Because of our decision to indicate sequences, the whole of our data needed to receive a tag. The stretches of text that were not speech/thought reports were marked as narration (N) (e.g. descriptions of actions, people and places). This also solved the problem of indicating the ends of categories: a category ends where the following one begins. Where we thought that a stretch of text was ambiguous between two categories, we adopted double tags. For example, the tag N-FIT indicates that the associated stretch of text is ambiguous between narration and FIT.

So far, we have only gone a small way in trying to develop a program for the automatic tagging of the corpus. Dodgson (1995) reports on an attempt to tag DS automatically in a subset of our corpus. The program was successful in that it captured all examples of DS and avoided phenomena like scare quotations, but some examples of FDS were also tagged as DS. This drawback may not, in the event, be a serious one. As indicated in 8.3.2 above, it may be argued that FDS should really be regarded as a sub-type of DS rather than as a category in its own right. DS is the easiest S&TP category to isolate automatically, as a consequence of the fact that there are fairly clear formal linguistic characteristics associated with it. Given that human researchers have difficulty in assigning tags unambiguously (see 8.6 below), automatic tagging of the other S&TP categories is bound to be more problematic. Indeed, until programs are developed which take into account pragmatic and contextual factors, progress in this area is likely to be limited.

8.4.1 Refining the model

The introduction of 'new' categories of S&TP

Inevitably, the attempt to code large amounts of authentic data with a relatively small number of categories leads to the discovery of inadequacies and ambiguities in the model that is being applied. Although Leech and Short's original categories successfully accounted for the majority of instances of S&TP in our corpus, we were also faced with phenomena that did not easily fit within their model. Our general principle was to avoid an excessive proliferation of categories, which would have resulted in an unhelpfully cumbersome framework. Where possible, therefore, we tried to redefine our categories and the boundaries between them in order to account for the complexity of our data. We did, however, find that two new categories were needed, both lying at the interface between narration (N) and the leftmost categories of S&TP on the clines given in section 8.3.1 above. These categories were provisionally called: Narrator's Report of Voice (NV), and Internal Narration (NI). These additions can then be made to the

S&TP clines as follows:

NV	NRSA	IS	FIS	DS	FDS
NI	NRTA	IT	FIT	DT	FDT

Narrator's Report of Voice (NV)

This category captures those instances where the report of speech is even more minimal than is the case with NRSA: the narrator simply tells us that some talk or speech event occurred, with no indication of the speech act(s) performed. Examples can be found in all the text types represented in our corpus. The relevant parts of the examples below are emboldened:

[12] He screwed the receiver close into his ear and sat still **while a low voice burred like a bee.**
(Graham Greene, *Brighton Rock*)

[13] **After talks in Belgrade**, Mr Milosevič said he fully agreed with the international peace plan …
(*The Guardian*, 'Milosevič Backs Hurd Peace Plea')

As the examples show, NV includes two main types of speech report: in [12] an individual person/character is reported to have spoken; in [13] a number of people are said to have taken part in the same speech event. No detail is explicitly provided as to what was said or even what speech acts were performed. As such, NV lies to the left of NRSA in the speech presentation cline, since it implies an even greater distance between the reader and the original speech situation.

Narration of Internal States in fiction (NI) and in the press (N-NI)

In fictional texts, narrators may provide reports of characters' cognitive activities and emotional states which do not fall under any of Leech and Short's categories for thought presentation:

[14] Her approval filled the military young man with happiness.
(Aldous Huxley, *Point Counter Point*)

[15] For a moment he was rendered motionless by surprise, a kind of respect.
(Rupert Thomson, *The Five Gates to Hell*)

In [14] we are given a report of the emotions experienced by a character at a particular point in the narrative. In [15] the references to 'surprise' and 'respect' suggest that the character's experience has both a cognitive and an emotional dimension. In each case, we are given insights into a character's internal states or changes, but no representation of specific thoughts of the character (see also Leech and Short 1981: 341–2). Examples such as these were coded as NI.

Clearly, NI lies at the interface between narration and thought presentation. As such, it falls to the left of NRTA on the thought presentation scale. In order for an internal report to qualify as NI, it needs to focus on *cognitive* or *emotional* experiences. In other words, NI does not include reports of characters' perceptions, whether the stimuli are internal ('She felt a pain in her stomach') or external ('She felt the softness of his hair'). These would be coded as narration (N).

NI is, not surprisingly, typical of fictional texts, where it is possible for narrators to have direct access to the consciousness of one or more of the characters. Newspaper reporters do, however, also use expressions that appear to reveal the internal states of the people whose stories are being reported. Consider the examples below:

[16] Diana, who had met Elizabeth through AIDS charity work, was shocked to learn she had lost 30lbs and could hardly walk.
(*The Daily Mirror*, 'Di's Tears and a Cuddle for Starsky's Wife')

[17] Right-wing ministers are also anxious to see the rebels back in the fold.
(*The Independent on Sunday*, 'Tory MPs want Rebels Reinstated')

Here, our source of information is not a potentially omniscient narrator, but journalists who must have inferred the internal states they are reporting from some kind of external evidence (unless, of course, they have made them up!). In fact, the rest of the report often indicates that the journalist's source is something that was *said*, either by the people involved, or by someone close to them. A few lines after [16], we are given the direct speech of 'a family friend' of Diana's, while [17] is immediately followed by an IS report of what one of 'the right wing ministers' is supposed to have said.

For the purposes of the tagging, these cases were classified as ambiguous between N and NI, and were therefore coded as N-NI. This was an attempt to capture the fact that, in semantic terms, examples like [16] and [17] are reports of internal states, but pragmatically they have to be interpreted as inferences about internal states that the reporter has incorporated within his or her own account of the event/s being reported. This decision, however limited and provisional, highlights an important dimension of the tagging process, namely the fact that many decisions are determined by pragmatic and contextual factors, including, as in this case, the status of the narrative voice in the discourse structure of the text under analysis. It is this kind of issue which makes the possibility of exhaustive automatic tagging very difficult.

8.5 Quantitative analysis

Due to lack of space, the discussion below of the quantitative results of our work will only concentrate on general tendencies and differences between categories. Finer analysis is left for future reports of our research.

8.5.1 Speech presentation frequencies for the whole corpus

The frequencies for speech presentation categories within the whole corpus are given in tables 8.1 and 8.2 below. Table 8.1 relates to the number of *instances of occurrence* of each category. Table 8.2 relates to the number of *words* included within each category. It should be noted that these figures do not include items which we coded as being ambiguous between categories. These ambiguities are briefly discussed in section 8.6 below.

Table 8.1 Instances of occurrence of speech presentation categories

	FDS	DS	FIS	IS	NRSA	NV
Number of instances	417	753	64	342	386	72
Number of instances as a % of the total number of instances of speech presentation	20.5	37.02	3.15	16.81	18.98	3.54

Table 8.2 Percentages of words in each speech presentation category

	FDS	DS	FIS	IS	NRSA	NV
Number of words as a % of the total number of words in the corpus	6.94	15.62	1.21	5.47	6.1	0.9
Number of words as a % of the total number of words of speech presentation	19.57	42.64	3.37	15.2	16.79	2.51

DS is clearly the most frequent speech presentation category, both in terms of number of instances and words. 37.02% of all instances of speech presentation in the corpus are DS, representing 15.62% of the total volume of words in the corpus. In considering these figures, we should also bear in mind that the distinction between DS and FDS is problematic. Although we cannot discuss the issue in detail here, a preliminary analysis suggests that FDS should indeed be regarded as a sub-type of DS.

Together, DS and FDS account for 57.52% of all instances and 62.21% of words of speech presentation, and represent 22.56% of the total number of words in the corpus. This finding lends quantitative support to the assumption made in Leech and Short (1981) that DS is the norm for speech presentation. The next most frequent speech presentation category, both in terms of number of instances and words, is NRSA. This result may be seen as surprising, given that traditionally DS and IS have been considered the main speech presentation categories. NRSA as a category was first coined in Leech and Short (1981). The fact that NRSA is so extensive in the corpus is largely, as we shall see in the section below, the result of its high frequency of occurrence in the press.

8.5.2 Speech presentation frequencies across text-types

The distribution of words in each speech presentation category according to the four sections of our corpus is represented in the table below:

Table 8.3 Number of words within each speech presentation category as a percentage of the total number of words for each text type

	'High' literature	Popular fiction	Broadsheets	Tabloids
FDS	10.89	14.04	0.92	1.91
DS	14.61	11.78	11.75	24.34
FIS	1.34	0.33	2.53	0.64
IS	0.36	0.50	14.05	6.98
NRSA	0.69	1.19	13.18	9.40
NV	0.45	1.27	1.03	0.84
Total	28.34	29.11	43.28	44.11

If we combine 'high' literature and popular fiction, 28.73% of the words in prose fiction are speech presentation. Taking broadsheets and tabloids together, 43.7% of the words in the press are speech presentation. This results in a difference of 14.97%. This difference can be explained by noting that on the one hand, the representation of speech is crucial in news report, and on the other hand, narration and thought presentation play a dominant role in prose fiction.

With regard to the speech presentation norm, there are some interesting differences between the text-types. For 'high' literature, popular fiction and the tabloids the quantitative norm is clearly at the DS/FDS end of the scale. However, this is not true of the broadsheets. Most broadsheet speech presentation falls into IS (14.05%) and NRSA (13.18%). Together they account for 27.23% of the words in the broadsheets. This compares with 1.05% of words in 'high' literature and 1.69% of words in popular fiction for the same categories. A possible reason for this difference is that the broadsheets do more by way of summarizing speech, sometimes whole series of utterances by several people. NRSA and IS are also the least 'dramatic' of the speech presentation forms, and so correspond best with the serious and balanced image that the broadsheets cherish. NRSA and IS, with their summarizing function, are also well represented in the tabloids, accounting for 16.38% of the words. However, the tabloids prioritize the more direct end of the speech presentation scale. Combined, FDS and DS account for 26.25% of the words in the tabloids. This compares with 12.67% of the words in the broadsheets for the same categories. This predominance of DS in the tabloids is presumably the result of a wish to present news stories in a vivid, dramatic and striking manner.

8.5.3 Thought presentation frequencies across text-types

The distribution of words in each thought presentation category according to the four sections of our corpus is represented in table 8.4 below.

Table 8.4 Number of words within each thought presentation category as a percentage of the total number of words for each text type

	'High' literature	Popular fiction	Broadsheets	Tabloids
FDT	0.29	0.85	0.00	0.00
DT	0.26	0.50	0.00	0.00
FIT	9.21	9.15	0.00	0.00
IT	0.87	1.21	0.00	0.11
NRTA	0.57	0.64	0.00	0.00
NI (and N-NI)	6.83	5.23	5.74	2.80

There is a clear difference between the occurrence of thought presentation in prose fiction and the press. As has been explained above, thought presentation is a widespread artifice in prose fiction, but does not play an important role in the press. However, reporters can infer what individuals think and this is reflected in the category N-NI which we felt the need to introduce in order to cope with the newspaper data (see section 8.4.1).

In quantitative terms, the largest category of thought presentation by far is FIT. Leech and Short argued that the norm for *speech* presentation is DS, and the quantitative evidence supports that claim. They suggested that the norm for *thought* presentation is IT. Clearly, the statistical evidence suggests that the norms for thought presentation and speech presentation cannot be at the same place on the clines. DT and FDT, when added together, still represent a very low proportion of the thought presentation total. The fact that the thought presentation norm in quantitative terms is FIT and not IT is presumably related to the 20th century novelists' preoccupation with representing the thoughts of characters empathetically. Although the quantitative evidence does not coincide with Leech and Short's semantically based arguments for the thought presentation norm being IT, the norm is clearly further to the indirect end of the scale than DT.

Table 8.4 also reveals some interesting facts about the relationship between 'high' literature and popular fiction. Firstly, all of the thought presentation categories occur in both kinds of fiction, and so it is not possible to argue that 'high' literature has linguistic thought presentation ingredients which popular fiction does not. Secondly, the figures for 'high' literature and popular fiction are remarkably similar for each category, and so no distinction can be made between the two text-types on quantitative grounds. We do feel, however, that there is a difference between the two text-types in terms of the abilities of authors to *control* and *use* the thought presentation categories effectively, but for reasons of space a discussion of this interesting matter will have to be postponed.

8.6 Conclusion and prospect

In this preliminary report we have outlined our basic approach, and described two main outcomes of our study so far: (i) the introduction of new S&TP categories to the Leech and Short model and (ii) the identification of some general tendencies in speech and thought reporting across the four text-types which constitute our corpus. Because our corpus is relatively restricted, confirmation of our suggestions will need to be provided by further work.

Lack of space has prevented us from discussing our project in more detail and from outlining other interesting phenomena and trends in our data:

(i) As well as the codings discussed above, we marked a number of category sub-types, which help to show interesting differences between the four text-types.

(ii) We identified a significant number of ambiguous codings (170, or 4.5% of total codings) and some other important areas of potential overlap between categories. This indicated the importance of pragmatic factors in assigning tags and provided interesting support for the notion of a *continuum* of S&TP categories, while at the same time suggesting that not all of the S&TP scale is clinal in nature.

(iii) The coding difficulties produced by our attempts to keep DS and FDS separate suggest that FDS should probably be thought of as a sub-type of DS.

(iv) The dominant patterns of sequences in S&TP categories (including the embedding of categories inside other categories) deserve careful examination in relationship to textual meaning and effect.

We would be happy to share our findings with other interested researchers, and in any case hope to publish further results in the near future.

Notes

1 We would like to thank the Social Sciences Faculty at Lancaster University for providing us with a small but essential grant to undertake this pilot project. The following students have helped us considerably in collecting, coding and analysing the material: Ruth Allen, Mike Dodgson, Markus Guadagnin and Martin Wynne. We are also grateful to Paul Baker for his help with the quantitative analysis. We owe all these people considerably more than we could pay them. Preliminary analysis of parts of the manually coded data can be found in Allen (1994) and Guadagnin (1994), and Dodgson (1995) is an account of an attempt to write software to 'parse' Direct Speech in part of the corpus.

2 Note that no attempt has been made in the present research to match the time periods within the 20th Century when the texts were produced.

3 As our corpus consists entirely of written English, we talk throughout this article of *writers* representing speech and thought. It should be remembered, however, that S&TP is also observable in speech (see Tannen 1989). Hence although 'writers' is an accurate representation of the reporters in our corpus in general terms it will be better to think of 'writers' as a convenient shorthand for 'writers or speakers'.

PART 3

Applications of corpus-based research to speech and language technology

9 A probabilistic LR parser of part-of-speech and punctuation labels

TED BRISCOE and JOHN CARROLL

9.1 Introduction

The work described here is part of an ongoing effort to develop a robust, domain-independent syntactic parser capable of yielding the one correct analysis for unrestricted naturally-occurring input. Our goal is to develop a system with performance comparable to extant part-of-speech taggers, returning a syntactic analysis from which predicate-argument structure can be recovered, and which can support semantic interpretation. Until the advent of substantial textual corpora of the type pioneered in the United Kingdom by Geoffrey Leech and his colleagues, exploration of robust parsing of real text would have been impossible. Today, however, practical robust parsing is critical for many tasks in natural language processing and information retrieval. In our view, the requirement for a domain-independent analyzer favours statistical techniques to resolve ambiguities, whilst the need for semantic interpretation favours a more sophisticated grammatical formalism than is typical in extant statistical approaches to robust analysis of corpus material.

Briscoe and Carroll (1993) describe a probabilistic parser using a wide-coverage unification-based grammar of English written in the Alvey Natural Language Tools (ANLT) metagrammatical formalism (Briscoe *et al* 1987), generating around 800 rules in a syntactic variant of the Definite Clause Grammar formalism (DCG, Pereira and Warren 1980) extended with iterative (Kleene) operators. The ANLT grammar is linked to a lexicon containing about 64K entries for 40K lexemes, including detailed subcategorization information appropriate for the grammar, built semi-automatically from a learners' dictionary (Carroll and Grover 1989). The resulting parser is efficient and capable of and Grover 1989). The resulting parser is efficient and capable of constructing a parse forest in quadratic time and efficiently returning the ranked *n*-most likely analyses for naturally-occurring sentences (Carroll 1993 1994). The probabilistic model is a refinement of probabilistic context-free grammar (PCFG) conditioning CF 'backbone' rule application on LR state and lookahead item. Unification of the 'residue' of features not incorporated into the backbone is performed at parse time in conjunction with reduce operations. Unification failure results in the reduce operation failing and the associated derivation being assigned a probability of zero. Probabilities are assigned to transitions in the LALR(1) action table via a process of supervised training based on computing the frequency with which transitions are traversed in a corpus of parse histories. The result is a probabilistic parser which, unlike a PCFG, is capable of probabilistically discriminating derivations which differ only in terms of order of application of the same set of CF backbone rules within the parse context defined by the LALR(1) table.

Experiments with this system revealed three major problems which our current research is designed to address. Firstly, although the system is able to rank parses with a 75% chance that the correct analysis will be the most highly ranked, further improvement will require a 'lexicalized' system in which (minimally) probabilities are associated with alternative subcategorization possibilities of individual lexical items. Currently, the relative frequency of subcategorization possibilities for individual lexical items is not recorded in wide-coverage lexicons, such as ANLT or COMLEX (Grishman *et al* 1994). Secondly, removal of punctuation from the input (after segmentation into text sentences) worsens performance as punctuation both reduces syntactic ambiguity (Jones 1994) and signals non-syntactic (discourse) relations between text units (Nunberg 1990). Thirdly, the biggest source of error on unseen input is the omission of appropriate subcategorization values for lexical items (mostly verbs) in the system's lexicon, which always prevent the system from finding the correct analysis. The current coverage of this system on a general corpus such as Brown or LOB is estimated to be around 20% by Briscoe (1994). Thus, we have developed a variant probabilistic LR parser which does not rely on subcategorization and utilizes punctuation to reduce ambiguity. The analyses produced by this parser could be utilized for phrase finding applications, recovery of subcategorization frames, and other 'intermediate' level parsing problems.

9.2 Part-of-speech tag sequence grammar

Several robust parsing systems exploit the comparative success of part-of-speech (PoS) taggers, such as Fidditch (Hindle 1989) or MITFP (de Marcken 1990), by reducing the input to a determinate sequence of extended PoS labels of the type which can be practically disambiguated in context using a PoS tagger (e.g. Church 1988). Such approaches, by definition, cannot exploit subcategorization, and probably achieve some of their robustness as a result. However, such parsers typically also employ heuristic rules, such as 'low' attachment of PPs to produce unique 'canonical' analyses. This latter step complicates the recovery of predicate-argument structure and does not integrate with a probabilistic approach to parsing.

We utilized the ANLT metagrammatical formalism to develop a feature-based, declarative description of PoS label sequences for English. This grammar compiles into a DCG-like grammar of approximately 400 rules. It has been designed to enumerate possible valencies for predicates (verbs, adjectives and nouns) by including separate rules for each pattern of possible complementation in English. The distinction between arguments and adjuncts is expressed, following X-bar theory (e.g. Jackendoff 1977), by Chomsky-adjunction of adjuncts to maximal projections (XP → XP Adjunct) as opposed to government of arguments (i.e. arguments are sisters within X1 projections; X1 → X0 Arg1 ... ArgN). Although the grammar enumerates complementation possibilities and checks for global sentential well-formedness, it is best described as 'intermediate' as it does not attempt to associate 'displaced' constituents with their canonical position / grammatical role.

The other difference between this grammar and a more conventional one is that it incorporates some rules specifically designed to overcome limitations or idiosyncrasies of the PoS tagging process. For example, past participles functioning adjectivally, as in [1a], are frequently tagged as past participles (VVN) as in [1b], so the grammar incorporates a rule (violating X-bar theory) which parses past participles in this context.

[1a] The disembodied head
[1b] The AT_disembodied_VVN head_NN1

Similar idiosyncratic rules are incorporated for dealing with gerunds, adjective-noun conversions, idiom sequences, and so forth.

This grammar has been developed and refined in a corpus-based fashion (e.g. see Black 1993) by testing against sentences from the Susanne corpus (Sampson 1994), a 138K word treebanked and balanced subset of the Brown corpus. The grammar currently covers more than 75% of the sentences. Many of the remaining failures for shorter text sentences are a consequence of the root sentence node requirement, since they represent elliptical noun or prepositional phrases in dialogue. Other failures on sentences are a consequence of incorporation of complementation constraints for auxiliary verbs into the grammar but the lack of any treatment of unbounded dependencies. Nevertheless, we tolerate these 'deficiencies', since they have the effect of limiting the number of analyses recovered in other cases, and will not, for example, affect unduly the recovery of subcategorization frames from the resulting analyses.

9.3 Text grammar and punctuation

Nunberg (1990) develops a partial 'text' grammar for English which incorporates many constraints that (ultimately) restrict syntactic and semantic interpretation. For example, textual adjunct clauses introduced by colons scope over following punctuation, as [2a] illustrates; whilst textual adjuncts introduced by dashes cannot intervene between a bracketed adjunct and the textual unit to which it attaches, as in [2b].

[2a] *He told them his reason: he would not renegotiate his contract, but he did not explain to the team owners. (vs. but would stay)

[2b] *She left — who could blame her — (during the chainsaw scene) and went home.

We have developed a declarative grammar in the ANLT metagrammatical formalism, based on Nunberg's procedural description. This grammar captures the bulk of the text-sentential constraints described by Nunberg with a grammar which compiles into 26 DCG-like rules. Text grammar analyses are useful because they demarcate some of the syntactic boundaries in the text sentence and thus reduce ambiguity, and because they identify the units for which a syntactic analysis should, in principle, be found; for example, in [3], the absence of dashes would mislead a parser into seeking a syntactic relationship between *three* and the following names, whilst in fact there is only a discourse relation of elaboration between this text adjunct and pronominal *three*.

[3] The three — Miles J. Cooperman, Sheldon Teller, and Richard Austin — and eight other defendants were charged in six indictments with conspiracy to violate federal narcotic law.

The rules of the text grammar divide into three groups: those introducing text-sentences, those defining text adjunct introduction and those defining text adjuncts. An example of each type of rule is given below:

a) T/txt-sc1 : TxtS → (Tu[+sc])* Tu[-sc] (+pex | +pqu)
b) Ta/dash- : Tu[-sc] → T[-sc, -cl, -da] Ta[+da, da-]
c) T/t ta-da- t : Ta[+da, da-] → +pda Tu[-sc, -da]

These rules are phrase structure schemata employing iterative operators, optionality and disjunction, preceded by a mnemonic name. Non-terminal categories are text sentences, units or adjuncts which carry features mostly representing the punctuation marks which occur as daughters in the rules (e.g. +sc represents presence of a semi-colon marker), whilst terminal punctuation is represented as +pxx (e.g. +pda, dash). a) states that a text sentence can contain zero or more text units with a semi-colon at their right boundary followed by a text unit optionally followed by a question mark or exclamation mark. b) states that a text unit not containing a semi-colon can consist of a text unit or adjunct not containing dashes, colons or semi-colons followed by a text adjunct introduced by a dash. This type of 'unbalanced' text adjunct can only be expanded by c) which states that it consists of a single opening dash followed by a text unit which does not itself contain dashes or semi-colons. The features on the first daughter of b) enforce dash adjuncts to have lower precedence and narrower scope than colons or semi-colons and block interpretations of multiple dashes as sequences of 'unbalanced' adjuncts.

The text grammar has been tested on Susanne and covers 99.8% of sentences. (The failures are mostly text segmentation problems.) The number of analyses varies from one (71%) to the thousands (0.1%). Just over 50% of Susanne sentences contain some internal punctuation, so around 20% of the singleton parses are punctuated. The major source of ambiguity in the analysis of punctuation concerns the function of commas and their relative scope as a result of a decision to distinguish delimiters and separators (Nunberg 1990: 36). Therefore, a text sentence containing eight commas (and no other punctuation) will have 3170 analyses. The multiple uses of commas cannot be resolved without access to (at least) the syntactic context of occurrence.

9.4 The integrated grammar

Despite Nunberg's observation that text grammar is distinct from syntax, text grammatical ambiguity favours interleaved application of text grammatical and syntactic constraints. The integration of text and PoS sequence grammars is straightforward and remains modular in that the text grammar is 'folded into' the PoS sequence grammar, by treating text and syntactic categories as overlapping and dealing with the properties of each using disjoint sets of features, principles of feature propagation, and so forth. The text grammar rules are represented as left or right branching rules of Chomsky-adjunction to lexical or phrasal constituents. For example, the simplified rule for combining NP appositional or parenthetical text adjuncts is N2[+ta] → H2 Ta[+bal] which states that a NP containing a textual adjunct consists of a head NP followed by a textual adjunct with balanced delimiters (dashes, brackets or commas). Rules of this form ensure that syntactic and textual analysis are mutually 'transparent' and orthogonal so, for example, any rules of semantic interpretation associated with syntactic rules continue to function unmodified. Such rules attach text adjuncts to the constituents over which they semantically scope, so it would be possible, in principle, to develop a semantics for them. In addition to the core text grammatical rules which carry over unchanged from the stand-alone text grammar, 44 syntactic rules (of pre- and post-posing, and coordination) now include (often optional) comma markers corresponding to the purely 'syntactic' uses of punctuation.

The approach to text grammar taken here is in many ways similar to that of Jones (1994). However, he opts to treat punctuation marks as clitics on words which introduce additional featural information into standard syntactic rules. Thus, his syntactic and textual rules are thoroughly intermixed and it would be harder to extract an independent text grammar or build a modular semantics.

9.5 Parsing the Susanne and SEC Corpora

The integrated grammar has been used to parse Susanne and the quite distinct SEC Corpus (Taylor and Knowles 1988), a 50K word treebanked corpus of transcribed British radio programmes punctuated by the corpus compilers. Both corpora were retagged with determinate PoS and punctuation labelling using the Acquilex HMM tagger (Elworthy 1993, 1994) trained on text tagged with a modified version of CLAWS-II labels (Garside *et al* 1987).

9.5.1 Coverage and average ambiguity

To examine the efficiency and coverage of the grammar we applied it to our retagged versions of Susanne and SEC. We used the ANLT chart parser (Carroll 1993), but modified just to count the number of possible parses in the parse forests (Billot and Lang 1989) rather than actually unpacking them. We also imposed a per-sentence time-out of 30 seconds CPU time, running in Franz Allegro Common Lisp 4.2 on an HP PA-RISC 715/100 workstation with 96 Mbytes of physical memory.

We define the 'coverage' of the grammar to be the inverse of the proportion of sentences for which no analysis was found — a weak measure since discovery of one or more global analyses does not entail that the correct analysis is recovered. For both corpora, the majority of sentences analyzed successfully received under 100 parses, although there is a long tail in the distribution. Monitoring this distribution is helpful during grammar development to ensure that coverage is increasing but the ambiguity rate is not. A more succinct though less intuitive measure of ambiguity rate for a given corpus is what we call the average parse base (APB), defined as the geometric mean over all sentences in the corpus of the formula $\sqrt[n]{p}$, where n is the number of words in a sentence, and p, the number of parses for that sentence.[1] Thus, given a sentence n tokens long, the APB raised to the nth power gives the number of analyses that the grammar can be expected to assign to a sentence of that length in the corpus. Table 9.1 gives these measures for all of the sentences in Susanne and in SEC.

Considering that the grammar was developed solely with reference to Susanne, coverage of SEC is quite robust. The two corpora differ considerably since the former is drawn from American written text whilst the latter represents British transcribed spoken material. The corpora overall contain material drawn from widely disparate genres/registers, and are more complex than those used in DARPA ATIS tests and more diverse than those used in MUC. The APBs for Susanne and SEC of 1.256 and 1.239 respectively indicate that sentences of average length in each corpus could be expected to be assigned of the order of 97 and 126 analyses (i.e. $1.256^{20.1}$ and $1.239^{22.6}$). Black *et al* (1993: 156) quote a *parse base* of 1.35 for the IBM grammar for computer manuals applied to sentences 1–17 words long. Although, as mentioned above, Black's measure may not be exactly the same as our APB measure.

Table 9.1 Grammar coverage on Susanne and SEC

	Susanne		SEC	
Parse fails	1745	24.9%	898	33.1%
1–9 parses	1566	22.3%	607	22.3%
10–99 parses	1306	18.6%	418	15.4%
100–999 parses	893	12.7%	299	11.0%
1K–9.9K parses	611	8.7%	197	7.3%
10K–99K parses	413	5.9%	108	4.0%
100K– parses	475	6.8%	189	7.0%
Time-outs	5	0.07%	1	0.04%
Number of sentences	7014		2717	
Mean sentence length	20.1		22.6	
Mean s.l. — fails	21.7		27.6	
Mean s.l. — time-outs	67.2		79.0	
Average Parse Base	1.256		1.239	

Black *et al* achieve a coverage of around 95%, as opposed to our coverage rate of 67–74 on much more heterogeneous data and longer sentences.

The parser throughput on these tests, for sentences successfully analyzed, is around 45 words per CPU second on an HP PA-RISC 715/100. Sentences of up to 30 tokens (words plus punctuation) are parsed in an average under 0.6 seconds each, whilst those around 60 tokens take on average 4.5 seconds. Nevertheless, the relationship between sentence length and processing time is fitted well by a quadratic function, supporting the findings of Carroll (1994) that in practice NL grammars do not evince worst-case parsing complexity.

9.5.1.1 Coverage, ambiguity and punctuation

We have also run experiments to evaluate the degree to which punctuation is contributing useful information. Intuitively, we would expect the exploitation of text grammatical constraints to both reduce ambiguity and extend coverage (where punctuation cues discourse rather than syntactic relations between constituents). Jones (1994) reports a preliminary experiment evaluating reduction of ambiguity by punctuation. However, the grammar he uses was developed only to cover the test sentences. These were drawn entirely from the SEC corpus, which was punctuated post hoc by the corpus developers (Taylor and Knowles 1988).

We took all in-coverage sentences from Susanne of length 8–40 words inclusive containing internal punctuation; a total of 2449 sentences. The APB for this set was 1.273, mean length 22.5 words, giving an expected number of analyses for an average sentence of 225. We then removed all sentence-internal punctuation from this set and re-parsed it. Around 8% of sentences now failed to receive an analysis. For those that did (mean length 20.7 words), the APB was now 1.320, so an average sentence would be assigned 310 analyses, 38% more than before. On closer inspection, the increase in ambiguity is due to two factors: a) a significant proportion of sentences that previously received 1–9 analyses now receive more, and b) there is a much more substantial tail in the distribution of sentence length vs. number of parses, due to some longer sentences being assigned many more parses. Manual examination of 100 depunctuated examples revealed that in around a third of cases, although the system returned global analyses, the correct one was not in this set (Briscoe and Carroll 1994). With a more constrained (subcategorized) syntactic grammar, many of these examples would not have received any global syntactic analysis.

9.5.2 Parse selection

A probabilistic LR parser was trained with the integrated grammar by exploiting the Susanne treebank bracketing. An LR parser (Briscoe and Carroll 1993) was applied to unlabelled bracketed sentences from the Susanne treebank, and a new treebank of 1758 correct and complete analyses with respect to the integrated grammar was constructed semi-automatically by manually resolving the remaining ambiguities. 250 sentences from the new treebank were kept back for testing. The remainder, together with a further set of analyses from 2285 treebank sentences that were not checked manually, were used to train a probabilistic version of the LR parser, using Good-Turing smoothing to estimate the probability of unseen transitions in the LALR(1) table (Briscoe and Carroll 1993; Carroll 1993). The probabilistic parser can then return a ranking of all possible analyses for a sentence, or efficiently return just the *n*-most probable (Carroll 1993).

The probabilistic parser was tested on the 250 sentences held out from the manually-created treebank[2] (with mean length 18.2 tokens, mean number of parses per sentence 977, and APB 1.252); in this test 85 sentences (34%) had the correct analysis ranked in the top three.[3] This figure rose to 51% for sentences of less than 20 words. Considering just the highest ranked analysis for each sentence, in Sampson, Haigh and Atwell's (1989) measure of correct rule application the parser scored a mean of 83.5% correct over all 250 sentences. We also analyzed the results of this test using the Grammar Evaluation Interest Group scheme (GEIG, see e.g. Harrison *et al* 1991). This compares unlabelled bracketings derived from corpus treebanks with those derived from parses for the same sentences by computing *recall*, the ratio of matched brackets over all brackets in the treebank; *precision*, the ratio of matched brackets over all brackets found by the parser; 'crossing' brackets, the number of times a bracketed sequence output by the parser overlaps with one from the treebank but neither is properly contained in the other; and *minC*, the number of sentences for which all of the analyses had one or more crossings. Using these metrics, the performance of the parsing system with respect to the original Susanne bracketings for the same 250 in-coverage sentences is given in table 9.2.

The table also gives an indication of the best and worst possible performance of the disambiguation component of the system, showing the results obtained when parse selection is replaced by a simple random choice, and the results of evaluating the manually-created treebank against the corresponding Susanne bracketings. In this latter figure, the mean number of crossings is greater than zero mainly because of compound noun bracketing ambiguity which our grammar does not attempt to resolve, always returning a right-branching binary analysis.

Black *et al* (1993: 7) uses the crossing brackets measure to define a notion of structural consistency, where the structural consistency rate for the grammar is defined as the proportion of sentences for which at least one analysis contains no crossing brackets, and reports a rate of around 95% for the IBM grammar tested on the computer manual corpus. The problem with the GEIG scheme and with structural consistency is that both are still weak measures (designed to avoid problems of parser/treebank representational compatibility) which lead to unintuitive numbers whose significance still depends heavily on details of the relationship between the representations compared (c.f. the compound noun issue mentioned above). The crossing bracket measure alone is particularly weak because in general the fewer the brackets inserted by the grammar/parser, the better it will score, whilst certain types of error such as incorrect level of attachment of constituents will not result in crossings.

Table 9.2 GEIG evaluation metrics for test set of 250 unseen sentences (lengths 3–56 words, mean length 18.2)

	minC	Crossings	Recall	Precision
Probabilistic parser analyses				
Top-ranked 3 analyses, weighted =	150	2.62	76.47%	42.35%
Random 3 analyses, weighted =	155	3.87	67.05%	37.40%
Manually-disambiguated analyses				
Single analysis	91	0.88	91.51%	50.73%

Schabes *et al* (1993) and Magerman (1995) report results using the GEIG evaluation scheme which are numerically superior to ours. However, their experiments are not strictly compatible because they both utilize more homogeneous and probably simpler corpora. In addition, Schabes *et al* do not recover tree labelling, whilst Magerman has developed a parser designed to produce identical analyses to those used in the Penn Treebank, removing the problem of spurious errors due to grammatical incompatibility. Both these approaches achieve better coverage by constructing the grammar fully automatically. No one has yet shown that any robust parser is practical and useful for some NLP task. However, it seems likely that say rule-to-rule semantic interpretation will be easier with hand-constructed grammars with an explicit, determinate ruleset. A more meaningful comparison will require application of different parsers to an identical and extended test suite and utilization of a more stringent standard evaluation procedure sensitive to node labellings, as well as evaluation in terms of applications.

9.5.2.1 *Parse selection and punctuation*

In order to assess the contribution of punctuation to the selection of the correct analysis, we applied the same trained version of the integrated grammar to the 106 sentences from the test set which contain internal punctuation, both with and without the punctuation marks in the input. A comparison of the GEIG evaluation metrics for this set of sentences punctuated and depunctuated gives a measure of the contribution of punctuation to parse selection on this data. (The results for the depunctuated set were computed against a version of the Susanne treebank from which punctuation had also been removed.) As table 9.3 shows, recall declines by 10%, precision by 5% and there are an average of 1.27 more crossing brackets per sentence. These results indicate clearly that punctuation and text grammatical constraints can play an important role in parse selection. The appendix contains examples of sentences for which the correct analysis was returned when punctuation was present, but for which an incorrect analysis was returned when these cues were removed.

Table 9.3 GEIG evaluation metrics for test set of 106 unseen punctuated sentences (mean length with punctuation 21.4 words; without, 19.6)

	minC	Cross-ings	Recall	Preci-sion
With punctuation Top-ranked 3 analyses, weighted=	78	3.25	74.38%	40.78%
Punctuation removed Top-ranked 3 analyses, weighted=	82	4.52	65.54%	35.95%

9.6 Conclusions

Briscoe and Carroll (1993) and Carroll (1993 1994) showed that the LR model, combined with a grammar exploiting subcategorization constraints, could achieve good parse selection accuracy but at the expense of poor coverage of free text. The results reported here suggest that improved coverage of heterogeneous text can be achieved by exploiting textual and grammatical constraints on PoS and punctuation label sequences. The experiments show quite clearly that a) grammatical coverage can be greatly increased by relaxing subcategorization constraints, and b) that text grammatical or punctuation-cued constraints can reduce ambiguity and increase coverage during parsing.

To our knowledge these are the first experiments which objectively demonstrate the utility of punctuation for resolution of syntactic ambiguity and improvement of parser coverage. They extend work by Jones (1994) and Briscoe and Carroll (1994) by applying a wide-coverage text grammar to substantial quantities of naturally-punctuated text and by quantifying the contribution of punctuation to ambiguity resolution in a well-defined probabilistic parse selection model.

Accurate enough parse selection for practical applications will require a more 'lexicalized' probabilistic model. Magerman's (1995) parser is an extension of the history-based parsing approach developed at IBM (e.g. Black *et al* 1993) in which rules are conditioned on lexical and other (essentially arbitrary) information available in the parse history. In future work, we intend to explore a more restricted and semantically-driven version of this approach in which, firstly, probabilities are associated with different subcategorization possibilities, and secondly, alternative predicate-argument structures derived from the grammar are ranked probabilistically. However, the massively increased coverage obtained here by relaxing subcategorization constraints underlines the need to acquire accurate and complete subcategorization frames in a corpus-driven fashion, before such constraints can be exploited robustly and effectively with free text.

Notes

1 Black *et al* (1993: 13) define an apparently similar measure, *parse base*, as the 'geometric mean of the number of parses per word for the entire corpus', but in the immediately following sentence talk about raising it to the power of the number of words in a sentence, which is inappropriate for a simple ratio.

2 See the appendix for sample sentences.

3 This is a strong measure, since it not only accounts for structural identity between trees, but also correct rule application at every node.

Appendix to Chapter 9

Sample of the 250-sentence test set, taken from the Brown genre categories: press reportage; belles lettres, biography, memoirs; and learned (mainly scientific and technical) writing.

'Yes, your honour', replied Bellows.
This is another of the modifications of policy on Laos that the Kennedy administration has felt compelled to make.
On Monday, the Hughes concern was formally declared bankrupt after its directors indicated they could not draw up a plan for reorganization.
Ierulli will replace Desmond D. Connall who has been called to active military service but is expected back on the job by March 31.
Place kicking is largely a matter of timing, Moritz declared.
Ritchie walked up to him at the magazine stand.
Hector Lopez, subbing for Berra, smashed a 3-run homer off Bill Henry during another 5-run explosion in the fourth.
That's how he first won the Masters in 1958.
Cooperman and Teller are accused of selling $4,700 worth of heroin to a convicted narcotics peddler, Otis Sears, 45, of 6934 Indiana av.
However, the system is designed, ingeniously and hopefully, so that no one man could initiate a thermonuclear war.
He bent down, a black cranelike figure, and put his mouth to the ground.
Those who actually get there find that it isn't spooky at all but as brilliant as a tile in sunlight.
Others look to more objective devices of order.
What additional roles has the scientific understanding of the 19th and 20th centuries played?
If we look at recent art we find it preoccupied with form.
Hence the beatniks sustain themselves on marijuana, jazz, free swinging poetry, exhausting themselves in orgies of sex; some of them are driven over the borderline of sanity and lose contact with reality.
Heidenstam could never be satisfied by surface.
Individual human strength is needed to pit against an inhuman condition.
The pressure gradient producing the jet is due to the nature of the magnetic field in the arc (rapid decrease of current density from

cathode to the anode).
At 100 Amp the 360 cycle ripple was less than 0.5 V (peak to peak) with a resistive load.

Highest-ranked analysis, firstly with punctuation (only one — correct — parse), and secondly with punctuation removed (incorrect attachment of the embedded sentence preferred). [Tu = text unit, all nodel labels represent aliases of feature sets].

the_AT aborigine_NN1 is_VBZ not_XX deceived_VVN ;_; he_PPHS1 knows_VVZ that_CST the_AT land_NN1 is_VBZ hard_JJ and_CC pitiless_JJ

```
(Tu
 (Tu
  (S (NP the_AT (N1 aborigine_NN1))
    (VP is_VBZ
      (VP not_XX (VP deceived_VVN))))
 ;_;)
 (S he_PPHS1
  (VP knows_VVZ
    (S that_CST
      (S (NP the_AT (N1 land_NN1))
        (VP is_VBZ
          (AP (A1 (A hard_JJ (A and_CC pitiless_JJ))))))))))

(Tu
 (S (NP the_AT (N1 aborigine_NN1))
  (VP is_VBZ
    (VP not_XX
      (VP deceived_VVN
        (S he_PPHS1
          (VP knows_VVZ
            (S that_CST
              (S (NP the_AT (N1 land_NN1))
                (VP is_VBZ
                  (AP
                     (A1 (A hard_JJ (A and_CC pitiless_JJ))))))))))))))
```

Highest-ranked analysis, firstly with punctuation (correct), and secondly with punctuation removed (incorrect structure preferred around the former positions of the commas). [Tu = text unit, Ta = text adjunct].

Moreover_RR ,_, it_PPH1 will_VM be_VB0 asymmetric_JJ until_ICS a_AT1 certain_JJ critical_JJ <formul>_&FO distance_NN1 is_VBZ reached_VVN ,_, below_II which_DDQ it_PPH1 will_VM become_VV0 symmetric_JJ

```
(Tu
 (S (AP (A1 Moreover_RR)) ,_,
  (S it_PPH1
   (VP
    (VP will_VM (VP be_VB0 (AP (A1 asymmetric_JJ))))
     (PP
      (P1 until_ICS
       (Tu
        (S
         (NP
          (NP a_AT1
           (N1 (AP (A1 certain_JJ))
            (N1 (AP (A1 critical_JJ))
             (N1 <formul>_&FO distance_NN1)))))
         (VP is_VBZ (VP reached_VVN)))
        (Ta ,_,
         (S (PP (P1 below_II which_DDQ))
          (S it_PPH1
           (VP will_VM
            (VP become_VV0 (AP (A1 symmetric_JJ))))))))))))))
```

```
(Tu
 (S (NP (A1 Moreover_RR) it_PPH1)
  (VP
   (VP will_VM (VP be_VB0 (AP (A1 asymmetric_JJ))))
   (PP
    (P1 until_ICS
     (S
      (NP
       (NP a_AT1
        (N1 (AP (A1 certain_JJ))
         (N1 (AP (A1 critical_JJ))
          (N1 <formul>_&FO distance_NN1)))))
      (VP is_VBZ
       (VP reached_VVN
        (PP (P1 below_II which_DDQ))
        (S it_PPH1
         (VP will_VM
          (VP become_VV0 (AP (A1 symmetric_JJ)))))))))))))
```

10 Machine learning from corpus resources for speech and handwriting recognition

ERIC ATWELL

10.1 Introduction: different perspectives on language learning

Geoffrey Leech's ideas have been inspirational both to Corpus-based computational linguists in general and to me personally: first as a student and Research Associate at Lancaster University, then as a Lecturer in Artificial Intelligence at Leeds University. This chapter focuses on research at Lancaster and Leeds building on Geoffrey Leech's ideas, looking in particular at how corpus resources can be applied as training data for 'intelligent' machine learning software systems, enabling them to 'learn' models of English language to use in Speech And Language Technology applications such as speech and handwriting recognition systems.

The pioneers of modern Corpus Linguistics saw their principal application areas as linguistic theory and English language teaching. For example, (Leech *et al* 1983a), an early paper on the LOB Corpus tagging project, cited 'the need for accurate textual evidence for statements about the language'; and (Leech 1986) discussed applications in computer-assisted language learning (CALL). Even today, the bulk of regular attenders at annual ICAME English Corpus Linguistics conferences[1] are from English linguistics and language teaching departments. Implicit in terms like ELT and even CALL is the assumption that the learners are humans.

With the growth of Information Technology has come growing demand for computers to process language in various ways, and this has led to a subfield of IT with a number of different names: 'Natural Language Processing' or 'Computational Linguistics' amongst academics (see Gazdar and Mellish 1989), 'Speech And Language Technology' (SALT) to UK research funding agencies such as DTI, EPSRC and HEFCs' NTI, and 'Language Engineering' to European Union funding agencies.[2] All SALT systems need some sort of language model, and one way to get this model into the computer system is to use a 'machine learning' algorithm, with a corpus as 'training data'. Much of the terminology has parallels with human language learning, but there are major differences in the underlying learning process. Most significantly, human learners of English as a second or foreign language start off knowing some other Natural Language; the learning task is one of mapping between the new and known languages. Learners obviously focus on the differences between English and their native tongue, but there is a great deal of overlap between any two Natural Languages which can be taken for granted. For example, when learning the English word COMPUTER the non-native speaker naturally relates this word to the native-language translation, and has mental lexical, syntactic, semantic and pragmatic concepts and structured interrelationships already available to 'hook onto'. In machine learning, by contrast, the computer starts from scratch. A word like COMPUTER is simply an ASCII character sequence or string, unless and until more complex language patterns are learnt and associated with the word.

The kinds of 'language patterns' which can be learnt may be quite different from those in human language processing. For SALT systems, this is not necessarily a failing: it may not be essential to mimic human language learning and processing functionality. SALT systems can achieve acceptable performance rates in their specific task without full human linguistic abilities. For example, the task of a speech recognition system is to map the input acoustic signal onto the corresponding sequence of ASCII strings; it is possible to do this surprisingly accurately without 'understanding' the speech signal, using models of vocabulary and grammar which are quite different to those learnt by EFL students. While general-purpose SALT systems generally have to be robust (able to cope with variations and 'ill-formedness' found in unconstrained English input), the level of linguistic analysis may be shallow or skeletal. To ensure computation in a reasonable time, it is more pragmatic to accept a minimally sufficient analysis, deliberately ignoring linguistic issues which are not essential or relevant to the application. Current successful SALT systems focus on tasks for which a robust shallow linguistic analysis suffices.

10.2 Speech recognition as disambiguation of 'noisy' English

Ambiguity resolution is a central issue in Speech And Language Technology. For large-vocabulary speech recognizers, not restricted to a small domain, the task of finding the correct ASCII transcription for the input acoustic signal can be seen as a disambiguation problem. The same perspective applies to systems for handwriting recognition and optical character recognition (OCR), and even grammar correction for word processors can be modelled in this way: in each case, the input must be assumed to be 'noisy', with several potential analyses (e.g. ASCII transcriptions) to choose between at each point.

This 'noisy English' representation inside a recognition system (be it for speech, handwriting or printed text input) is typically a sequence of sets of candidate-words, referred to as a word recognition lattice. Atwell (1993a) gives the following illustration (much simplified compared to realistic systems). On 'hearing' the sentence 'Stephen left school last year', an English speech recognition system may produce the following lattice of word-candidates (in order of decreasing similarity to input speech signal):

stephen	stiffen	stiffens
left	lift	loft
school	scowl	scull
lest	last	least
yearn	your	year

In speech recognition, alternative candidates at each point are phonetically similar; in script recognition, candidates are graphemically similar. The task of detecting errors in word-processed English text can also be cast in terms of a word recognition lattice, if the system artificially 'ambiguates' each word as it is typed in: Atwell (1987a) proposed that '... this could be done by generating COHORTS for each input word, and then choosing the cohort-member word which fits the context best'. If the 'best' choice is not the word actually typed in, this becomes the suggested replacement for an error.

The language model's task is to find the best sequence of words, so that the chosen sequence of words is the most linguistically plausible. Most language models for lattice disambiguation provide only a limited coverage of the linguistic knowledge available (Jelinek 1990, Young 1995). This is because the system has to search through all possible combinations of candidates; in the above example this amounts to 3*3*3*3*3 = 243 possible sentences. Analysis of recognition lattices involves traversing a much larger search space than when analysing 'known' sentences. Because of this, sophisticated language analysis systems may be too slow and unwieldy to disambiguate recognition lattices in reasonable time. For example, Atwell (1994) found that a probabilistic context-free chart parser (based on the outline implementation in Gazdar and Mellish 1989) required impractically long computation times to discover a very large number of ambiguous analyses of even simple word recognition lattices. Similarly Keenan (1992) reported impractically-long compute times when attempting to use the Alvey Natural Language Toolkit (ANLT) chart parser (Phillips and Thompson 1987) to disambiguate handwritten word recognition lattices. There is arguably a need for language models which strike a pragmatic balance, incorporating a range of linguistic knowledge while remaining computationally practical.

10.3 What aspects of language can computers learn from corpus resources?

Generally models extracted or learnt from corpus resources are lexically-oriented; not for linguistic-theoretic reasons, but because machine learning is data-driven, and in 'bottom-up' learning the words in the training text are the baseline. A wide range of information about words and how they combine can be gleaned from corpus resources. This is particularly true if corpus resources are not limited to raw text samples, but also richer text resources (Atwell *et al* 1993). A widening range of annotated corpora are also available, including Part-of-Speech wordtagged text (see chapter 11, also Taylor *et al* 1991), treebanks with sentences annotated with syntactic phrase structure (see chapter 9, also Souter and Atwell 1994), spoken corpora with graphemic and/or phonetic transcriptions aligned with digitized acoustic signal (see chapter 4, also Arnfield 1994), parallel corpora with English sentences aligned with their translations in another language, e.g. French or German (see chapter 13, Taylor *et al* 1991), error corpora, English text with spelling or grammatical errors flagged or marked, and annotated with preferred corrections (see Atwell and Elliott 1987);

lattice corpora, the output of speech or handwriting recognition systems, where each word is annotated with a cohort or word-candidate set (see Modd and Atwell 1994, Hanlon 1994), and even parallel-annotated corpora, with words and sentences annotated with several types of linguistic analysis (see Arnfield and Atwell 1993, Hughes *et al* 1995). For machine learning purposes, it can be useful to regard the machine-readable version of a printed dictionary (such as the Longman Dictionary of Contemporary English, LDOCE) as a special sort of annotated corpus, where headwords have complex annotations including grammatical classes and sense-definition text (see Demetriou and Atwell 1994). Given this wider range of training data, a wider range of linguistic information is machine-learnable, including the following:

- A list of words in English, together with frequencies or likelihoods;
- Word classes or categories: syntactic, semantic, or composite;
- Recurring word combinations: idioms and collocation patterns;
- Word-tuples (word-pairs, word-triples, ...) with frequencies or likelihoods;
- Wordclass- or wordtag-tuples (tag-pairs, tag-triples, ...) with frequencies or likelihoods;
- Higher-level syntactic constituent structures, with constituent likelihoods;
- Recurring combinations of words and grammatical contexts: collegation patterns;
- Dictionary word-sense (lexical semantics) collocation likelihoods;
- Thesaurus semantic field collocation likelihoods;
- Semantic structures, with constituent likelihoods;
- Pragmatic discourse structures, with constituent likelihoods;

- Word-candidate lattice traversal models, for speech or written script input;
- Error-correction models for 'noisy English', e.g. word-processed text;
- Mappings or transducers between annotations at different levels, e.g. prosody to/from syntax;
- Mappings or transducers between rival syntactic annotation schemes advocated by different research teams;
- Mappings or translators between sentences in two languages in a parallel corpus.

Some of these models are well-known and used by linguists and ELT researchers; while others have no immediate analogy in human language learning, but may still be useful in applications like speech word-lattice traversal.

10.4 Advantages of machine learning from corpus resources

Within the wider field of Knowledge Based Systems (see, for example, Atwell 1993b), the 'knowledge acquisition bottleneck' problem is widespread. A Knowledge Based System or KBS must somehow acquire its knowledge from human experts in the field or domain. Instead of requiring domain experts to write down their knowledge directly as program code, a common approach is for a Knowledge Engineer to elicit a comprehensive set of examples of the knowledge being applied, and then to reprocess these examples into a Knowledge Base. Machine learning from corpus resources is essentially the same process: examples of linguistic expertise are captured in corpus annotations and lexical database entries, to be reprocessed into a language model usable in a SALT system.

The alternative to machine learning of language models is for linguists to 'hand-craft' their linguistic expertise into SALT systems, directly encoding their knowledge about language into software. As a half-way house between these two extremes, the linguist can be guided by corpus examples in building a grammar; or, starting from the other end, the results of machine learning can be improved and fine-tuned by augmenting or merging with linguists' hand-crafted resources.

Even the watered-down use of machine learning has advantages over purely hand-crafted language modelling. The main advantage is that the building of SALT language models is broken into two separate subtasks: building corpus resources, and then extracting computable models from these corpus resources. For many linguists, annotating examples in a corpus or lexical database is more straightforward and 'natural' than encoding linguistic knowledge in a computable formalism. Both subtasks yield recyclable resources: an annotated corpus has uses other than machine learning of language models (e.g. lexicography, ELT, ...); and a successful language-model-learning algorithm can in principle be re-applied to other annotated corpora to extract models of rival tagging/parsing schemes. For example, Atwell (1988) described how a context-free phrase-structure grammar and parser were learnt from the Lancaster/Leeds Treebank (see below); essentially the same technique was used in Souter and Atwell (1992) to glean a context-free phrase-structure grammar from the Polytechnic of Wales treebank (annotated with Systemic Functional Grammar parsetrees) and in Atwell (1994) to extract a third context-free phrase structure grammar from the Spoken English Corpus Treebank (annotated using Lancaster/IBM skeletal grammar). Furthermore, a machine learning algorithm which works on English corpus resources should work with minimal modifications with corpora in other languages. For example, the IBM research team led by Jelinek (Jelinek 1990) has been highly successful at gleaning corpus-based language models for English speech recognition; Gros *et al* (1994) reused the same machine learning techniques to learn corpus-based language models for a Slovene speech recognizer.

A concept related to learning is adaptation. It is desirable that SALT systems can automatically adapt to variations of language style, genre, accent, etc, even single-speaker variations and degradations over time. Once a basic default language model has been learnt, a machine learning system can be transformed into a user-adaptive system by adding a 'feedback-loop'. The system then incrementally updates the initial language model from its own analyses. For example, Atwell *et al* (1988) report on a probabilistic parser which learnt its grammar model from the Polytechnic of Wales treebank; Hughes (1989) described a modified version of this parser, which adapted its learnt grammar to account for parses of new sentences. In contrast, grammars hand-crafted by linguists must be explicitly updated or maintained by linguists.

Corpus-based approaches force awareness of practical issues which are important in working, reusable SALT systems. In hand-crafting a language model, linguists can overlook issues such as punctuation and/or prosodic markers, capitalization, neologisms or 'out-of-vocabulary' unknown words, segmentation into words and sentences, etc. A machine learning system must have ways of coping with these in processing its training set, and these 'low-level' routines can be re-used in the end-product SALT system. The prime example is the attention to detail of punctuation, capitalization etc in the Constituent Likelihood Automatic Wordtagging System Claws, used to wordtag the LOB Corpus (Leech *et al* 1983a and b, Atwell *et al* 1984, Johansson *et al* 1986). The wordtag-pair model (also known as wordtag N-gram or Markov model) at the heart of the Claws wordtag-disambiguation routine is learnt from a tagged corpus training set, and the routines for handling punctuation etc are also used in analysing new text.

Last but not least, I find machine learning intellectually challenging because it allows researchers to explore an undiscovered country of novel models of language, quite different to those dreamt up by traditional theoretical linguists.[3] Some of these are illustrated below.

10.5 Problems with machine learning from corpus resources

Of course, machine learning is not a panacea. Probably the main disadvantage is that current machine learning techniques require copious training datasets, and current corpus resources may not be adequate. Furthermore, even a large corpus resource is unlikely to cover all possible instances of a linguistic feature. The simplest example of this is lexicon-extraction: a list of words in English, along with frequencies of usage, can be directly extracted from a raw-text English corpus. A wordtagged corpus can yield a wordlist with words coupled with possible parts of speech. However, wordlists derived even from a very large corpus are not complete: for example, many words do not appear in all the inflected and derived forms given in a dictionary. A solution is to merge or combine corpus-derived lexical resources with human-expert-crafted dictionary resources. For example, the original wordlist and suffixlist used in the Claws system to wordtag the LOB Corpus were in part derived from the tagged Brown Corpus, but supplemented by cross-checking with printed dictionaries (and linguistic intuition) to ensure all words in LOB were fully covered. More recently, Souter (1993) describes how the Systemic-Functional Grammar wordlist extracted from the SFG-annotated Polytechnic of Wales corpus was merged with the CELEX lexical database to derive a large-vocabulary SFG lexical resource. This principle of merging machine-learnt models with linguists' intuitions applies to higher levels of language modelling. For example, Howarth (1995) argued that corpus-derived collocations need to be supplemented with idiomatic and collocational word-patterns from expert intuition for a more complete picture; Haigh *et al* (1988) showed how linguistic knowledge can be applied to modify a corpus-derived grammar model to improve parser accuracy.

A rather more insidious problem is that machine-learnable syntax and semantics models tend to focus on what is learnable, and tend to be skeletal or non-compositional; it is difficult to see how to learn models based on the more esoteric linguistic theories such as GPSG, HPSG, LFG. The tendency to take due account of punctuation, capitalization, etc, was listed above as a positive advantage of corpus-based machine learning; however, this could also be seen as undue attention to 'trivia', at the possible expense of overlooking theoretically significant linguistic issues. A related problem is that these theories aim to translate a parse-tree into a semantic or knowledge representation amenable to inferencing and 'understanding' — the kinds of machine-learnt skeletal language models currently in use do not readily deliver rich representations to pass to semantic interpretation or inferencing modules of an intelligent Natural Language Understanding system. There is a need for further research to extend machine learning algorithms to cover richer linguistic formalisms, and language processing beyond skeletal parsing and semantics. Leech and Fligelstone (1992) note: 'A context-free phrase structure grammar is manifestly too weak a model for good results, and one direction of progress is in developing more sophisticated models, such as a probabilistic unification grammar. ... Another direction in which to advance is to integrate a corpus parser within a grander scheme for corpus analysis, including semantic analysis.'

10.6 Examples of novel machine-learnt language models

At present, most large-vocabulary speech or script recognition systems use very simple language models. For example Young (1995) reports that most current research on speech recognition systems attempts to constrain the search through word-candidate lattices using N-gram models of word-tuples: essentially a list of all word-pairs, word-triples, etc found in a training corpus, along with frequencies or likelihoods. Such models, when manipulated with smart statistical techniques, have proved surprisingly successful for certain tasks (such as transcribing passages read out loud from the Wall Street Journal); but some less constrained tasks may call for higher-level linguistic modelling.

This success of word N-gram language models may seem counterintuitive and even implausible to some linguists. An analogy with computer chess may be helpful. Grand Masters become chess experts by learning thousands of specialized move-sequences and strategies; but computer chess programs generally work by 'brute force' computation of all possible combinations of moves and their relative scores, within a constrained 'look-ahead'. The Grand Master may well perceive a 'best score' move sequence predicted by a chess program as a structured sequence of moves following one or more known generalized strategies; but the chess program does not need this higher-level knowledge. The lack of 'psychological validity' in the computer approach to chess is irrelevant, as long as the models used yield the required results. Both human and computer approaches to chess are suited to respective processing capabilities. In language modelling for speech recognition, the computer must compute all possible sequences of words and their relative scores, using word sequence patterns in a training corpus as a guide. Speech recognition researchers have shown empirically that a word N-gram model can approximate the score of a word-sequence without recourse to higher-level knowledge, at least for some tasks. It is up to linguists to find speech recognition tasks where their wares are needed!

However, given that high-level linguistic knowledge MAY be useful, at least it may be worth developing some machine-learnt language models to try out. The following are some novel models of language which contrast with traditional linguistic concepts. Because of space limitations, these models can only be described here in outline; but see the references for fuller details.

10.6.1 Word-classes

Word N-gram models do not make use of the generally-accepted linguistic generalization that words can be grouped into classes with similar linguistic behaviour. At least this minimal linguistic concept ought to be of use in speech and handwriting recognition. Traditionally English words have been grouped into Parts of Speech (noun, verb, adjective, ...); corpus linguists have refined these into much more detailed wordclass or wordtag sets for corpus annotation. However, below the coarse categories, there is fuzziness or disagreement on class-boundaries; the current corpus tagsets for LOB, Brown, SEC, POW, ICE, BNC, UPenn etc are all incompatible.

One possible response is to start again from scratch, formulating computable machine learning criteria for putting words into wordclasses. For example, Atwell (1987b), Atwell and Drakos (1987) and Atwell and Elliott (1987) computed new wordclasses for words in a training corpus by clustering words with similar collocational behaviour; other researchers have experimented with other clustering and similarity metrics. However, these machine learning experiments also led to a range of incompatible results: different algorithms for clustering, and different definitions of collocational criteria, led to different word-classes. As a further response, Hughes (1994) and Hughes and Atwell (1994) proposed an algorithm for automatically evaluating a range of competing word-classifications against a specific 'target'.

In practice, many researchers would prefer to reuse an existing tagged corpus and corpus tagset. At present, this means they are restricted to a single corpus; but (Atwell *et al* 1994, Hughes *et al* 1995) discuss experiments with machine learning a mapping between corpus tagsets, using a Parallel Annotated Corpus as a training set.

10.6.2 Phrase-structure syntax

Grammatical sentence structure is traditionally captured in a two-dimensional phrase-structure syntax tree. The standard baseline way of defining phrase structure for parsing is in terms of context-free rules: each non-terminal node in the syntax-tree corresponds to the application of a context-free rule, which has the node-label as its left-hand-side, and the node's immediate daughters as its right-hand-side. For example, in the Lancaster/IBM Spoken English Corpus treebank, the parse-tree for the sentence 'Stephen left school last year.' is:

[S [N Stephen_NP1 N][V left_VVD [N school_NN1 N][Nr last_MD year_NNT1 Nr]V] ._. S]

This is a compact textfile encoding of the following 2-dimensional syntax tree diagram:

```
                     S
                   / | \
                  /  |  \
                 N   V   \
                /   /|\   \
               /   / | \   \
              /   /  N  Nr  \
             /   /   |  | \  \
            /   /    |  |  \  \
           NP1 VVD NN1 MD NNT1 .
          /   /      |  |   |   \
   Stephen left school last year .
```

This phrase structure tree can be generated by, or broken down into, a set of context-free rules:

S --> N V .
N --> NP1
V --> VVD N Nr
N --> NN1
Nr --> MD NNT1

There is also a set of lexical rewrite rules: 'NP1 --> Stephen', etc. In this way, a context-free grammar and parser can be 'learnt' from a treebank: for each sentence-tree, extract a context-free rule for each non-terminal node. If the machine learning algorithm also keeps a count of how frequently each context-free rule is found in the treebank, this yields a probabilistic context-free grammar (see Atwell 1988b, 1994, Souter and Atwell 1992, Leech and Fligelstone 1992). However, as mentioned above, a probabilistic context-free chart parser can require impractically long computation times for speech recognition applications, so alternative grammar-extraction methods may be worth investigation.

One alternative approach to parsing involves a Markov or tag-N-gram model; this was originally proposed as an extension to the Claws wordtagging algorithm (Atwell 1983, Atwell *et al* 1984), but could not be implemented until training resources such as the SEC treebank became available (Atwell 1993c, 1994). The model used is a variant of standard N-gram theory, in that both the training set and desired output are required to be an alternating sequence of wordtags and labelled bracket combinations; for example, the above parse-tree (leaving off the words for simplification) is processed as the tag-sequence:

[S [N NP1 N][V VVD [N NN1 N][Nr MD _ NNT1 Nr]V] . S]

Whereas the standard word N-gram model learns word-pairs, word-triples etc (see above), the tag-N-gram parser learns tag-triples such as:

[S	[N	NP1
NP1	N][V	VVD
VVD	[N	NN1
NN1	N][Nr	MD
MD	_	NNT1
NNT1	Nr]V]	.
.	S]	[S

The parser implementation uses this adapted model for a 'bracket-insertion' procedure. First, the words are wordtagged, using a Claws-like tag N-gram model; then phrase-structure-brackets are inserted between pairs of wordtags, guided by the tag-triples table. There is a final 'tree-closing' procedure to ensure parse-trees are correctly balanced. With experiments in parsing lattices, using equivalent sized training sets, Pocock and Atwell (1993) and Atwell (1994) found that the Markov Model based parser is much faster and more robust than a probabilistic chart parser developed using the same training treebank. Its optimal parsetree is not always structurally correct, but it is more likely to dominate the correct word-sequence, which is adequate for lattice disambiguation.

A variant N-gram approximation to phrase-structure syntax is used in the Vertical Strip Parser VSP (O'Donoghue 1993). In learning from a treebank, syntax trees are chopped into a series of Vertical Strips from root to leaves; for example, the above syntax tree is analysed into:

S	S	S	S	S	S
|	|	|	|	|	|
N	V	V	V	V	.
|	|	|	|	|	
NP1	VVD	N	Nr	Nr	
		|	|	|	
		NN1	MD	NNT1	

The VSP learning algorithm stores the set of vertical strips occurring with each wordtag. In analysing new sentences, the parser finds a vertical strip for each wordtag which is compatible with its neighbours, and combines these into a well-formed syntax tree by merging nodes from the root down until they diverge.

10.6.3 Semantic constraints

All word sense-definitions in the Longman Dictionary Of Contemporary English (LDOCE) are written in terms of the Longman Defining Vocabulary, a closed set of approximately 2000 words. This effectively means that LDOCE sense definitions are stated in terms of 'semantic primitives', and as a crude measure of semantic relatedness we can count the number of 'semantic primitives' the two definitions have in common. For example, Demetriou (1992, 1993) and Demetriou and Atwell (1994), use the LDOCE definitions as the basis for semantic constraints by maximizing semantic overlap in a word recognition lattice. In analysing the earlier illustrative lattice, Demetriou's algorithm looks up the LDOCE definition of each candidate, to calculate a semantic overlap score for every possible path through the lattice. For example, in evaluating 'stiffen lift scowl last year', the algorithm notes that the LDOCE definition of 'last' includes:

> '... (in time) one or ones before the one mentioned or now ...'

and the LDOCE definition of 'year' includes:

'... a measure of time equal to about 365 days ...'

These definitions both contain the 'semantic primitive' 'time', indicating a semantic overlap favouring cooccurrence of these two candidates; so the score of all word-lattice sequences including 'last year' is incremented. This procedure is applied to all candidate-pairs in a sequence to evaluate each possible sequence, and the highest-scoring candidate sequence should be the most semantically consistent.

LDOCE also has a set of semantic field markers which provide a hierarchical taxonomic semantics at a higher-level of abstraction than the sense-definitions. Words have associated a small number of semantic field markers and Jost and Atwell (1993) and Jost (1994) showed that these can be used as semantic tags in a Markovian disambiguation algorithm. An alternative semantic tag set has been produced at Lancaster University (Wilson and Rayson 1993, Eyes and Leech 1993) and this may also prove applicable to semantic constraints for speech and handwriting recognition.

10.6.4 Discourse structure

The principles of pragmatics are particularly difficult to 'pin down', not just for SALT systems, but even in theoretical linguistics: Leech (1983) warned against '... a tendency to compartmentalize and hierarchize units of discourse, as if they were constituents in an immediate constituent analysis ... the fault of "overgrammaticization" can be observed not only in the paradigmatic rigidity of a set of mutually exclusive categories, but also in the syntagmatic rigidity of a segmentation of discourse into discrete non-overlapping units'. Machine learning researchers in particular should heed this warning! However, there is at least a passing resemblance between N-gram modelling and empirical analysis of adjacent pairs of utterances in dialogue, called 'adjacency pairs' (see Heritage 1988, McKevitt 1991). Atwell and McKevitt (1994) discuss how such empirical intention models might be applied to speech recognition. Intention models are more tangible in a specific, constrained domain; for example Atwell *et al* (1995) describes an empirical speech recognition discourse model trained on a constrained corpus of transcribed dialogue between Air Traffic Control and small aircraft around Leeds/Bradford Airport.

10.6.5 Conclusions

Machine learning of language models from corpus resources is a fledgling research field, with much to learn![4] The pioneering developers of corpus resources had backgrounds in English linguistics and language teaching, so naturally saw this as the prime application area for corpus linguistics. Lancaster University continues to be the leading centre for the production of corpus resources (see, for example, Leech and Garside 1991, Eyes and Leech 1993, Black *et al* 1993). The rapidly-growing field of Information Technology, and specifically Speech And Language Technology, is finding new uses for corpus resources as training data for machine learning of robust large-scale language models; Geoffrey Leech's work is finding applications in a whole new field of research.

Notes

1 ICAME = International Computer Archive of Modern English, an international network of corpus linguists, with a base at Bergen University. ICAME publishes an annual Journal, and holds annual International Conferences; see Souter and Atwell (1993) for a list of past venues and proceedings.

2 DTI = Department of Trade and Industry, which subsidises Industrial SALT research and development projects; EPSRC = Engineering and Physical Sciences Research Council, which funds University SALT research projects; HEFCs' NTI = Higher Education Funding Councils' New Technologies Initiative, which funds IT infrastructure for UK Universities, including SALT training resources.

3 As fellow Star Trek fans will know, the Undiscovered Country is the Future.

4 The Association for Computational Linguistics has recently set up a Special Interest Group on Natural Language Learning, ACL-SIGNLL; for further details, contact its President, David Powers, Flinders University (powers@cs.flinders.edu.au) or Secretary, Walter Daelemans, Tilburg University (walter@kub.nl).

11 The robust tagging of unrestricted text: the BNC experience

ROGER GARSIDE

11.1 Introduction

The production of annotated machine-readable corpora has been a central activity of the UCREL team at Lancaster University, led by Geoffrey Leech, since the early 1980s. This commenced with the annotation of the LOB (Lancaster-Oslo/Bergen) corpus with part-of-speech information over the period 1981–84 (Garside, Leech and Sampson 1987). The work has continued with corpora which introduced syntactic annotation at the constituent level (Leech and Garside 1991) and at the level of anaphora (Fligelstone 1992; Garside 1993), with corpora marked with word sense and key semantic relationship information (Wilson and Rayson 1993), and with aligned multi-lingual corpora (McEnery *et al* 1994). Most recently it has resulted in the development of the British National Corpus (BNC), a corpus of one hundred million words of varied written and spoken texts annotated with part-of-speech information (Leech 1993). The BNC was constructed by a team of publishers (Oxford University Press, Longman, and Chambers Harrap), academic institutions (Lancaster University and Oxford University Computing Services) and the British Library, over the period 1991–94; Lancaster was responsible for the grammatical tagging of the corpus.

The various types of annotation listed above have always been inserted in the text by a mixture of automatic and manual procedures, generally making use of some form of probabilistic technique to assign an analysis to a text at the appropriate linguistic level, and this can then be manually post-edited if necessary to achieve the desired level of accuracy. Because large quantities of text are involved, the post-editing will always involve some assistance by the computer to minimize the time taken to implement the analyst's decision, and to check the validity of each change. The results of the manual correction check the validity of each change. The results of the manual correction (for example, revised probability values) can also be used to improve the subsequent automatic processing of other similar texts.

A preliminary task in all the work described above has been the preparation of the texts (tokenization, explicit marking of sentence breaks, etc.) and the assignment of part-of-speech markers (word-tags or, often, simply 'tags'). Since the early 1980s this has been carried out at Lancaster by a program or suite of programs called Claws (Constituent Likelihood Automatic Word-tagging System). This was one of the first part-of-speech taggers to make use of probabilistic information, achieving a 95–6% accuracy rate (Marshall 1983; see also Church 1988 for another early system). A consequence of the assignment of part-of-speech markers is the wish to associate a single tag with a sequence of two or more contiguous words, such as 'Preposition' with 'according to' or 'Conjunction' with 'as well as' (at least in some cases). For historical reasons we use the term 'dittotag' for this concept, making use of it (for instance) to assign an appropriate tag to a sequence of foreign words; for example, the tag 'Plural Common Noun' would be assigned to 'hoi polloi'.

11.2 The history of Claws

The first version of Claws (in retrospect called Claws1) was developed for tagging the LOB corpus over the period 1981–84. It incorporated what we have since referred to as the C1 tagset of 133 tags, a revision of the tagset used by Greene and Rubin in their work (Greene and Rubin 1971). Over the period 1983–86 parts of this suite of programs were rewritten (as Claws2), mainly to allow the program to make various decisions (such as the positioning of sentence breaks) which Claws1 did not have to make, since the information had already been explicitly encoded by hand in the LOB corpus. This development was part of a general attempt to avoid requiring manual pre-processing of the text before it could be processed by Claws, replacing it by optional manual post-editing to correct the automatic annotation if the required accuracy rate warrants it. The tagset used was a rationalization of the C1 tagset, the C2 tagset, subsequently modified to form the C2a tagset.

Preliminary work was carried out in 1987 on a further development of Claws to make use of verb subcategorization. This work was never developed further than a lexicon containing verb subcategorization information, referred to as the Claws3 lexicon. Thus the next (and current) version of Claws is Claws4, first written in 1988, and incorporating the earlier suite of five programs into a single program. Claws4 has been further developed (we are currently at revision 19) to allow for the extensive changes required by the BNC project. One fundamental change has been to attempt to make the Claws program as independent as possible of the tagset, since the BNC uses two tagsets — a main tagset (C5) with 62 tags with which the whole of the corpus has been tagged, and a larger (C7) tagset with 152 tags, which has been used to make a selected 'core' sample corpus of two million words.

11.3 Issues concerning orthography

In early versions of Claws various different forms of annotation were used to mark special features of the text (such as new paragraphs, or a change of font) and for indicating special characters, such as the accented letters. The LOB corpus had a specially devised coding scheme (Johansson, Leech and Goodluck 1978) which was used for Claws1. Subsequent work used other coding schemes, largely based on the TeX text mark-up system (Knuth 1984). A major revision of the Claws system was entailed by the use of SGML (Standard Generalized Mark-up Language: see Goldfarb 1990) for the BNC, and the current version of Claws assumes that the input text is either in straight-forward ASCII with no special text coding conventions, or makes use of coding conventions based on SGML. Because other forms of annotation are commonly found in the more readily available collections of machine-readable text (such as in electronic mail and on the World Wide Web), we have written various pre-processing programs to convert these formats automatically into an SGML-based format which Claws can handle.

An attempt has been made to retain flexibility in the range of SGML annotation to be expected in a text, and its interpretation. Thus one of the resources read by the Claws program when it starts up is a list of SGML tags and entities, together with an indication of how each item is to be processed by Claws.

If accented letters are represented in the text it is assumed that the SGML form is used; for example the SGML entities 'À' and 'à' respectively represent upper and lower case 'a' with a grave accent. The SGML entity table used by Claws indicates what would be the equivalent letter or letters without the accent, and words are held in the Claws lexicons without accents. Thus the word 'naïve' would be represented as 'naïve' in the input text, and would be transformed to 'naive' before it is looked up in the Claws lexicon. This mechanism allows Claws to handle more complicated cases of transliteration into a conventional character set before look-up in the lexicon, for example '&oelig'; representing the ligature 'œ', or even 'þ', representing 'þ' or 'ð' transliterated as 'th'. Since accents are represented erratically in English text, and are not usually significant in part-of-speech marking, we have chosen to use this rather straight-forward procedure; an alternative, suggested in Sampson (1989b), is to have the lexicon indicate the position of all possible accented letters in a word, and then perform a look-up with and without the accents. In principle the above transliteration scheme could be used for Greek characters as well, but these are marked as such in the SGML entity table, and are used to indicate that this is not an orthographic word in the conventional sense, but a foreign word or mathematical formula.

Other possible interpretations of special characters recognized by Claws are 'noise symbols' (such as the copyright mark '©'), which are treated as if they are not present during lexical look-up; 'formula symbols' which indicate that the immediate stretch of surrounding text is likely to be a mathematical formula (as, for example, in 'a≤3'); 'currency symbols' and 'unit symbols' which indicate that the immediate stretch of text is probably a number and an indication of a unit of measurement (as in '£5' and '70°'); and 'punctuation symbols' (such as '¡') which are to be treated like the normal punctuation marks. It is also possible to indicate to Claws in this way alternative representations for different types of quotation marks, dashes, ellipsis marks, etc., all of which are to be treated in the same way as the normal forms of these characters. Thus this facility allows unusual characters to be represented in a text, and for Claws to be able to treat them in an appropriate way.

SGML 'tags' are used to mark the beginning and end of an element of text of a certain type (a paragraph, a chapter, a heading), perhaps together with one or more attributes with particular values for each instance of the element (identifying number, rendition information, and so on). On the whole Claws did not make use of these in any significant way during the processing of the BNC. Most SGML beginning and end tags were treated as items of text which were to be passed directly to the output and not assigned part-of-speech tags.

Furthermore, when Claws is disambiguating a sequence of text words, intervening SGML tags should normally be treated as if they were not there. Thus the sequence

<hi r=it>Don't</hi> call me that.

which represents italicized *Don't* for emphasis, is tagged and disambiguated as if it were

Don't call me that.

Some SGML tags, such as for the beginning and end of a paragraph (in written text) or of an utterance (in spoken text), indicate the position of a sentence break, even if the orthography of the text at this point does not warrant it. This information is specified in the list of SGML tags, and actioned by Claws.

A text in the BNC generally begins with an extensive set of header information, indicating the provenance of the text, its coding conventions, the editorial process, etc. There follows the text proper, and then possibly some trailer information. The text to be tagged could also consist of several separate segments of text, each with its own header information. In order for Claws to be able to distinguish sections of text to be tagged from header information to be transferred to the output unchanged, the list of SGML tags can indicate that certain beginning SGML tags mark the start of the text for part-of-speech tagging, with the corresponding end tag marking the end of the current stretch of tagging.

We have made an attempt in Claws to allow for normal variation in orthographic practice, particularly in the area of capitalization and the presence or absence of abbreviational full stops. All words are held in the lexicon in lower case, and each tag associated with a word includes a notation specifying the normal orthography associated with that tag. Thus a tag would be indicated as appropriate for a word which was all in upper case, or with an initial capital, or all in lower case; and as appearing with a final abbreviational full stop, with internal full stops, or with no full stops. The lexicon look-up procedure attempts to extract a suitable list of potential tags based on these markers and the orthography of the word in the original text. There has to be some flexibility in this extraction, because (for example) of changing patterns in the use of abbreviational full stops, and of course because of the presence of sentence-initial capitalization. So the list of potential tags for a word will in appropriate cases include tags marked for a different orthography than that present in the text. This includes the case of a text appearing all in upper case, as for example in a heading. Since headings are explicitly marked in the BNC, it would have been possible to have the tag extraction procedure make use of this information. However we did not do this, since texts can also appear set all in upper case (particularly in electronic mail) and we wanted Claws to be able to handle this type of situation. Because Claws attempts to make use of normal conventions in orthography, it is less successful in handling text all in lower case, which also occasionally occurs in electronic mail.

Claws does not attempt to retain the exact word spacing of an original text, assuming that the 'normal' conventions of spacing between words and between preceding and following punctuation marks apply. In order to retain the convention of there being only a single word-tag associated with any individual unit of text, we have chosen to split into two or more separate textual units certain character strings which are conventionally written as a single orthographic word, such as 'cannot' and 'don't'. In cases like this Claws inserts a marker in the output text to show that the separate units were a single word in the original text. In the BNC project a much expanded range of words was treated in this way (for example, 'gonna', 'gorra', 'gotta'), and in the final version of the corpus the markers introduced by Claws were used to recover the spacing of the original text. There were a small number of mainly mathematical texts where the layout of word spacing was unconventional, and the system discussed above did not work. It would have been possible for Claws to insert in its output an explicit indication in all cases of the exact form of the spacing between units, but the frequency of this phenomenon did not warrant the change.

Since the BNC contains a section of spoken texts, Claws has to be able to handle textual representations of whatever speech phenomena are transcribed. This turned out not to be a major problem, since the transcription of the spoken parts of the BNC does not attempt to transcribe such speech phenomena as stuttering, etc., although such things do occur occasionally in representations of direct speech in some parts of the written part of the BNC. The coding conventions of the spoken part of the BNC incorporate a marker for truncated words, and these are simply marked with the 'unknown word' tag. Code was also incorporated into Claws to handle dropped initial 'h' and final 'g', by modifications to the lexical look-up which would, for example, match ' 'avin' ' to 'having'. Procedures were considered to handle representations of other speech phenomena in the written texts, such as 'm-m-must' and 'zooooooom', but were not implemented because of their relative rarity in the BNC.

11.4 The structure of the Claws tagging system

The Claws tagging program is divided into six main sections, as follows:

1. the input running text is read in, divided into individual tokens, and sentence breaks are recognized.

2. a list of possible tags is then assigned to each word, the main source being a lexicon.

3. a number of words in any text will not be found in the lexicon, and for these there is a sequence of rules to be applied in an attempt to assign a suitable list of potential tags.

4. since the lists of potential tags from steps 2 and 3 are based solely on individual words, the next step uses several libraries of template patterns to allow modifications to be made to the lists of tags in the light of the immediate context in which a word occurs.

5. the next step is to calculate the probability of each potential sequence of tags, and to choose the sequence with the highest probability as the preferred one.

6. finally the text and associated information about tag choice is output.

In this section we briefly discuss each of these steps, and the modifications as a result of the BNC project. The output from Claws may be manually post-edited, and possibly re-formatted; this is discussed further in section 11.5.

For the BNC project we had a large quantity of texts of various kinds to be tagged over a relatively short period of time. The tagging of the texts was carried out by a team of analysts, who, as well as running the tagging system over the texts, were also post-editing selected portions of the BNC, particularly the early sections of a new genre of texts, which might indicate places where the tagging system was not working as well as it might. The results of this post-editing would be a series of proposed changes to the resources used by the tagging system, such as the lexicon and libraries of patterns, and occasional changes to the code of the Claws program itself. For this reason we attempted to hold the resources used by Claws in as flexible form as possible, so as to ease the problem of updating them, particularly given the fact that two tagsets were in use.

The resources used by the Claws system are as follows:

1. the list of tags to be used for the current text.

2. the list of SGML tags and entities and an indication of how each is to be processed.

3. the lexicon of words and potential tags.

4. a list of word-endings and potential tags.

5. a set of other miscellaneous lists, including such things as the list of words to be split (such as 'don't' and 'gotta'), how they are to be split, and the tag to be assigned to each portion of the word.

6. the libraries of template patterns.

7. the matrix of probabilities of tag combinations, from which the probability of a tag sequence can be calculated.

In order to make the lexicon easy to handle by the analysts it has been split into several sections, which are merged when Claws begins to run. One of these sections is arranged to allow it to overwrite entries in the other sections. Thus a normal run of Claws would make use of a set of standard sections, perhaps together with a supplementary section for the particular type of text being processed. A standard use of the supplementary section has been to hold words which have to be treated differently in the spoken part of the BNC. Because of the success of the rules for dealing with words not in the lexicon, it has been possible to keep the lexicon fairly small. The main part of the lexicon contains some ten thousand words, and a separate section holds a list of some five thousand proper names of various types. The lexicon currently in use holds for each word a list of potential tags and associated orthographic information. It also holds information as to the frequency of use of a word-tag combination, and this can be in either of two forms; there is either a set of markers for the analyst to indicate a rough frequency (in the range 'common', 'rare', 'very rare'), or a set of frequency figures can be inserted from a tagged text. For the BNC tagging project the former hand-annotation of frequency information was used, but in a follow-up project we are experimenting with probability figures extracted from the 'core' part of the BNC for re-tagging other parts of the BNC.

Some 65–70% of words are assigned a set of potential tags from the lexicon. An important source of tags for other words is the list of word-endings. Claws attempts to match an unknown word against the word-ending list, working from longest to shortest, and assigns the tags indicated. A relatively recent addition to this has been the possibility of distinguishing word-endings with a particular significance for words with an initial capital from word-endings with a general significance. There are a number of further procedures for textual items which fail to match both the lexicon and the word-ending list. These include procedures for words which consist of digits, of a mixture of digits and letters, or contain special characters apart from accented letters — this third type is assumed to be either a combination of a number and an indication of the unit involved, or an arithmetic formula. If all else fails, a word will be assigned an appropriate list of the possible open-class tags, taking into account capitalization and whether or not the word ends with an 's'. These procedures are described in detail in Garside (1985).

Our early experience with the first version of Claws suggested that there were a number of simple patterns of words which the probabilistic disambiguation was getting wrong, or where it could be helped by eliminating one of the tags where we could be certain it was contextually inappropriate. Furthermore there was a requirement to assign a single tag to a sequence of orthographically distinct words, the 'dittotag' mentioned in the first section. We chose to handle this by having Claws match a library of templates against each sequence of words, a successful match requiring a modification to the list of potential tags already assigned to a word. The modification could involve deletion of some, or all but one, of the potential tags; or it could involve the assigning of a tag distinct from all the tags previously assigned to this word, such as a dittotag. We originally referred to the library of templates (incorrectly) as an 'Idiomlist', and we have tended to continue to use this term. In Claws we have treated the dittotag as a special type of template matching; of course it could instead, and perhaps more logically, have been treated as a part of the lexicon, given an extended form of lexicon look-up.

This simple type of template matching has been extensively developed in more recent versions of Claws. One of the problems present in all versions of this mechanism is how to deal with overlapped patterns. On the one hand the matching of a shorter pattern might cause a tagging change which would allow a longer pattern to match; thus a decision to assign to the sequence 'as yet' a dittotag indicating that it is an adverb might allow the matching of a longer sequence containing 'as yet' to a template consisting of the various parts of a potential verb phrase. On the other hand, we will generally want to look for longer matches in preference to shorter matches. There are a number of ways of handling this, none of which is entirely satisfactory; in Claws it is handled by scanning from left to right through the text, searching simultaneously for all matching templates starting at each position in the text. If there are several matches at a certain point then one is chosen, using a value function which involves the length of match and also the type of match, since it could be on the word, on one of the potential tags, or simply an unspecified intervening word (and in later versions of Claws it could further be a part of a word, such as 'any word ending -ing', or a part of a tag, such as any of the noun tags). Then the tag changes associated with the preferred template are implemented, any unfinished template matches in the scope of this successful match being abandoned.

To allow more flexibility Claws now has three separate libraries of templates (although the same template can appear in more than one library if required). The first set of templates is matched to the input text, and the changes for any matched template are implemented. The second set of templates is then matched against the resulting text, and again the actions of any matched templates are implemented. The basic idea is that all the more-or-less fixed phrases, including dittotags, will be dealt with on the first pass, and the more general patterns will be searched for on the second pass, making use of the tags corrected by patterns on the first pass. A third pass is then made with a third library of templates, but this takes place *after* the probabilistic disambiguation phase. If a template specifies a tag to be matched on the first or second pass, it is allowed to match against any of the list of potential tags associated with a word; but on the third pass the match must be against the tag preferred by the probabilistic disambiguation. Thus the third pass can be used for templates which would overgenerate matches if allowed to match against *any* potential tag. The above describes the rationale for the design of the template matching system, but because of the complex interactions possible within a text the decision as to how to write and place the individual templates depends on a degree of judgement and experimentation; this is discussed from a more linguistic point-of-view in chapter 12.

Within this multi-pass generalization of the template matching, other smaller changes have been made to allow more flexible forms of matching. We have already mentioned matching against part-words and part-tags; it is also possible to require the match against the word or tag to fail if a template match is to succeed, to require that an (otherwise unspecified) word has a word-initial capital, to specify alternative word or tag matches in the same template, and to allow repeated optional matches (to some specified maximum) against a portion of the template. The current version of Claws has some three thousand template patterns (eighteen hundred in the first pass, nine hundred in the second, and three hundred in the third). To allow the analysts to update the template libraries easily, template lists of different types are held separately and merged at run-time; for example, expressions involving compound nouns, foreign phrases, expressions involving proper names, and patterns involving verb sequences are all held as separate lists.

The probabilistic disambiguation phase is essentially the same technique that was used in earlier versions of Claws. The Viterbi alignment procedure is used to indicate the most likely sequence of tags where there is a sequence of one or more alternatives. The Viterbi calculation is now also used to estimate the probability of each alternative tag assigned to a word, since this value is required to implement the 'portmanteau tag' evaluation described in section 11.5. These probabilities are calculated from the word-tag probabilities in the lexicon, whether estimated by the analysts or extracted from tagged text, and from tag-tag probabilities, extracted from tagged data and read in as one of the Claws resources. The current version of Claws can make use of first- or second-order tag-tag probabilities; for the tagging of the BNC we have used first-order probabilities, but we are currently investigating the use of second-order probabilities (i.e. tag trigrams) (Leech, Garside and Bryant 1994a).

While performing the Viterbi alignment certain textual items can be treated as if they were not present in the sequence. Thus all SGML tags are ignored, as are all words in a list supplied as part of the Claws resources — generally this includes only 'fillers' in spoken text such as 'er' and 'erm'. This list of items to be ignored is also used during the template matching described earlier.

One other form of contextual disambiguation can be carried out by Claws; this is the recognition of repetitions in spoken texts. A repeated sequence of words (perhaps including one or more fillers) is tagged as if the repetition and the fillers were absent; this is discussed in more detail in Garside (1995).

11.5 The post-processing of tagged output

The output from the Claws program is in what we term 'vertical' format, with a line per textual item. Each line contains a reference number (linking the item back to the original input line), the textual item itself (word, punctuation mark, SGML tag, or whatever), the list of potential part-of-speech tags with the preferred tag listed first, some information about the tagging process (such as the source of the list of potential tags, whether lexicon, word-ending list, hyphenation procedures, etc.), and some subsidiary information, such as markers for textual items joined together in the input, and a marker for cases where internal checks during the tagging procedure indicate that the tagging of a word may be insecure (such as where the orthography of an input word does not match the possible orthographic forms of the word listed in the lexicon). This form of output is recognized by all the post-processing programs, including the editing software.

A problem for the BNC project was that an input file might contain a certain amount of data which cannot be fitted into this format; there will be an extensive set of header information which is not to be tagged, there may be SGML tags which contain extended lists of attribute and value pairs, etc. Because of this the output from Claws was redesigned so that the normal tagged output was still produced in the above format, so that the post-processing programs did not have to be changed. But the data which cannot be put in this format are output to a supplementary file, and a cross-reference to it is inserted in the primary output file. This is also how long textual items are now processed. Earlier versions of Claws simply truncated long textual items at the twenty-fifth character with an error message;

now the long word is inserted in the supplementary file, with a cross-reference in the primary file so that it can be extracted by the post-processing programs as required.

One form of post-processing performed to varying degrees on different output texts is post-editing by human analysts, to correct erroneous tagging and other decisions by Claws. The 'core' part of the BNC has been post-edited in full, while only selected portions of the rest of the corpus have been post-edited, to establish the types of error occurring in different genres. During most of the BNC project a special purpose text editor, called the LB editor and written by Tony McEnery, was used to perform this task.

More recently the LB editor has been replaced by an X-Windows-based editor called Xanthippe, which carries out essentially the same tasks. A section of the text being post-edited is presented on the screen, together with the tag preferred by Claws and a list of the other potential tags considered but rejected. Because the information per word is fairly large, only a small number of words can be displayed in this format. So a separate window displays the same words and surrounding text, but without the tagging information so that a larger context can be seen; the two windows are linked, so that they scroll together.

The most common type of tagging error is one where the list of potential tags is correct, but Claws has selected the wrong one. In this case the analyst selects the correct tag, and it is promoted to the preferred tag position. If the correct tag is not among the list of potential tags for this word, Xanthippe displays a menu of all possible tags from which the correct tag can be selected; a supplementary list allows a sequence of words to be tagged with a selected dittotag. These tag-correcting operations are the most frequent tasks carried out using Xanthippe, but there are facilities for correcting a textual item (for example, if it is a typographic error), for splitting or joining words (and adjusting the link markers, if necessary) if the Claws tokenization is in error, for inserting and deleting sentence breaks, and for inserting notes of various types to comment on the text or the tagging decisions.

For the BNC project a suite of programs was run after Claws to check various features of the SGML structure of the document, to match the spacing of the original to the final text, and so on. A further program converts the text into the final form of the corpus at the completion of processing at Lancaster, with the words back in 'horizontal' running text format, and with the tags represented as

SGML entities. A number of further reformating procedures were required at this stage. One example was that, with the insertion of an SGML tag to indicate a sentence break, certain parts of the SGML structure of the original document might be invalidated; for instance, a <hi> tag indicating a font change (perhaps for emphasis) which crossed a sentence boundary. In situations like this the post-processing program has to replicate the <hi> tag on either side of the sentence break. Another issue was the use of 'portmanteau tags'. This is a tag indicating that the Claws choice between two tags is particularly uncertain, so that the tag allocated to the word is a combination of the two possibilities. The post-processing program recognizes such situations (of a pair of tags with probability figures from Claws lying within a certain range of each other) and adjusts the tag accordingly (for more details see Leech, Garside and Bryant 1994a).

11.6 Conclusion

An error analysis has been performed on the automatic tagging of a portion of the BNC, using the smaller (C5) tagset (Leech and Smith 1995). This shows that there is an error rate of about 1.7%, and about 4.7% of the tags are portmanteau tags. The report gives further details, such as error rates for particular tags and for particular tag pairs.

We are currently engaged in an EPSRC-funded project (GR/K14223) to improve the tagging of the BNC, making use of the manually post-edited 'core' corpus. This is being used as a source of revised Claws resources which will be used to re-tag the BNC; it is also being used as a source of information about error patterns, from which we are developing 'patching' techniques for correcting the main corpus.

12 Template analysis: bridging the gap between grammar and the lexicon

STEVE FLIGELSTONE, PAUL RAYSON and NICHOLAS SMITH

12.1 Introduction

Since the late 1970s, Geoffrey Leech and the UCREL team at Lancaster have made a notable contribution to the field of Natural Language Processing (NLP) through the development of probabilistic techniques of grammatical analysis. Claws, which has been developed continuously[1] throughout this period, is not only regarded as a pioneering program, but is still one of the most accurate part-of-speech taggers available. Geoffrey Leech has also been involved in, and to a large extent responsible for, various projects leading to significant progress in the more complex problem of automatic syntactic parsing (see Garside, Leech and Sampson 1987; Black, Garside and Leech 1993).

A central feature of all these efforts, which to a certain extent defines the UCREL probabilistic paradigm, has been the use of Hidden Markov Model (HMM)-based statistical algorithms. Though many researchers were slow to embrace them, such empirically oriented statistical techniques have gained currency as a primary means of facing the challenges posed by the complexities of 'real language'. This focus on statistical techniques notwithstanding, since the early days of Claws development, UCREL NLP systems have used additional strategies to achieve accurate output. In this paper we consider what is perhaps the most significant supplementary methodology, which has emerged as an important facet, not only of Claws, but of a number of other software development projects undertaken by UCREL, and which is increasingly showing signs of becoming a practically and theoretically significant approach to NLP in its own right. We refer to this method as 'template analysis', and the best-known example of UCREL's use of the approach in question is the 'idiom-tagging' module of Claws itself.

In the following sections we explain what we mean by 'template analysis', and report on a number of projects in which the method has featured prominently. We consider also some of the reasons why such techniques are useful. We argue that the template analysis paradigm is a useful means of (partially) modelling language, which blends in a pragmatic and conceptually plausible way, aspects of language processing conventionally regarded as belonging to two distinct, albeit interwoven, domains, the lexicon and the grammar.

12.2 Template analysis

The basic template analysis paradigm is a simple one, and differs from conventional parsing techniques in that there is no in-built concept of sentence 'structure', but rather an emphasis on the tagging of fragments of text, be these single words, whole phrases, part-phrases or even fragments of text spanning part of one phrase and also part or all of another. The tagger uses a table of template rules to identify significant sequences of text, and apply some specified annotation to that text. A rule consists of a sequence of one or more patterns, each specifying, somewhat in the manner of a standard regular expression, a set of possible input strings which may match that part of the rule in question. A second component of each rule is an action or set of actions to be carried out if the pattern specifications of the rule are met in full. This action is normally specified explicitly within the rule itself, so that each rule may be said to consist of a pattern and an action. Thus a rule applying to a sequence of three input strings, has the canonical form:

pattern ACTION, *pattern* ACTION, *pattern* ACTION

Note that for any of the actions in the rule to be carried out, the entire template, i.e. each *pattern* in the rule, must be matched by something in the input. Although in theory all *actions* are optional, at least one action is specified somewhere within the rule (or is implicitly associated with the rule).

In its simplest form, such a rule may consist just of a sequence of words to be matched, and a sequence of labels, or *tags*, to be applied:

word TAG, *word* TAG, *word* TAG

In practice, however, many rules have greater coverage than this. For example, a 'wild card' may be used in the pattern, so that it could match any of several strings. For example, the pattern *depart** would match any of the strings *depart, departs, departed, departing, departure,* etc. Furthermore, in most current applications template rules are used not with raw text as input, but with pre-analyzed text, so that any existing annotations, such as part-of-speech (POS) tags, are also available as target patterns for a rule template.

Thus a rule

word-tag NEWTAG, *word-tag* NEWTAG, *word-tag* NEWTAG

or even:

word NEWTAG, *tag* NEWTAG, *word* NEWTAG

could be used to modify the tagging of some partially specified pre-analyzed input. This can produce quite broad coverage rules, such that a template *N**, *N**, *V** will match any sequence of words bearing tags indicating (any class of) noun, noun and verb, respectively.[2]

The action component of a rule may also be used to mark other linguistic features in text such as syntactic information or semantic field tags (this is described in section 12.5, below).

12.3 Template analysis as a corrective to Claws

We make no claim for the originality of a template approach. Indeed, a system using 'context frame rules' was the tag disambiguation method used in the first major corpus-tagging project, that undertaken with the Brown Corpus (Greene and Rubin 1971, Francis 1980), and as we shall see (section 12.8, below) very fruitful lines of enquiry are currently being pursued by several investigators in the field.

Whilst UCREL set about the task of developing statistical methods for disambiguating tag sequences, it was nonetheless found useful to apply template analysis techniques in order to enhance the performance of the Claws word tagging system. Various template rules, in the guise of an 'idiom-tagging' module, were applied to effect an analysis preferred over that which the Claws HMM-based algorithm would otherwise produce. At various times this part of the tagging system received relatively little attention, whist the 'real work' of developing the statistically driven software progressed. But in recent years the emphasis on idiom-tagging has strengthened once more (see section 12.4, below). The initial development and uses of this part of the Claws system are described in Blackwell (1987), but below we offer a brief summary for the benefit of readers unfamiliar with the basic design of Claws.

If we imagine a Claws system without its idiom-tagging module, and without some of its pre-processing functions, we could represent it schematically thus:

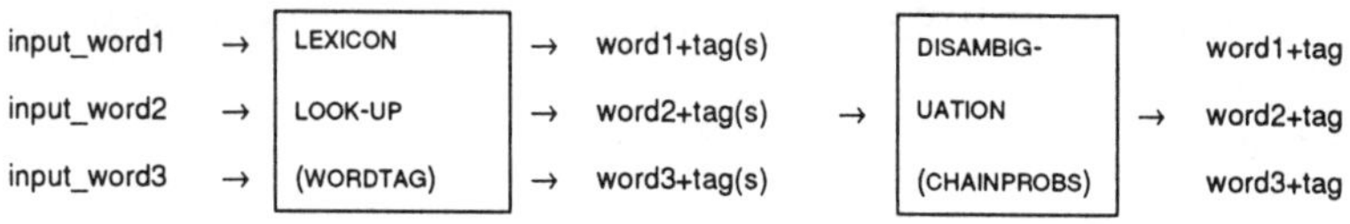

The word-tagging module would use the lexicon and various morphologically oriented rules to produce a list of 'candidate tags' (or, in the case of a grammatically unambiguous word, a single tag) for each word of input. An ambiguously tagged sequence of words would then be input to the probabilistic CHAINPROBS module,[3] which outputs for each word the most likely of the candidate tags, based on a calculation of the probabilities of the various possible tag sequences.

The point of application of the idiom-tagging rules is between the word-tagging module and the probabilistic disambiguation. Any part of WORDTAG's output, that is to say, the words themselves or any of the candidate tags assigned by the program, may be tested against the idiom-tagging rules for a match. It is thus used to influence the actions of the disambiguator by altering the output from WORDTAG which would otherwise be fed to it. In order to achieve this it may execute a number of actions. For a given word:

- it may delete one or more of the candidate tags assigned by WORDTAG
- it may alter the probabilities associated with the tags assigned to it

- it may replace or augment the pre-assigned tags with different tags, not given in the lexicon

Examples of the first case would be the 'strong' rules:

every, little DA1, helps VVZ
shocked JJ, at

Here there is only a single candidate tag for the grammatically ambiguous words *little*, *helps* and *shocked* and the idiom-tagging rule is taking precedence over the other parts of the system, effectively dictating what the output will be.

A common use of the third case is the assignment of 'ditto tags' to sequences regarded for tagging purposes as single entities, such as compound prepositions or certain adverbial expressions (e.g. *at large*, *of course*).

The following rule incorporates all of the aforementioned IDIOMTAG devices, and still leaves work for the probabilistic disambiguator to do:

in II% RR21, vain JJ RR22

Here, the rule eliminates any lexicon-derived candidate tags other than II (preposition) and JJ (adjective) for *in* and *vain*, respectively. Furthermore, it introduces as new candidates the ditto tags RR21 and RR22 (for a compound adverb), and finally, whilst confirming the candidature of the II and JJ tags, it adjust the probability associated with II (the percentage sign indicates a downgrading of the normal probability of a given tag). Since the likelihood of II RR22 or RR21 JJ being selected as sequences is set to zero, the CHAINPROBS program will be left to decide on the basis of the broader context which of the sequences II JJ and RR21 RR22 is the more likely, taking into account the adjustment in probabilities brought about by the rule.

The primary motivation for introducing these rules into the Claws system was to reduce the error-rate associated with the main procedures of lexicon look-up followed by HMM disambiguation. For several years, the number of such rules used at any one time was just a few hundred, but more recently, the number, power and flexibility of the idiom-tagging rules has increased substantially.

What these rules enable Claws to achieve, in a way which

eludes the first-order HMM, is to base tagging decisions on information concerning word or word-class sequences with characteristics that cannot be adequately modelled on the basis of adjacency likelihood. This is particularly useful with longer spans of text with some dependency operating between non-adjacent words, and with sequences of words which, due to lexically specific factors are not in fact as ambiguous as they might appear, as it were, to a HMM. In this way, Claws may be said to contain a phraseological component, and thereby a means of dealing with what have been termed 'prefabricated patterns' (Hakuta 1974) or 'speech formulas' (Pawley and Syder 1983)

Because it has been developed to fulfil a specific role in a particular piece of software, the precise workings of the IDIOMTAG module are a little more complex than presented here, and the formalism has developed subtleties which are rather task-specific and not always entirely transparent to the casual observer (the use of implicit actions being a case in point). However, we have presented the essentials in sufficient detail to illustrate the basic mechanism, which is common to all the work described in this paper.

In order to imagine a template analysis module in a more general way, one might envisage the idiom tagger in Claws being brought into play not before the CHAINPROBS disambiguation, but afterwards, as the final processing stage. In this case, the resulting output can be seen as a direct consequence of the actions specified in the template rules. In fact, such a system has been implemented, as a means not of pre-empting, but of correcting errors induced by the probabilistic disambiguation process, and is described in the following section. In other contexts, too, where template analysis has been introduced, development has concentrated on systems where the output is determined directly by actions specified in the template rules.

12.4 Recent development of Claws idiom-tagging

The main impetus in expanding the functionality of the Claws Idiomlist in recent years has been the need to tag increasingly large corpora with little or no manual correction. This was particularly the case in the tagging of the 100 million word British National Corpus (BNC).[4] A short passage from the corpus is reproduced below, showing (in bold) a significant proportion of tag assignment decisions that have been made as a result of an idiom rule:

We_PPIS2 passed_VVD the_AT lay-by_NN1 near_II the_AT **Cowal_NP Road_NNL1** junction_NN1 doing_VDG **about_RG** ninety_MC ._. I_PPIS1 watched_VVD as_CSA we_PPIS2 went_VVD by_RP ._. Nothing_PN1 ;_; it_PPH1 was_VBDZ just_RR a_AT1 damp_JJ ,_, deserted_JJ **parking_NN1** place_NN1 with_IW a_AT1 big_JJ new_JJ concrete_JJ litter_NN1 bin_NN1 (_(replaced_VVN with_IW unusual_JJ alacrity_NN1 ,_, in_II **less_RR21 than_RR22** six_MC months_NNT2)_) ._.
(from BNC, CrowRd:1–7)

12.4.1 Extended rules: modular development

The template rules which effected the highlighted taggings above were developed in sections arranged on loosely thematic principles, such as geographical and titular nouns, verb strings, foreign expressions and compound nouns. Taking this modular approach analysts can more easily identify gaps and tagging inconsistencies in the coverage of a particular class. While quite a wide catchment is ensured in tagging unseen texts, new patterns or templates identified in sample error analyses can quickly be added to the lists.[5] In this section we explore the wide-ranging nature of the rules in the context of the various thematic modules, while section 12.4.3 deals with the facility of adding or deleting whole lists of entries specific to a particular genre or domain.

The Core list

A miscellany of items encountered in general English constitute the so-called *Core* Idiomlist. Typical entries disambiguate known problematic words, for example *as*, and idiosyncratic sequences, for example *for certain*, by specifying the appropriate tag(s) in a particular context:

(i) as CSA, follows
(ii) as RG, ([ ])5, as CSA, possible JJ
(iii) for RR21, certain RR22, ![N*]

The first entry is straightforward in that it forces any instance of *as* to be treated as a subordinating conjunction when it precedes the word *follows*. The second rule is more flexible, allowing between up to five unspecified tags (or words) to come in between the *as* ... *as possible* of a comparative construction, assigning the tags RG and CSA to the first and second instances respectively of *as*. The number of unspecified tags can be adjusted for different templates, capturing various long-distance relationships that Markov modelling may treat as ambiguous.

According to the third rule, provided that there is no form of noun tag following it, the sequence *for certain* is taken as an adverbial idiom. Here we employ ditto tagging to capture the integrated quality of the expression with a single duplicated tag. The negation operator '!' is a means of preventing the idiom being applied unrestrictively to cases where ordinary lexical tags (for *IF*, certain *JJ*) would be preferred.

Naming expressions

Our approach to dealing with multiple word sequences representing geographical, personal and titular names — a problematic area in NLP — has been to capture such entities in one of three ways; expressing them either (i) in full, (ii) as a series of alternative words sharing the same tag, or (iii) as word and/or tag templates with options:

(i) Buenos NP1, Aires NP1
Chief NNB, Buthelezi NP1

(ii) New NP1, England/Guinea/Hampshire/Haven/Hebrides NP1

(iii) Fort NNL1, ([WIC])2 NP1, [WIC] NP1
[WIC] NP1, ([WIC])2 NP1, Lake/Lane/Loch/Mill NNL1
Doctor/Dr NNB, ([WIC])2 NP1, [WIC] NP1

The last option is applied in cases where a key word such as *Fort* or *Lane* is regularly followed or preceded by at least one, and up to three, words with initial capital letter (WIC), which can be tagged as Proper noun.[6] Rules such as these have obviated the need to specify individually in the Idiomlists many thousands of multi-word place and titular names, many of which are little heard of (such as *Fort Perch Rock*) or lexically ambiguous (*Dr Bill Smart*).

Naturalized foreign expressions

Ditto tagging has proved especially useful in the area of foreign expressions naturalized into English (cf. Johansson 1986:131):

(i) viva NN121 JJ21 RR21%, voce NN122 JJ22 RR22%
je NN141, ne NN142, sais NN143, quoi NN144

Thus *viva voce*, for example, can function as a nominal, adjectival or adverbial compound. To reflect the comparatively rare usage of this last tag it is given a lower probability (%) marking. We have endeavoured to extend the coverage of this set of expressions as far as possible, to overcome tagger difficulties in guessing an appropriate English POS tag for each of a sequence of generally unfamiliar word forms.

Verb strings

Idiomlist entries have frequently helped to correct the tags assigned by HMM to various phrasal verbs[7] (particularly the particle component):

(i) calm VV0, down RP
switch/switched/switches/switching, off/on/out RP

We have also found templates to distinguish, for example, a past participle (VVN) from a simple past form (VVD), and an infinitive (VVI) from a base form verb (VV0), to be effective:

(ii) [VH*], ([XX/R*])3, [VVD] VVN
(iii) [VM], ([XX/R*])3, [VV0] VVI

Rule (ii) changes VVD to VVN after any form of auxiliary *have*, rule (iii) changes VV0 to VVI after a modal verb. A fair degree of flexibility is allowed in the specification of verb sequences. In these instances up to three negative or adverb tags are permitted in the medial position, while in other templates the permutations of optional tags are more varied. It is, moreover, possible to link rules together, as discussed in the next section.

12.4.2 Pre- and post-HMM idiomlists

In the past all idioms were processed by Claws in one pass, *before* probabilistic disambiguation. One occasional consequence of this was that some templates designed to improve tagged output actually introduced errors. As an example, a rule from the verb string section:

to TO, ([XX/R*])3, [VV0] VVI

would match on the text sequence *I refer to Report 2a.* — because *Report* is capable of being a verb (as indicated in the lexicon), and it is preceded by *to*. The resultant tagging would be

I_PPIS1 refer_VV0 to_TO Report_VVI 2a_FO ._.

If, on the other hand, one were to place the same rule *after* Markov disambiguation, the action to change a base form verb to infinitive would not occur, since *Report* would already have been disambiguated as a singular noun (NN1). Thus a pass of the idiom-matching routine after HMM does not consider the full set of candidate tags as supplied by the lexicon (or the list of suffixes), but performs an action only on the *preferred* tag as assigned by HMM.

In operational terms Claws merges the thematic lists described above into three sets, two being matched against the text before Markov disambiguation and one after. Some general principles of distribution are: (i) entries which filter the choice of tags, while still leaving it ambiguous, must go in one of the first two sets; (ii) entries which are fairly safe in that they do not require the help of HMM are generally placed before it; (iii) entries which do require HMM should follow it, in the third set.[8]

In this way output of a rule in an early stage of processing may feed into the probability matrix or into a later rule, or both. For example, in the sentence: *You should at least watch!* the first idiom below would mark *at least* as an adverbial, which in turn would ensure that *watch* is disambiguated by HMM as a verb. Application of the second rule below would then ensure that the verb be assigned the infinitive tag:

at RR21, least RR22
[VM], ([XX/R*])3, [VV0] VVI

12.4.3 Genre-specific adaptations

As an extension of the componential approach to Idiomlist development, we now have the facility to 'slot in' additional or substitutional lists, or to change the way Claws handles the lists, to deal with constructions peculiar to a particular domain or genre.

Scientific/technical

In tagging two corpora of technical data, the IBM corpus of computer manuals,[9] and the ITU Corpus[10] consisting of telecommunications texts, we added to the Idiomlists entries to improve the accuracy and consistency of tagging of technical terms, such as:

> to TO, IPL VVI [11]
> the, power NN1, on RP, light NN1
> control NN1, channel/device/echo NN1
> signalling NN1, [NNT1]

Conversely, certain idioms which may operate in general varieties of English can be omitted, or assigned a lower probability, when processing texts like the ITU. We found, for example, that the informal adverbial sequence

a RR21, bit RR22 was redundant in the telecommunications corpus, and occasioned errors if retained in the Idiomlists:

> In_II this_DD1 mode_NN1 it_PPH1 is_VBZ expected_VVN that_CST behaviour_NN1 of_IO the_AT link_NN1 at_II **a_RR21 bit_RR22** level_JJ is_VBZ not_XX of_IO interest_NN1 ._.

Informal conversational texts

Approximately five million words of the BNC are of casual, generally unprepared conversation.[12] A set of Idiomlist entries has been compiled to capture colloquial patterns such as slang expressions and non-standard verb forms:

> fair JJ, do NN221, 's NN222 (and: fair JJ, does NN2)

cotton VV0, on/onto
did VDD, n't XX, used VMK, to TO

For the processing of spoken texts Claws has been modified to enable idiom pattern-matching in cases of interruption, hesitation and repetition. For example, ditto tags identifying a prepositional unit *according to* no longer need to be contiguous when certain items such as intervening pauses, whether vocalized (e.g. *er* and *erm*) or empty (marked by the SGML <pause> tag), occur between the individual elements:

According_II21 er_FU to_II22 the_AT latest_RRT weather_NN1 report_NN1 ...

Handling of repetition and other features of spoken texts is discussed further in Garside, Chapter 11, this volume.

12.4.4 Future developments

We are currently increasing the coverage and refinement of the rules outlined above within the existing Claws Idiomlist formalism. One aspect of this work will be to improve, for example, the probability weightings assigned to entries that contain ambiguous taggings.

However, the main area of growth in the future is to be in extending the formalism further, by adopting some of the more powerful template tagging techniques described in subsequent sections of this paper; the principle application of this work will be to produce an enhanced version of the tagged BNC.[13]

12.5 Template analysis for Key Syntactic Links (MATRIX)

In a project called 'The Automatic Content Analysis of Spoken Discourse' [14] (see Wilson and Rayson 1993), and continuing in a current project, 'Automatic Content Analysis of Market Research Interview Transcripts'[15] (ACAMRIT, see Chapter 7, this volume), UCREL aims to produce computer-based tools to assist with the linguistic analysis of product surveys of a Market Research company.

We have developed a system which automatically assigns semantic field tags to large bodies of transcribed spoken interviews conducted between the market researchers and members of the public.

Our aim is to allow qualitative analysis to be carried out on a larger scale than is normally possible, along with traditional quantitative evidence only usually found by using fixed multiple choice questionnaires.

The text is POS tagged by Claws, and then semantically tagged. The projects have developed various ways of disambiguating word senses based on rank ordering and domain of discourse. We use a template analysis method to link degree modifiers to adjectives, adjectives to the nouns they modify, and deal with transferred negation. A program called MATRIX (see Rayson 1994) reads user-defined template rules and automatically assigns links between the appropriate words or phrases. The MATRIX formalism is also used for marking auxiliary verbs within the semantic tagger (see below). In the current project we are planning to extend the linguistic analysis to a limited resolution of anaphoric references, and identify key argument-predicate relations using enhanced template analysis techniques.

Previous content analyzers such as General Inquirer have simply provided frequency counts on the content categories for the texts being studied. However, mere frequency counts on individual categories cannot provide information about the referents of adjectives, whether and how adjectives are modified by intensifiers or downtoners, and whether or not assertions are negated. In the past these have had to be annotated by hand.

It should perhaps be said that template analysis here is not intended as a competitor to the method of a full syntactic parse and semantic analysis: rather, it is an attempt to link together the most important descriptive and modifying words in a corpus without the additional computation and manual intervention that the former kind of analysis would require.

Based on the analysis of a preliminary corpus of just over 200,000 words of market research interviews, template rules were developed for the following:

- Linking adjectives to the nouns they modify, e.g.

  The STAFF are HELPFUL

  This is achieved with the template:

  VB*, (XX), (RG*/RR*), J*[<P*/DD1/N*]

where the sequence in square brackets means link the adjective (J*) to the previous pronoun (P*), singular determiner (DD1) or noun (N*).

- Linking degree modifiers to adjectives, e.g.

  The staff are VERY HELPFUL

- Ensuring that negative words are linked to the items which they negate (cf. Wilson 1991), e.g.

  I do NOT LIKE mushrooms

  This also includes transferred negation, where in an indirect statement a negative structurally negates one of a set of introductory verbs (e.g. *think*) but semantically negates the main verb or adjective in the indirect statement, e.g.

  I do NOT think (that) asparagus is TASTY
  I do NOT think (that) Paula LIKES it

  The first example is marked by the template:

  VD*, XX[>J*/V*], (RG*/RR*), think/seem/see, DD*

  where the sequence in square brackets means link the negative (XX) to the following adjective (J*) or verb (V*).

The links for the various kinds of relation form chains connecting the relevant negatives, adjectives, modifiers, and nouns, which are interpreted and applied in producing the final output. These template rules have a success rate of over 90% when run over Claws tagged interview text. With manual postediting of Claws tags, the results are even more satisfactory.

12.5.1 The auxiliary/content problem

A large number of semantic ambiguities in the text are caused by the very common verbs *be, do* and *have*, which are treated as syntactically unambiguous by Claws, but which may have either an auxiliary function or one or more 'content' (main verb) senses. Rank frequency ordering in these cases is unhelpful as, for example, auxiliary *be* has approximately the same frequency of occurrence as content *be*. However, given that each of the auxiliaries collocate with a particular form of the lexical verb, we have been able to develop template rules based on characteristic sequences of Claws POS tags within which these collocations occur. These rules distinguish the auxiliary uses of these verbs with a high degree of accuracy. For example, the rule:

VH*, (XX), (RR*), V*N

is used to distinguish the auxiliary use *she HAS arrived* from the content sense *she HAS a new car*.

12.5.2 Semantic idiom tagging

The semantic tagger we developed also identifies semantic phrasal idioms such as *all in all* and *up the creek without a paddle* which we mark as one multi-word unit with a particular semantic tag. A human analyst updates a list of templates as new idioms are found (currently we have over 11000 templates). The analyst is able to define which intervening items are allowed between words of the idiom by use of a special template rule, for example:

hand*, {Np/P*/R*}, over RP

which will mark the phrasal verb *handed over* in the sentence *Laura handed the £50 reward money over* because it is interrupted by a noun phrase (Np).[16] The use of templates is an improvement on our previous technique which set a limit on the number of words which could intervene between parts of an idiom but didn't allow us to specify what the words were.

12.6 Sharpening Claws (JAWS)

The JAWS[17] program (see Fligelstone, in preparation) applies techniques derived from those in MATRIX (see section 12.5, above) to the task of refining Claws output in such a way as to produce a Claws-like output, but with an enhanced tagset in which there is greater precision in a number of areas. Contextual template rules are used to distinguish not only the main and auxiliary uses of *be, do, have* and *get* (see MATRIX, above), but also to distinguish active past participles from passive participles (identically tagged by Claws), and to distinguish between pronominal and determiner uses of such dual-purpose words as *this, that, more, some, all,* etc. In Claws analysis, no attempt is made to make this distinction, with the tags applied to them being inherently ambiguous. Further rules are used to mark relative pronouns, also indicating case in most instances. In the JAWS variation of the Claws tagset, the pronoun, determiner and verb tags are substantially reworked to take account of the extra information that JAWS is able to include in the output.

The program also carries out lemmatization of the input text[18] so that lexemes, rather than specific word forms, can be used in the formulation of templates, leading to greater economy of rule-writing.

JAWS has also been used experimentally to identify noun phrase heads to a high degree of accuracy, and a further layer of analysis utilizes the linking algorithm of MATRIX to identify a large number of phrasal verbs, linking their roots to their adverbial particles in the form of a dependency link.

12.7 Towards a generalized template analysis tool

The above descriptions relate to a number of separate but related language analysis projects in which software development and formalisms have been developed specifically to meet the requirements of each project. However, it is apparent that there is a broad similarity in the approaches, and consequently we feel it is desirable to move towards adopting a standard 'language' for the writing of template rules. The goal is not simply one of notational uniformity, but that of developing more flexible software.

Central to this task is the making explicit of that which is implicit in earlier systems. Whereas it is easy to envisage the use of template rules for the manipulation of various kinds of information, e.g. part of speech, semantic, or dependency, at present each program developed is tailored to work only on levels of annotation relevant to the particular purpose for which it has been written. Insofar as it is possible to define a single set of functions, or actions, which could be used to do all, or at least most, of the template-driven tagging and linking work of the programs discussed in this paper, and a formalism developed for expressing these functions, then by explicitly stating within a rule the nature of any input or output items specified within it, it should be possible to develop a program which can be used for a variety of analytical purposes, all based on the template analysis approach. For example, a rule cited in section 12.3 could be schematically represented as:

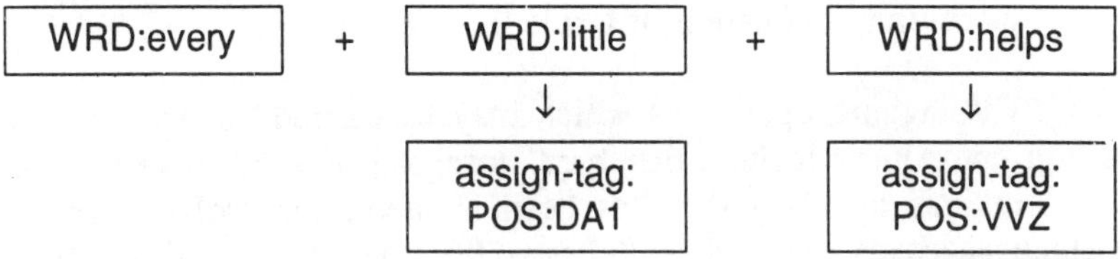

By allowing the user to inform the program what levels of analysis (i.e. types of tag) will be used for a particular task, a linguistically naïve program can be conceived. The only restrictions on its effectiveness will be the range of tag manipulation functions available, and the appropriateness of the template rules themselves. As well as offering considerable versatility, such a program will provide a useful experimental tool for exploring the scope of template-based methods, as the user is free to invent at will any number of tagsets for simultaneous use, representing an open-ended range of analytical levels.

The task of developing such software is currently being undertaken in the writing of the successor program to JAWS, which is required to carry out a much fuller dependency analysis than merely the identification of phrasal verbs and noun phrase heads. As well as identification of a broad range of dependencies, we are seeking to label heads and adverbials with information concerning their semantic type and semantic role. The 'Template Tagger' is devoid of any 'hard-wired' information concerning tags, their types and their interrelations.

This open-endedness is handled by the use of a user-edited configuration file in which various parameters are set to control the operation of the program:

- a list of the levels of annotation to be matched and/or applied in rules (e.g. POS, lexeme, semantic and head identifying)

- restrictions on the range of valid tokens for any given level (for example, a file may be specified which contains the tagset for use with the level 'POS')

- which rule tables to apply, and in what sequence
- whether (and how many) consecutive passes through a given table should be made
- (for each rule set) whether the program should attempt to apply every rule in the list to a given input, or terminate on the first successful application of a rule.[19]

The tagging operations which may be carried out by a rule's action component include the 'hard' insertion of a tag (overwriting any previous labelling that has been applied), the 'soft' insertion (which succeeds only when the new tag does not conflict with a previously assigned annotation), various operations to apply additional tags, thus increasing ambiguity in the output, and functions which actually modify existing labelling, e.g. in order to subscript major category labels.

At the time of writing a working version of the Template Tagger has been developed[20] incorporating most of the functions referred to above. The Template Tagger at present is essentially a powerful rule-driven 'word-tagging' program, but in due course 'linking' functions, similar to those described in section 12.5 will be added in order to increase its versatility.[21]

12.8 Conclusions

The task of text analysis or mark-up is first and foremost a task of disambiguation. A parsing tool which is heavily biased towards grammatical categories of a general kind, and away from individual lexical and collocational knowledge may provide a concise means of defining a set of legal constructs which may be appropriate to the text fragment in question, but it will be prone to generate a large number of legal, but contextually inappropriate, analyses.

But as scholars are increasingly aware, means for rejecting such spurious analyses are available, not only to the human, but also to the machine equipped with some knowledge about what is typical in language use. As currently implemented, probabilistic techniques such as HMMs represent a very useful, but flawed 'catch-all' method of modelling typicality as represented in the likelihood of various sequences, but typically these sequences, too, are defined in terms of broad grammatical categories and tend to be short-range on grounds of computability.

The template tagging approach allows rules of greater and lesser degrees of coverage to prefer one or a small number of analyses over all others, insofar as they enable typicality, rather than merely 'legality', to be modelled, and also in that such patterns of typicality can be represented efficiently in terms of a combination of lexical, syntactic and semantic features. Whilst it is not argued that a template-based approach described here can ultimately provide a complete method for the automatic analysis of language samples, it does provide a powerful means of ambiguity reduction which can usefully complement other methods of analysis. In the case of Claws we have seen that such methods complement the HMM disambiguation strategy both by altering the input fed to it, and by checking its output for likely defects.

A highly developed and impressive template rule-based methodology is Helsinki's 'Constraint Grammar' approach to syntactic (part-of-speech, dependency and function) analysis (Karlsson *et al* 1995). One point of contrast between our approach and the Constraint Grammar approach concerns the division of labour between the lexicon and the grammar. In the Helsinki approach this distinction is a clear one, with the lexicon being the source of candidate analyses, and the role of the grammar (or rules) being to reduce the ambiguity by eliminating inappropriate analyses. We tend to pay less respect to this distinction. We may use a rule not only to select between conflicting analyses, but to apply an appropriate analysis in the first instance. That is to say, analytical tags may be supplied by the lexicon, or they may be supplied by template rules themselves, and there is no logical necessity in our approach for the lexicon to be the initial source of information. Indeed, it could be argued that there is some merit in allowing more holistic, contextually rich rules to do some processing before the lexicon is consulted, in order to preclude the introduction of unnecessary ambiguity into the analysis. Another way of looking at this is to consider the lexicon as simply a list of very short (normally single element) templates, but not fundamentally different from a more complex template rule, and for the question of the optimal ordering of rules to be based on less abstract considerations that whether something is 'part of the lexicon' or 'part of the grammar'.

Pawley and Syder (1983) suggested that idiomaticity and fluency posed 'two puzzles' for the generative grammarian, and questioned the appropriateness of a strict distinction between grammar and lexicon. In their view, there must be some redundancy in the means to handle a wide variety of language strings, whereby a given string could be produced either by the use of productive grammar rules plus lexicon, or by the invocation of some under-investigated means of producing lexicalized or semi-lexicalized utterances. The template tagging approach turns this around and suggests that exploiting knowledge about 'prefabricated chunks of language' or 'speech formulas' (which might take the form of fixed expressions, but could equally well be stereotypical grammatical constructions) can provide an efficient means of disambiguating text input for the purpose of automatic analysis. In a set of template rules or 'mini-grammars' (Pawley and Syder, op cit., p. 216) which are neither wholly lexical nor wholly grammatical, we may be able to bridge the traditional gap between the grammatical and the lexical components of the NLP system.

Another line of investigation which underlines in a different way the importance of the template approach is that undertaken by Brill (1992 and 1993). Whilst work in Lancaster and Helsinki has depended heavily on the expertise of the linguist to construct meaningful and useful rules, Brill has demonstrated how much can be achieved within a relatively constrained template framework, and, moreover with remarkably little input from the linguist, by developing a tagging system in which an automatically induced set of 'transformation rules' achieve a level of accuracy comparable with HMM-based systems.

At the time of writing, work is under way at Lancaster to apply similar rule-induction techniques (based on a comparison of corrected and uncorrected corpus texts) to create 'patches' (Brill's term) for the task of correcting and enhancing the annotations in the British National Corpus.

We mentioned at the outset that statistical methods had proved strikingly, and perhaps also surprisingly, effective in analysing continuous natural language samples. They achieve this usually in spite of demonstrable weaknesses in their capacity to model human cognitive language production and recognition processes themselves. If the latter term is taken to mean, as is often assumed, the human cognitive 'grammar', then this success may well be connected with the fact that grammar in itself does not provide an adequate explanatory framework for the production and comprehension of human language. Pawley (1994) suggested four other types of knowledge that must be used in the production and comprehension of language by humans: subject matter knowledge, fixed and productive speech formulae and discourse rules. At least as far as the central pair is concerned (and to some extent also subject matter knowledge), a template approach may provide NLP with a tool that has some features of psychological plausibility. At any rate, it provides a potentially powerful means of modelling 'typicality' features of real language, and thus improving our automatic analyses.

While in the past the primary focus of our NLP research has been on statistical techniques, in recent years template analysis methodologies have gained significantly in prominence. Finding the right blend of rule-based and statistical methods will be one of the interesting challenges for researchers in the coming years.

Acknowledgements

The authors acknowledge Roger Garside for implementing all programming changes in Claws with regard to idiom processing described here, and for his comments on this paper.

Notes

1 Although only one version of Claws has been made generally available to the research community, numerous modifications have been made in subsequent versions. The current development version is known as Claws4 (see Leech, Garside and Bryant 1994b), and may be used with a number of different tagsets.

2 Examples concerning part-of-speech tagging are based on the Claws2 tagset, or subsequent variations thereof. In the Claws1 (LOB) tagset, not all verb tags began with 'V'.

3 In Claws1, WORDTAG, IDIOMTAG and CHAINPROBS are actually separate programs. In recent versions, they are distinct modules within a single program.

4 The BNC, compiled between 1990–94, is the result of a collaborative project between two academic institutions (UCREL and Oxford University Computing Services), three publishing companies (Longman Group, Chambers-Harrap and Oxford University Press) and the British Library. The corpus contains 90 million words of written and 10 million words of spoken text, from a wide range of types. Part-of-speech tags (see Appendix to this chapter) were

assigned at Lancaster using Claws.

5 A special-purpose Idiomlist editing tool has been written (by Mark Walsh of the Computing Department, Lancaster University) to enable accurate entering of increasingly complex templates.

6 WICs are usually nouns identified by the lexicon or list of suffixes as being capable of nominal function.

7 But for a more extended catchment of phrasal verbs see section 12.5.2.

8 The actual distribution is not straightforward since rules which apply to the same span of text may need to be separated to avoid problems of overlap (see discussion by Garside in Chapter 11).

9 The IBM Corpus was tagged and parsed by UCREL in collaboration with the IBM T.J. Watson Research Center, New York, USA. See Black *et al* 1993.

10 The proceedings of meetings of the International Telecommunications Union (ITU) were POS-tagged as part of the EU-sponsored ET10-63 and CRATER projects. UCREL collaborated with the University of Essex, IBM Paris, the Paris software house (C2V), and the Universidad Autonoma de Madrid. The projects aimed to provide high quality annotated multi-lingual corpus resources.

11 Where *IPL* means 'Initial Program Load'.

12 These conversations have been sampled demographically from all over the British Isles, and orthographically transcribed with SGML markup. For details see Crowdy 1993.

13 In a EPSRC/DTI-funded project at UCREL called the BNC Tagging Enhancement Project, started in January 1995. (Grant reference GR/K14223).

14 This work was supported by SERC/DTI grant number GR/F36385 to Prof. G. N. Leech, Dr J. A. Thomas and Mr R. G. Garside and ran for 24 months from July 1990.

15 This work is supported by EPSRC/DTI grant number GR/J93733 for 33 months from November 1993.

16 Noun phrases are identified by a separate program called NPEXT, developed by Paul Rayson in the EU-sponsored ET10-63 project at

Lancaster University.

17 JAWS and Template Tagger (see section 12.7) have been developed within the ESRC-funded project 'Lancaster Database of Linguistic Corpora'. The support of the ESRC is gratefully acknowledged.

18 The lemmatization routines were developed by Beale (1989).

19 Other user-configurable features which are being experimented with include a) the ability to make certain input items 'disappear' from the tagger's view in certain circumstances (e.g. quotation marks unless they are explicitly cited in a rule) and b) the assignment for a given rule table of a default tagging function, to allow for greater economy in rule-writing, and to provide the means to compare (by switching the default) different basic tagging strategies.

20 Thanks are due to Mike Pacey of the Computing Department, Lancaster University, for his considerable contribution to the creation of code for the Template Tagger.

21 An early vindication of the Template Tagger approach came with the program's very first run using a full rule set. Independently, Geoff and Fanny Leech had compiled a set of template rules designed to apply partial syntactic bracketing to tagged text as a first stage in a multi-phase approach to automatic parsing. These rules were then translated into the Template Tagger formalism and were applied successfully without any changes being required to the program code. The Template Tagger thus fulfilled the role of obviating the need for special software to be written for each new task, providing the rules can be expressed in the form allowed for by the program.

Appendix to Chapter 12

Claws7 Tagset

!	punctuation tag — exclamation mark
"	punctuation tag — quotes
(	punctuation tag — left bracket
)	punctuation tag — right bracket
,	punctuation tag — comma
-	punctuation tag — dash
-----	new sentence marker
.	punctuation tag — full-stop
...	punctuation tag — ellipsis

:	punctuation tag — colon
;	punctuation tag — semicolon
?	punctuation tag — question mark
APPGE	possessive pronoun, pre-nominal (e.g. my, your, our)
AT	article (e.g. the, no)
AT1	singular article (e.g. a, an, every)
BCL	before-clause marker (e.g. in order (that), in order (to))
CC	coordinating conjunction (e.g. and, or)
CCB	adversative coordinating conjunction (but)
CS	subordinating conjunction (e.g. if, because, unless, so, for)
CSA	as (as conjunction)
CSN	than (as conjunction)
CST	that (as conjunction)
CSW	whether (as conjunction)
DA	after-determiner or post-determiner capable of pronominal function (e.g. such, former, same)
DA1	singular after-determiner (e.g. little, much)
DA2	plural after-determiner (e.g. few, several, many)
DAR	comparative after-determiner (e.g. more, less, fewer)
DAT	superlative after-determiner (e.g. most, least, fewest)
DB	before determiner or pre-determiner capable of pronominal function (all, half)
DB2	plural before-determiner (both)
DD	determiner (capable of pronominal function) (e.g any, some)
DD1	singular determiner (e.g. this, that, another)
DD2	plural determiner (these, those)
DDQ	wh-determiner (which, what)
DDQGE	wh-determiner, genitive (whose)
DDQV	wh-ever determiner, (whichever, whatever)
EX	existential there
FO	formula
FU	unclassified word
FW	foreign word
GE	germanic genitive marker — (' or 's)
IF	for (as preposition)
II	general preposition
IO	of (as preposition)
IW	with, without (as prepositions)
JJ	general adjective
JJR	general comparative adjective (e.g. older, better, stronger)
JJT	general superlative adjective (e.g. oldest, best, strongest)
JK	catenative adjective (able in be able to, willing in be willing to)

MC	cardinal number, neutral for number (two, three ...)
MC1	singular cardinal number (one)
MC2	plural cardinal number (tens, hundreds)
MCGE	genitive cardinal number, neutral for number (two's, 100's)
MCMC	hyphenated number (40–50, 1770–1827)
MD	ordinal number (e.g. first, second, next, last)
MF	fraction, neutral for number (e.g. quarters, two-thirds)
ND1	singular noun of direction (e.g. north, southeast)
NN	common noun, neutral for number (e.g. sheep, cod, headquarters)
NN1	singular common noun (e.g. book, girl)
NN2	plural common noun (e.g. books, girls)
NNA	following noun of title (e.g. M.A.)
NNB	preceding noun of title (e.g. Mr., Prof.)
NNJ	organization noun, neutral for number (e.g. council, department)
NNJ2	organization noun, plural (e.g. governments, committees)
NNL1	singular locative noun (e.g. island, street)
NNL2	plural locative noun (e.g.islands, streets)
NNO	numeral noun, neutral for number (e.g. dozen, hundred)
NNO2	numeral noun, plural (e.g. hundreds, thousands)
NNT1	temporal noun, singular (e.g. day, week, year)
NNT2	temporal noun, plural (e.g. days, weeks, years)
NNU	unit of measurement, neutral for number (e.g. in, cc)
NNU1	singular unit of measurement (e.g. inch, centimetre)
NNU2	plural unit of measurement (e.g. ins., feet)
NP	proper noun, neutral for number (e.g. IBM, Andes)
NP1	singular proper noun (e.g. London, Jane, Frederick)
NP2	plural proper noun (e.g. Browns, Reagans, Koreas)
NPD1	singular weekday noun (e.g. Sunday)
NPD2	plural weekday noun (e.g. Sundays)
NPM1	singular month noun (e.g. October)
NPM2	plural month noun (e.g. Octobers)
NULL	the null tag, for words which receive no tag
PN	indefinite pronoun, neutral for number (none)
PN1	indefinite pronoun, singular (e.g. anyone, everything, nobody, one)
PNQO	objective wh-pronoun (whom)
PNQS	subjective wh-pronoun (who)
PNQV	wh-ever pronoun (whoever)
PNX1	reflexive indefinite pronoun (oneself)
PPGE	nominal possessive personal pronoun (e.g. mine, yours)
PPH1	3rd person sing. neuter personal pronoun (it)

PPHO1	3rd person sing. objective personal pronoun (him, her)
PPHO2	3rd person plural objective personal pronoun (them)
PPHS1	3rd person sing. subjective personal pronoun (he, she)
PPHS2	3rd person plural subjective personal pronoun (they)
PPIO1	1st person sing. objective personal pronoun (me)
PPIO2	1st person plural objective personal pronoun (us)
PPIS1	1st person sing. subjective personal pronoun (I)
PPIS2	1st person plural subjective personal pronoun (we)
PPX1	singular reflexive personal pronoun (e.g. yourself, itself)
PPX2	plural reflexive personal pronoun (e.g. yourselves, themselves)
PPY	2nd person personal pronoun (you)
RA	adverb, after nominal head (e.g. else, galore)
REX	adverb introducing appositional constructions (namely, e.g.)
RG	degree adverb (very, so, too)
RGQ	wh- degree adverb (how)
RGQV	wh-ever degree adverb (however)
RGR	comparative degree adverb (more, less)
RGT	superlative degree adverb (most, least)
RL	locative adverb (e.g. alongside, forward)
RP	prep. adverb, particle (e.g about, in)
RPK	prep. adv., catenative (about in be about to)
RR	general adverb
RRQ	wh- general adverb (where, when, why, how)
RRQV	wh-ever general adverb (wherever, whenever)
RRR	comparative general adverb (e.g. better, longer)
RRT	superlative general adverb (e.g. best, longest)
RT	quasi-nominal adverb of time (e.g. now, tomorrow)
TO	infinitive marker (to)
UH	interjection (e.g. oh, yes, um)
VB0	be base form (finite i.e. imperative, subjunctive)
VBDR	were
VBDZ	was
VBG	being
VBI	be infinitive (To be or not ... It will be ...)
VBM	am
VBN	been
VBR	are
VBZ	is
VD0	do base form (finite)
VDD	did
VDG	doing
VDI	do infinitive (I may do ... To do ...)

VDN	done
VDZ	does
VH0	have base form (finite)
VHD	had (past tense)
VHG	having
VHI	have (infinitive)
VHN	had (past participle)
VHZ	has
VM	modal auxiliary (can, will, would, etc.)
VMK	modal catenative (ought, used)
VV0	base form of lexical verb (e.g. give, work)
VVD	past tense of lexical verb (e.g. gave, worked)
VVG	-ing participle of lexical verb (e.g. giving, working)
VVGK	-ing participle catenative (going in be going to)
VVI	infinitive (e.g. to give ... It will work ...)
VVN	past participle of lexical verb (e.g. given, worked)
VVNK	past participle catenative (e.g. bound in be bound to)
VVZ	-s form of lexical verb (e.g. gives, works)
XX	not, n't
ZZ1	singular letter of the alphabet (e.g. A, b)
ZZ2	plural letter of the alphabet (e.g. A's, b's)

PART 4

Wider applications of Corpus-based research

13 Sentence and word alignment in the CRATER Project

TONY MCENERY and MICHAEL OAKES

13.1 Introduction

It seems reasonable to imagine that Napoleon, when he invaded Egypt in 1798, had no idea that his actions would ultimately provide a bright idea for corpus and computational linguists to exploit in the late twentieth century. Much to the chagrin of his troops, Napoleon brought with him an army of intellectuals as well as an army of soldiers. It was these intellectuals, travelling around the country, who discovered an artifact which was to ensure that the invasion would, in some sense, have a lasting effect. They discovered the so-called 'Rosetta Stone'. This was a highly unusual artifact. A stone tablet, containing the same message in Hieroglyphs, Greek and Demotic. A **parallel text** — three languages used to express the same ideas. When the task of deciphering the stone was completed later in the century in Britain, a lasting result was achieved — the hieroglyphs of ancient Egypt were at last understood and translated. This translation was possible only because the *unknown* hieroglyphs were present in parallel with two other *known* languages. Once the hieroglyphs were roughly aligned with the other languages — a process of finding what translates to what — the key to the language of the pharaohs was turned. How does this relate to modern text corpora?

Parallel corpora, such as the Canadian Hansard corpus and the ITU (International Telecommunications Union) corpus, provide the same text in two or more languages,[1] and are said to be the 'Rosetta Stone of modern corpus linguistics' (McEnery and Wilson 1994). Yet rather than being the key to an unknown language for human translators, the hope is that eventually they may provide important clues to natural language processing systems dealing with a variety of mono and multilingual tasks. In short, they promise to be of use in both automatic lexicon construction and text translation, though it is mainly on their use in multilingual lexicon construction that this paper will concentrate.

13.2 Background: aligned parallel corpora and their uses

The use of parallel corpora within computational linguistics is burgeoning, permeating all levels of the discipline, and even being used as the basis of statistical machine translation systems by researchers such as Brown *et al* (1993).

Parallel corpora also provide an ideal test bed for translation tuition, as described by Catizone, Russell and Warwick (1989). The advantage of a multilingual parallel aligned corpus is that it stores existing mutual translations of the same text in two or more languages. The corpora can be used to call up sets of words or grammatical features in one language for their examination, and/or for the call up of the foreign language equivalents in parallel aligned segments. This process of alignment and retrieval is made easier through the annotation of the aligned corpus with part-of-speech, syntactic and semantic information. One such translator's aid is the Bilingual Knowledge Bank of the DLT project of Sadler *et al*, as reported in (Hutchins and Somers 1992).

Another developing use of multilingual aligned corpora is in automatic bilingual lexicon construction, which is one of the major goals of the CRATER project ('Corpus Resources and Terminology Extraction', funded under the MLAP initiative of the CEC, grant number MLAP-93/20). Current research on the CRATER project concerns automatic alignment of parallel texts both at the sentence and word level, and it is that work which will be reported in this paper. As part of the process of word and sentence alignment, a major investigation of methods of searching through the corpus for lexical cognates has been undertaken on the project. Consequently this paper will begin with a brief discussion of the alignment procedures used on the project to date, and then move on to a discussion of various similarity metrics used to evaluate the lexical similarity of words which are possibly translations of each other.

13.3 Purely statistical methods of automatic sentence alignment

During the initial stages of the CRATER project, our task has been to develop core statistical alignment methods to achieve sentence level alignment of parallel corpora. We have re-implemented the method of Gale and Church (1993), which is based on the facts that:

- longer sentences in one language tend to be translated into longer sequences in the other and
- certain types of alignment are more commonly encountered than others, where for example single sentence substitutions are considered more likely than 2:2 or other alignments.

Gale and Church rank potential sentence alignments using a score based upon these two components. A probabilistic model first produces an approximation to the probability that two segments are mutual translations, given the lengths in characters of the two segments, and this is then summed with the logarithm of the likelihood of the translation pattern that connects them relative to the probability of a 1:1 alignment or *penalty* as shown in Table 13.1.

Table 13.1 *A priori* likelihood of the alignment types considered by Gale and Church

Type	1-1	1-0 or 0-1	2-1 or 1-2	2-2
Probability	.89	.0099	.089	.011
Penalty	0	450	230	440

In order to demonstrate the extent to which the Gale and Church statistical alignment algorithm is language-pair independent, sample outputs for alignments of English and five other languages were evaluated. The results are given in Table 13.2. The values given are the percentage of aligned regions in the output which were entirely correct. The success rates appear both language and domain dependent, with approximately equal success rates for Polish, which is distantly related to English, and the three Western European languages. Genre seemed another factor which had an impact upon the results of the Gale and Church algorithm. Gale and Church's technique produces impressive results for the language pairs tested, but there is no disguising the fact that the results gained using the algorithm vary across genres and language pairs. To push this point a little further we decided to try to align two widely differing language pairs: Chinese and English.

Using the GB (Zimin and White 1990) code, single Chinese characters can be represented by a sequence of two extended ASCII characters. It was found that, on average, a single Chinese character corresponded with about 5 English characters, and thus a single extended ASCII character corresponded with about 2.5 English characters. This ratio was incorporated into the Gale and Church program. The results for Chinese were less encouraging, because the translation involved relatively few 1:1 alignments. Simard *et al* (1992) suggest that one possible explanation for Gale and Church's high rate of success is that most of the time the program is solving the trivial 1:1 alignment. For more difficult alignments, errors may occur. For example, they obtained 5 times the error rate for 2:1 alignments, and 1:0 alignments were often missed altogether. The Chinese/English result seems in line with this finding, possibly leading to the observation that the *a priori* likelihood of alignment figures used by Gale and Church are in fact language pair and possibly genre specific. The Gale and Church algorithm is surprisingly successful, it is not entirely language independent.

Table 13.2 Success rates for the Gale and Church algorithm

Language Pair	Domain	Regions Tested	% Correct
English-French	ITU corpus	100	98.0
English-German	Economics	36	75.0
English-Polish	Fiction (School)	89	100.0
English-Polish	Fiction (Tigers)	132	64.4
English-Polish	Medical	72	66.7
English-Polish	Finance	27	85.2
English-Spanish	ITU corpus	222	93.2
Chinese-English	Newspaper	171	54.5

13.4 The incorporation of language pair specific cognates

The accuracy of the original Gale and Church (1993) method, which employs statistical data alone, as shown in Table 13.2, has been found to be in the range 54% to 100% for our data. Various authors feel that just a small amount of linguistic knowledge would help improve that value.[2] The best results should come from a combination of statistical and simple linguistic techniques. While statistical approaches provide a language-free core technique, linguistic filters are specific to a given language pair. Part of the CRATER project is to produce filters specifically for French to Spanish translation and also those for French to English translation.

One means used on the project to improve alignment is to redefine the notion of anchor point. An anchor point is a point of known correspondence between two texts, the identification of which assists in the alignment process. The anchor points we have considered so far, in line with the views of Gale and Church, are the terminations of sentences and paragraphs. We now wish to examine the use of more linguistically motivated anchor points. We feel intuitively that proper nouns, numeric data and mark-up keywords should prove reliable in this respect, but more sophisticated linguistic rules have been suggested by Papageorgiou *et al* (1994) and Simard *et al* (1992).

Papageorgiou *et al* (1994) suggest the incorporation of surface linguistic information into the Gale and Church algorithm, where sentence length is determined by assigning a score for each part-of-speech identified in the sentence. Simard *et al* (1992) stated that 'a small amount of linguistic information is necessary in order to overcome the inherited weaknesses of the Gale and Church method.' They employ the notion of cognate words which 'provides a source of knowledge for a minimal price.' Cognates are defined here as pairs of tokens in different languages which share 'obvious' phonological or orthographic and semantic properties, with the result that they are likely to be used as mutual translations e.g. 'generation / génération', 'error / erreur'. Cognates are pairs of words which are reliable translations of each other, and provide 'anchor' points for text alignment in bilingual corpora. Simard *et al* suggest that likely cognates might be

- question marks (a question in English will probably align with a question in French)
- words in both languages which are identical for the first *n* characters, e.g. 'tax' and 'taxe'
- proper nouns
- numerical expressions
- parentheses.

They consider three types of candidate cognates:

- numerical expressions, entirely composed of letters and digits, but containing at least one digit, and identical in each language
- non-function words exclusively composed of letters and identical for at least the first four letters
- single punctuation characters, on the intuition that the translation process has a tendency to preserve punctuation.

Candidates of the first and third types are cognates if they are completely identical, and candidates of the second type are cognates if the first four letters are identical. They measure the *cognateness* of two text segments by Dice's similarity coefficient; n and m are the number of tokens in each segment and c is the number of pairs of cognates in that segment without using the same token twice, the cognateness is $2c / (n+m)$. They found significantly more cognates in aligned sentences than in random pairs. Cognateness was 0.21 for mutual translations and 0.06 for random pairs. Simard *et al* employ a binary classification, where a pair of words either are or are not cognates, but we use real-valued metrics which allow the assignment of intermediate degrees of cognateness.

The method employed at Lancaster of identifying cognates is to examine pairs of words which are lexically similar (have many characters in common), as identified by *approximate string matching* techniques (Hall and Dowling 1980). We have performed experiments to determine the reliability of this idea for English and French, including:

- the production of a histogram plotting Dice's similarity coefficient based on character structure for a sample of English and French terms against the probability of these two terms being translations of each other
- a repeat of this experiment for various term truncation lengths.

Oakes and Taylor (1992) have shown that truncation is more effective than Dice's similarity coefficient for pharmaceutical term clustering, but this technique will result in the confusion of such word pairs as *mice* and *micelle* and the loss of such pairs as *gouvernement* and *government* (Simard *et al* 1992).

Approximate string matching techniques have traditionally been employed in information retrieval for the recognition of different grammatical forms of the same root word or lemma. We have extended their use to the identification of word clusters in different languages which are related in meaning, and have employed the resulting information to assist in the task of identifying language-pair specific cognates for sentence alignment in our multilingual corpora. The approximate string-matching techniques we have examined to date are Dice's similarity coefficient, truncation, and dynamic programming (Hall and Dowling 1980) These techniques are language specific in that a greater number of true cognates will be discovered for more closely related language pairs.

13.5 Dice's similarity coefficient

Dice's similarity coefficient (Dice 1945) is a metric originally developed for the comparison of biological specimens, which returns a real numeric value in the range 0 to 1. This metric can be employed to assign a value to describe the lexical similarity between two words, in this case one word from the English token or lemma list, and one from the corresponding French token or lemma list produced from the International Telecommunications Union (ITU) corpus. Two terms which are totally dissimilar in their character structures would return a Dice score of 0, while two lexically identical terms would return a Dice Score of 1. Using the technique of Adamson and Boreham (1974), the comparison of words depends on the number of matching bigrams or consecutive pairs of characters. The formula for Dice's similarity coefficient, S, is then

$$S = 2a / (b + c),$$

where *a* is the number of matching bigrams and *b* and *c* are the total number of bigrams in each term. For example, the English word 'colour' yields the bigrams 'co-ol-lo-ou-ur', while the French word 'couleur' yields the bigrams 'co-ou-ul-le-eu-ur'. The total number of matching digrams is three, while the total number of digrams is eleven. The coefficient of similarity between these terms is then 6/11, about 0.55.

An experiment was performed in which Dice's similarity coefficient was found for each term pair in the English and French ITU corpus token lists, which consist of one occurrence of every single lexical item in the corpus. The term pairs were divided into bands according to their respective Dice scores, each band having a bandwidth of 0.1. In Tables 13.3 and 13.4, the lower limits of the bands are given. All term pairs with a Dice score of less than 0.4 were disregarded. A pseudo-random sample of 200 pairs from each band was printed out, and the pairs were each scored 1 if they were considered either exact translations or useful grammatical variants of each other (i.e. a sentence containing one of the pair might conceivably contain the other in its translation), or 0 if the terms were either unrelated, matching only in their prefixes and suffixes, or terms where an identical root had given rise to variants of considerably different meaning (e.g. 'recover', 'découvrir'). The proportion of pairs with a score of 1 in each band is given in the row labelled 'tokens' in Table 13.3.

The experiment was repeated using the corresponding ITU lemma lists, which differ from the token lists in that plurals and inflexional variants of a word are all considered as a single word rather than separate items. The results are shown in the row labelled 'lemmas' in Table 13.3.

Table 13.3 Success rate for determining cognates by Dice's similarity coefficient: all pairs considered

Dice	0.4-0.49	0.5-0.59	0.6-0.69	0.7-0.79	0.8-0.89	0.9-0.99	1.0
Tokens	0	.07	.205	.475	.89	.98	1
Lemmas	.005	.02	.175	.535	.525*	.965	1

In most cases, better results were obtained for the token lists than for the lemma lists. This was because the lemmatization process results in the removal of suffixes which often correspond in true cognates in English and French, since the suffix 's' denotes plurality in both languages. The asterisk * denotes that unexpectedly poor results were obtained in the 0.8 band for the lemmas, due to a repeated phenomenon, namely the comparison of a four character acronym in one language with a three character acronym in the other, the two acronyms in question not being translations of each other. In order to circumvent this problem, the experiments were repeated considering only those term pairs in which both members consisted of at least 4 characters. The results for this evaluation are given in Table 13.4.

Table 13.4 Success rate for determining cognates by dice's similarity coefficient: pairs in which both terms consist of 4 or more characters

Dice	0.4-0.49	0.5-0.59	0.6-0.69	0.7-0.79	0.8-0.89	0.9-0.99	1.0
Tokens	0	.07	.215	.49	.816	.97	1
Lemmas	0	.05	.225	.48	.71	.95	1

From the results given in Tables 13.3 and 13.4, it was decided that Dice's similarity coefficient should be used in conjunction with the token list rather than the lemma list for cognate matching, and only terms with 4 or more characters should be considered. When matching pairs across the entire corpus, a Dice score of at least 0.9 is required to ensure 95% accuracy for cognate identification. As shown in Table 13.5, the estimated number of true cognates in the corpus (found by multiplying the number of word pairs retrieved in each band by the percentage correct in that band) is greatest in the lower scoring bands. However, as will be expanded upon later, lower Dice scores can identify cognates accurately when only those word pairs which occur in corresponding regions of text are considered.

Table 13.5 Potential numbers of cognates retrievable from each Dice band

Score	*Number in Band*	*% Correct*	*Est. No. Cognates*
1.0	29259	100	29259
0.9-0.99	20142	97.0	19538
0.8-0.89	57150	81.6	46634
0.7-0.79	118080	49.0	57859
0.6-0.69	372528	21.5	80094
0.5-0.59	1547289	7.0	108310
0.4-0.49	5508639	0.0	0

13.6 Truncation

Term truncation is commonly employed in the field of Information Retrieval to enable searching for clusters of related terms as a single unit. The technique is simply to regard two terms which commence with the same *n* characters as equivalent. For example, the common truncation length for *colour* and *couleur* is 2. An experiment was performed in which each term in the English token list was compared with each term in the French token list, and the number of initial common characters in each case was recorded. All term pairs with fewer than three initial characters in common were disregarded. All other pairs were divided into bands according to their number of common initial characters, and a pseudo-random sample of 200 pairs was then taken from each band for evaluation. As before, a score of 1 for each pair was assigned if the two terms were considered useful grammatical variants of each other, and a score of 0 otherwise. The proportion of pairs which were considered true cognates is given in Table 13.6.

Table 13.6 Accuracy of cognate determination using truncation data without stoplisting

Length	3	4	5	6	7	8	9	>9
Correct	.01	.075	.14	.685	.925	.975	.995	1

The results in Table 13.6 show that cognates can be found with 95% reliability if both terms commence with the same eight characters.

As shown in Table 13.7, an estimation of the number of true cognates in the corpus which could potentially be found at each truncation level was made by multiplying the number of matching pairs for each truncation length by the percentage of correct pairs found in each sample of 200.

The resulting values show that the bulk of true cognates are to be found using truncation lengths in the range 5 to 7. Thus it was necessary to devise some means of rendering the truncation matching process more accurate in this range. The estimated number of true cognates retrieved by truncation at the 95% accuracy level (sum of the estimated numbers of true cognates retrieved by truncation to eight characters or more) was 13,328 compared with the corresponding value for Dice's similarity coefficient (derived from Table 13.5, with scores -0.9) of 48,797. We feel that both techniques should be used in conjunction, to maximize the number of retrieved cognates.

Table 13.7 Potential numbers of cognates retrievable at each truncation level

Truncation Length	Total Matches	% Correct	Est. no. Cognates
20	3	100	3
19	9	100	9
18	14	100	14
17	19	100	19
16	16	100	16
15	71	100	71
14	175	100	175
13	231	100	231
12	539	100	539
11	891	100	891
10	1987	100	1987
9	3516	99.5	3498
8	6025	97.5	5874
7	10591	92.5	9797
6	17685	68.5	12114
5	71875	14	10063
4	112423	7.5	8432
3	506420	1	5064

The observed inaccuracy at shorter truncation lengths resulted from overlap of initial character sequences in unrelated word families, such as in the case of 'computer' and 'compulsion'. To overcome this problem, stoplists were created for each truncation length. In the example given here, a rule should be created to the effect that 'if both terms truncate to the same five characters, and these characters are "compu", then the word pair should not be considered a cognate'. The procedure for creating the stoplists for each truncation length was as follows:

- Examples of word pairs with the same initial *n* characters were examined manually.
- All initial character sequences for incorrect pairs were placed in the stoplist.
- All initial character sequences which produced at least ten correct pairs and no incorrect pairs were placed in a 'go' list.

- Return to (1) employing the current stop and go lists.
- Stop when all pairs allowed through by the stop and go lists have been examined.

Since fully comprehensive stoplists would be unduly large, it was decided to restrict the stoplists to the 100 most commonly employed entries, as determined by a version of the truncation program which kept a record of the number of times each stoplist entry was employed. All stoplist items of length 7 or more were retained, as were items of length 6 firing 4 times or more, length 5 firing 42 times or more, length 4 firing 120 times or more and length 3 firing 360 times or more. The lists of most commonly employed stoplist items for each truncation length are available from the authors.

To estimate the accuracy of truncation after stoplisting, a pseudo-random sample of 200 pairs from each truncation length band was taken. The results are given in Table 13.8. The accuracy of truncation matching in the range 5 to 7 is somewhat improved relative to the values given in Table 13.6. Accuracy at 5 and 6 might be increased to the 95 % level by the inclusion of further stoplist items.

Table 13.8 Accuracy of truncation after stoplisting

Length	3	4	5	6	7	8	9	10	11
Correct	4.5%	19.5%	73.5%	93.5%	97.5%	99.5%	99%	99.5%	100%

One possibility originally considered was that the truncation matching procedure might depend solely on the presence of the matching sequence in the go lists, and thus an estimation was made of the retrieval potential and accuracy of truncation using only items in the go lists firing 10 or more times.

In this experiment, only term pairs which commenced with character sequences given in the go lists were considered. A sample of over 200 output pairs was examined for each truncation length, and the results are given in Table 13.9. The go lists employed are available on request from the authors. It was found that the use of go lists was over 95% accurate for truncation lengths of 4 or more, but this method yielded relatively few cognates. The danger of go lists, even if found to be sufficiently accurate in one domain, is that counter examples might be found in another domain. With stop listing, the knowledge that confusion of certain word families is possible will be applicable in all domains.

Table 13.9 Effectiveness of 'go' lists

Length	Number of Rules	Total Matches	% True Cognates	Est. No. Cognates
9	58	1827	96.2	1757
8	72	2348	98.3	2308
7	80	3390	98.5	3339
6	73	3571	98.4	3514
5	72	3368	97.7	3291
4	27	1211	95.4	1155
3	13	317	77.6	246

13.7 Dynamic programming

The Damerau-Levenshtein metric (reported by Hall and Dowling 1980) was originally developed to examine the problem of misspellings in words. It is a procedure for checking whether two character strings differ in any of the following respects, which correspond to the most common errors: single character omissions, insertions, substitutions and reversals. By using sequences of such operations any character string can be transformed into any other character string. Dynamic programming enables one to determine the least number of such transformations required to convert one string into another, and thus provides a measure of the lexical similarity of two strings. For example, the conversion of *couleur* into *colour* would require two transformations: c = c, o = o, *u deleted*, l = l, *e substituted by o*, u = u, r = r. We employed the dynamic programming approach to measure the similarity between each English term and each French term in the ITU token lists. In order to convert the integral score produced by this method into a real valued metric in the range 0 to 1, we employed the following formula:

DP Score = 1– (Minimum number of substitutions required / Number of characters in the longer term.)

In order to evaluate the effectiveness of the Dynamic Programming technique, we found the DP Score for each token pair in the two language lists, and then determined manually the percentage of true cognates in a pseudo-random sample of 250 term pairs in each score band with bandwidth 0.1 in the range 0.4 to 1.0. The results are given in Table 13.10. Although it was expected that dynamic programming would produce results similar to Dice's similarity coefficient both in retrieval effectiveness and in terms of the actual token pairs retrieved, we discovered that Dynamic Programming performed less well than Dice's similarity coefficient. The advantage of using Dynamic Programming, however, is that we will be able to maintain counts of which character substitutions regularly occur when examining related terms in two languages.

Table 13.10 Accuracy of dynamic programming compared with Dice's similarity coefficient

DP Score	0.4-0.49	0.5-0.59	0.6-0.69	0.7-0.79	0.8-0.89	0.9-0.99	1.0
DP %	.008	.016	.124	.388	.728	.948	1
Dice %	.000	.070	.205	.475	.890	.980	1

13.8 Repetition of the Dice and truncation experiments for restricted regions of text

The results obtained in Tables 13.3 to 13.10 were obtained when matching pairs from all regions of the corpus were considered. However, it was expected that when matching pairs in which each member originated from a corresponding region of text such as an equivalent paragraph or sentence, a higher proportion of matching pairs would be true cognates. Thus the experiments were repeated, considering only those pairs found in matching regions of the text.

The two levels of granularity employed were the 'hard' and 'soft' regions defined by Gale and Church. Hard regions are those regions, often corresponding to paragraphs, within which their alignment algorithm is constrained. No sentence may be aligned with a region of text unless it occurs within the corresponding hard region. Soft regions are the smallest unbreakable region of text considered by the alignment algorithm. For the purposes of these experiments, the hard and soft regions in the test corpus were determined manually. The programs for these evaluations were produced by Eric Gaussier at IBM Paris, and the results are given in Tables 13.11 and 13.12.

The 'Best Match' criterion of Gaussier *et al* (1992) ensures that an English word can only be assigned to a French word if the French word is not associated with another English word with a higher score. In this way, only the term pair with the highest matching score is retained out of all term-pairs with a matching coefficient above threshold.

The results given in Tables 13.11 and 13.12 show that for truncation and Dice's similarity coefficient, the narrower the region in which term pair comparison is constrained, the more likely it is that two terms with a given score of association are indeed true cognates. A similar effect is produced by employing the best match criterion of Gaussier *et al.* In the case of truncation, the results could be improved yet further by making use of the stoplist. When the experiments were repeated for truncation for comparisons within soft regions, no false matches were produced in the samples at any truncation length, irrespective of whether hard or soft regions or the best match criterion were employed.

With regard to sample size, the entries in Table 13.11 were obtained with an average of 194 token pairs per cell, the entries in Table 13.12 were obtained with an average of 162 token pairs per cell.

Table 13.11 Dice's similarity coefficient

Comparison within Hard Regions, All matches considered:							
Dice	0.4-0.49	0.5-0.59	0.6-0.69	0.7-0.79	0.8-0.89	0.9-0.99	1.0
Accuracy	.049	.334	.660	.942	.961	.992	.993
Comparison within Soft Regions, All matches considered							
Dice	0.4-0.49	0.5-0.59	0.6-0.69	0.7-0.79	0.8-0.89	0.9-0.99	1.0
Accuracy	.146	.693	.706	.971	1.00	1.00	1.00
Comparison within Hard Regions, Best Match Criterion employed							
Dice	0.4-0.49	0.5-0.59	0.6-0.69	0.7-0.79	0.8-0.89	0.9-0.99	1.0
Accuracy	.26	.715	.805	1.00	1.00	1.00	
Comparison within Soft Regions, Best Match Criterion employed							
Dice	0.4-0.49	0.5-0.59	0.6-0.69	0.7-0.79	0.8-0.89	0.9-0.99	1.0
Accuracy	.411	.927	.902	1.00	1.00	1.00	1.00

Table 13.12 Truncation

Comparison within Hard Regions, All matches considered, No Stoplist employed					
Length	3	4	5	6	7
Accuracy	.315	.829	.622	.979	1.00
Comparison within Hard Regions, All matches considered, Stoplist employed					
Length	3	4	5	6	7
Accuracy	.848	.987	1.00	.992	1.00
Comparison within Hard Regions, Best match criterion, No Stoplist employed					
Length	3	4	5	6	7
Accuracy	.622	.960	.955	1.00	1.00
Comparison within Hard Regions, Best match criterion, Stoplist employed					
Length	3	4	5	6	7
Accuracy	.886	1.00	1.00	1.00	1.00

As shown in Tables 13.4 and 13.6, when comparisons are made across the entire corpus, with no Best Match criterion or stoplist, to obtain 95% accuracy requires that thresholds of 0.9 for Dice and 8 for truncation length must be employed. However, under optimal conditions, this level of accuracy can be obtained for Dice Scores of 0.7 and truncation lengths of 3. If these measures were employed under these conditions for the entire corpus, the estimated number of true cognates retrieved, derived from Tables 13.3 and 13.5, would be about 153,000 for Dice and 59,033 for truncation, these values being the sums of the estimated number of cognates in acceptable bands.

13.9 The production of cognate data for other language pairs

Our original data for determining the reliability of English-French cognate pairs according to the degree of lexical similarity is given in Tables 13.4 and 13.6. These experiments using the English-French token lists were repeated using the Spanish-French and Spanish-English token lists. The lists of Spanish-French and Spanish-English candidate cognates were evaluated by Fernando Sanchez-Leon. The results are shown in Table 13.13.

Table 13.3 Accuracy of Dice and truncation for Spanish-English and Spanish-French word pairs

Spanish-English Truncation			
Truncation Level	Number Correct	Total Tested	% Correct
10 or over	139	139	100
9	107	107	100
8	257	257	100
7	262	268	97.8
6	159	203	78.3
5	119	219	54.3
4	147	213	69.0
3	7	205	3.4
Spanish-English Dice			
Dice Score Band	Number Correct	Total Tested	% Correct
1	262	262	100
0.9-0.99	95	95	100
0.8-0.89	309	332	93.1
0.7-0.79	176	218	80.7
0.6-0.69	151	249	60.6
0.5-0.59	38	209	18.2
0.4-0.49	12	277	5.3
French-Spanish Truncation			
Truncation Level	Number Correct	Total Tested	% Correct
10 or over	147	147	100
9	162	162	100
8	281	281	100
7	334	353	94.6
6	192	275	69.8
5	126	239	52.7
4	143	221	64.7
3	5	204	2.5
French-Spanish Dice			
Band	Number Correct	Total Tested	% Correct
1	289	289	100
0.9-0.99	117	117	100
0.8-0.89	311	347	89.6
0.7-0.79	231	285	81.1
0.6-0.69	118	222	53.2
0.5-0.59	43	200	21.5
0.4-0.49	10	198	5.1

These results vary relatively little from those for English-French given in Tables 13.4 and 13.6, with the English-Spanish and French-Spanish token lists performing slightly better than the English-French token lists.

We wish to repeat these experiments for English-Polish term pairs, in order to discover whether the fact that Polish is less related to English than the other languages under study affects the shape of the curve relating lexical similarity to the probability of true cognateness. It may be that the shape of the curve remains unchanged, the only difference being the number cognates found in each band. We plan also to obtain similar data for English and German. However, even the Pin-Yin representation of Chinese in which a Romanized alphabet is employed would certainly yield too few cognates to produce such an evaluation for English and Chinese.

13.10 The production of a program to incorporate cognate information into the Gale and Church algorithm

We have produced a program which incorporates cognate data into the Gale and Church algorithm. As described in Section 13.2, the original Gale and Church algorithm depends on two statistical criteria, namely the relative lengths of the two alignable regions and the likelihood of alignment type relative to a simple 1:1 substitution. We have now included a third factor in the calculation — the measure of the degree of overlap between the sets of cognate terms contained within the alignable regions.

The procedure will be to first produce token lists for each language within a given hard region. By using the Best-Match procedure, one or all of the metrics Dice, truncation and Damerau-Levenshtein, will be employed to create a table of term pairs with an associated probability of true cognateness, obtained using an experimentally derived baseline curve derived from the values given in Tables 13.4 and 13.6. As dynamic programming considers each putative alignment, a variant of Dice's similarity coefficient designed to deal with real values will again be used, this time to consider the degree of match between the number of cognates present in each segment of text. Dice's original formula in this case has been modified slightly to allow for the real values associated with each cognate pair. The top line of the equation is now twice the sum of the weights of all cognate pairs where both words occur in the putative alignment;

the bottom line of the equation is the sum of the weights associated with individual terms occurring in the putative alignment, irrespective of whether the corresponding term in the other language is present or not.

Figure 13.1 Sample output from the sentence alignment program which incorporates cognates

```
exp d = 311 ------------------------------------------
----------------------------------&

general   -   describes   individually   a   number   of   the
transmission impairments which can affect the quality of
speech transmission in telephone connections

information is provided on the general nature of each
impairment on methods which have been recommended to
measure the impairment and on the acceptable ranges for the
impairment

--------------------------------------------------&

consideraciones generales - se describen por separado
varias de las degradaciones de transmission que pueden
influir desfavorablemente en la calidad de transmision de
la  palabra  por  conexiones  telefonicas  facilitandose
informacion sobre la natureleza general de cada degradacion
los metodos que se han recomendado para medirla y sus
limites aceptables

consideraciones   --->   connections
sect   --->   affect
describen   --->   describes
transmision --->   transmission
conexiones   --->   connections
telefonicas   --->   telephone
informacion   --->   information
naturaleza   --->   natural
general   --->   general
metodos   --->   methods
recomendado   --->   recommended
aceptables   --->   acceptable
------------------------------------------------------------
----------------------------------------
```

For example, consider a putative alignment in which two sentences of English are to be aligned with one sentence of French. Suppose that English sentence 1 contains the terms *a* and *b*, English sentence 2 contains *c* and *d*, while the French sentence contains the terms *a′*, *b′* and *c′*. According to the cognate table, *a* and *a′*, *b* and *b′*, *c* and *c′* are all cognate pairs with a probability of 0.9, while *d* and *d′*

(absent from the French sentence) are a cognate pair with a probability of 0.5. Dice's similarity coefficient between the two alignable regions is then 2 * (0.9 + 0.9 + 0.9) / (0.9 + 0.9 + 0.9 + 0.9 + 0.9 + 0.9 + 0.5), i.e. the sum of the probability scores for each individual term involved in a match divided by the sum of the probabilities of each individual term which occurs in the putative alignment, resulting in a score of .915.

Sample output from this program is shown in Figure 13.1. The notation *exp d = 311* shows that the alignment type is *expansion*, where one sentence of Spanish has been expanded to form two sentences of English. The value *311* is the sum of the penalties for the difference in region lengths, the non-1:1 alignment and the degree of non-overlap between the cognate lists. Although no full evaluation of this cognate-enhanced approach has yet been performed, our initial observation is that the incorporation of too much cognate information will result in noise leading to less accurate alignment. This is in accordance with the findings of Knut Hofland (personal communication). We must therefore work on methods of pruning down the number of cognates used in the alignment calculation, probably based on frequency or some other measure of uniqueness, which will leave us only with cognates with high information content.

13.11 Conclusions

We have produced a language free statistical sentence alignment package which employs the basic Gale and Church algorithm, which depends both on sentence lengths and the *a priori* probability of each alignment type. We have discovered, however, that the results of the Gale and Church technique as it stands are not invariant for language pair and genre.

We have employed approximate string matching techniques to demonstrate empirically that the higher the degree of lexical match between two words, each taken from two languages, the greater the probability that these two words are translations of each other. Word pairs thus deemed to be likely mutual translations can be regarded as cognates, and we have described methods of employing cognate information to enhance the performance of the Gale and Church statistical sentence alignment algorithm.

Since cognates are terms which are lexically similar in both languages, and our method for their identification is language independent, their extraction constitutes a step towards the construction of a language free term extraction package. As part of the work of CRATER, IBM France are looking at the use of cognates in the extraction of terms which consist of more than one word.

The concluding note of the paper must be this: lexical cognates are potentially terrifically useful. Within the context of parallel corpora, the automated extraction of cognates may be a significant development for many areas of corpus-based computational linguistics; cognates of this sort can contribute towards sentence alignment, word alignment and term extraction. Given the high degree of success that standard similarity measures seem to enjoy in lexical cognate extraction, we envisage their increased use in multilingual corpus building and exploitation.

Acknowledgements

Spanish-English alignment evaluated by Ruthanna Barnett (Lancaster University). Dynamic programming module written by Roger Garside (Lancaster University). Polish-English alignment evaluated by Barbara Lewandowska (Lodz University). Spanish-English cognate list evaluated by Fernando Sanchez (Universidad Autónoma de Madrid). German-English alignment evaluated by Hildegard Schäffler (Chemnitz University). Chinese-English alignment evaluated by Xu Xunfeng (Lancaster University).

Notes

1 The Canadian Hansard is available in English and French, while the ITU is available in French, Spanish and English.

2 One piece of linguistic data that the authors feel would certainly help, though will not be pursued here, is the incorporation of language pair and genre-specific *a priori* likelihood alignment figures.

14 English corpus linguistics and the foreign language teaching syllabus

DIETER MINDT

14.1 Introduction

The results of corpus linguistics have spread from dictionaries (e.g. *Collins COBUILD English Language Dictionary* 1987) to the grammatical description of English (cf. Mindt 1987, de Haan 1989, Mindt 1992). One very important area of English, however, (at least in Germany) seems to have been almost totally unaffected by the findings of corpus-based studies: teaching materials and especially textbooks for teaching English as a foreign language.

A comparative study of authentic language data and textbooks for teaching English as a foreign language has revealed that the use of grammatical structures in textbooks differs considerably from the use of these structures in authentic English (Mindt 1992: 186). Ljung has shown that this is also true of the vocabulary of textbooks (Ljung 1990).

Although compiled by different teams of authors and launched by different publishers, the textbooks share a number of features which make them very similar to each other. There is obviously a kind of school English which does not seem to exist outside the foreign language classroom. As a result, learners who leave their school surroundings very often find it hard to adapt to the English used by native speakers. Learners who communicate with native speakers constantly have to reshape their linguistic behaviour in those areas of the language which were not taught properly.

14.2 Syllabuses

Most language teaching syllabuses are structural syllabuses. A structural or grammatical syllabus is based on a careful selection and gradation of grammatical items (cf. Richards, Platt and Platt 1992: 358). The use of grammatical syllabuses has a long tradition. Even before machine-readable language corpora became available, there was research on the distribution of grammatical constructions and lexical elements which are important for foreign language teaching (e.g. George 1963a and George 1963b, Perebejnos *et al* 1986).

The possibilities of large-scale and effective research using the traditional methods of linguistics were, however, limited. Prohibitive amounts of working time were necessary for relatively simple tasks such as collecting the data and sorting them. The availability of large language corpora in machine-readable form and the possibility of exploring them by means of computational procedures will enable research with far-reaching implications for foreign language teaching.

A small but practical example is a learning list of irregular verbs in English that was compiled on the basis of machine-readable corpora of British and American English (Grabowski and Mindt 1994). In this list the verbs are ordered according to the frequency of their occurrence in English texts. After learning the forms of the first ten verbs of the list (*say, make, go, take, come, see, know, get, give, find*) the learner has mastered more than 45% of all forms of irregular verbs in English.

Textbooks in Germany are normally based on a structural syllabus without disregarding notional and situational criteria. The syllabus is, however, not openly discussed. Even though there are no commonly accepted criteria for the selection and gradation of grammatical items in a syllabus, it is either tradition or a tacit agreement by the authors of textbooks or the authors' anticipations about the grading expected by foreign language teachers that makes these syllabuses very often strikingly similar to each other.

The overriding objective of English language teaching in German schools is communication in everyday life situations. Hence it is claimed that a syllabus should be based on the spoken language before taking written English into account.

German textbooks are mostly designed for a 6-year course (classes 5 to 10, age 10 to 15 or 16). There are also 5-year courses. Normally one volume of a textbook is intended to cover one year.

In the following I should like to look at syllabus decisions concerning modal verbs, future time orientation in English and conditional clauses. I shall mainly be dealing with the first three years of the syllabus. In each case the results of corpus-based studies will be contrasted with the treatment of these grammatical items in current textbooks.

The following textbooks (both widely used in Germany) have been selected:

GOS1: for class 5 in comprehensive and similar schools.
GOS2: for class 6 in comprehensive and similar schools.
GA3: for class 7 in *Gymnasien* (grammar schools) (follow-up volume for learners who have used GOS1 and GOS2 in classes 5 and 6 and change to a grammar school for class 7: normal procedure in states like Berlin, Brandenburg, Hesse, and others).[1]

LEOL1: for class 5 in comprehensive and similar schools.
LEOL2: for class 6 in comprehensive and similar schools.
LEOL3: for class 7 in comprehensive and similar schools.[2]

(For bibliographical details, see *Notes 1 and 2*, below).

In order to comply with the precedence of spoken English over written English in the first teaching years, the corpus selected to illustrate authentic English is the surreptitious part of the London-Lund Corpus: Svartvik and Quirk 1980, henceforth: CEC (cf. Svartvik 1990: 19).

14.3 Modal verbs

From the point of view of their form central modals (cf. Quirk *et al* 1985: 135) fall into two different groups:

- so-called present forms: *can, may, must, shall, will*
- so-called past forms: *could, might, should, would.*

This distinction is purely formal and cannot be taken to imply that the forms invariably express present or past time (cf. Leech 1987: 72). The present forms occur more frequently in main clauses than the past forms (cf. Mindt 1995: 180). A syllabus should start with main clauses before introducing subclauses. For this reason it would be appropriate to introduce *can, may, must, shall, will* before *could, might, should. Would*, which is the most frequent modal verb in spoken conversation, should be treated separately and will therefore not be considered here.

The relative frequency of central modals in the first twelve conversations of CEC is displayed in figure 14.1.

Figure 14.1 Relative frequency of central modals (percentages)

27.5%	*would*
22.4%	*can*
18.3%	*will*
10.4%	*could*
6.5%	*must*
5.4%	*should*
3.4%	*may*
3.3%	*might*
2.9%	*shall*

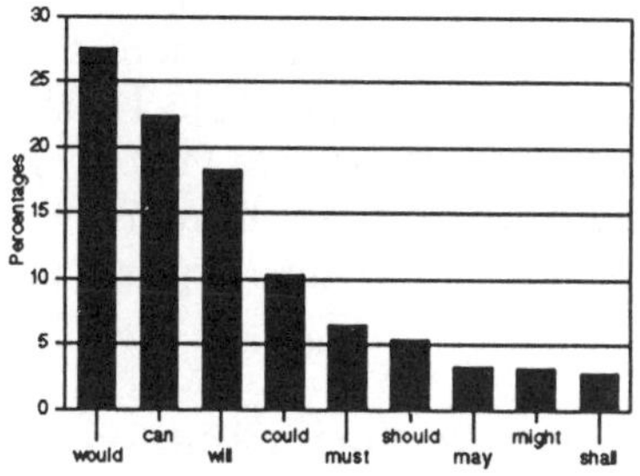

Taking only frequency data into account the following order of modals (present form) would be expected in a syllabus: *can, will, must, may, shall.*

For modal verbs with present forms textbook authors further distinguish modals which mainly express present time orientation or timelessness on the one hand (*can, must, may*)

they ***can*** *read it*
you ***must*** *do that*
you ***may*** *think that's extremely stupid*

from modals which are often used to express future time orientation on the other (*will, shall*)

there ***will*** *be two questions only*
I ***shall*** *see you at ten o'clock on Wednesday morning*

In a syllabus, present time orientation and timelessness normally precede future time orientation. For this reason members of the group containing *can, must, may* are expected to precede the group containing *will* and *shall.*

How do textbooks grade central modals with present tense forms? In GOS1 and GOS2 we find the order: *can, may, must* (first year). *Will* is introduced at the end of the second year. In LEOL1 and

LEOL2 we find the order *can, must* (first year). *May* and *will* are introduced in the second year in this order.

Both textbooks postpone *will* in favour of the infrequent modal verbs *must* and *may*. It is very difficult to see why *will* should be introduced only in the middle or at the end of the second year when it is so frequently used by native speakers in spoken conversation.

The prominence of *will* is certainly due to the fact that it is mostly used to express future time orientation. It is vital for the foreign language learner to be able to understand and to produce utterances which refer to the future at a comparatively early stage of the curriculum. It is, therefore, interesting to have a look at the treatment of future time orientation in textbooks.

14.4 Future time orientation

14.4.1 Will vs. going to

The two most prominent constructions expressing future time orientation are:

- *Will* + infinitive: *The parcel* ***will*** *arrive tomorrow.*
- *Going to* + infinitive: *The parcel is* ***going to*** *arrive tomorrow.*

Other constructions (the present progressive, the simple present, *will/shall* + progressive infinitive (cf. Leech 1987: 56) are less important than *will* and *going to.*

A comprehensive study of future time orientation in authentic English and in textbooks for teaching English as a foreign language (Mindt 1987 and Mindt 1992) has confirmed the prominence of *will* and *going to* both in spoken and written English.

The relative frequency of *will* and *going to* within a core area of spoken English (cf. Mindt 1987: 94f. and Mindt 1987 *Darstellungen*: 16) is displayed in figure 14.2.

Figure 14.2 Percentages for the minima and maxima of *will* and *going to* in a core area of spoken English

	will	*going to*
max	74.95%	15.82%
min	49.89%	10.65%

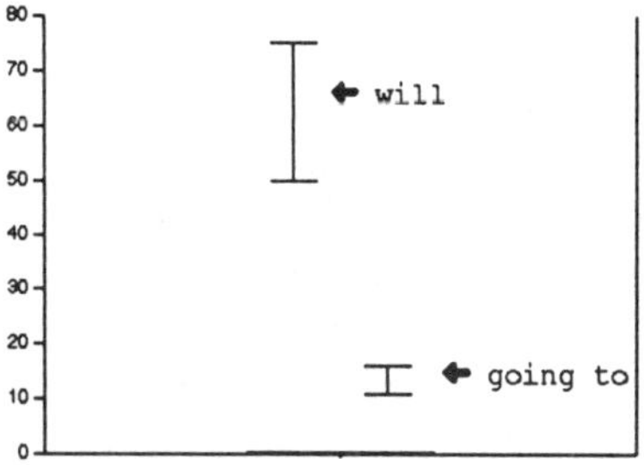

The findings of this study correspond to other corpus-based studies on written English (Kirsten 1972, Wekker 1976).

In addition, studies on the order of acquisition in the mother tongue (Wells 1979, Perkins 1983, Larsen-Freeman 1976 and Larsen-Freeman 1978) have shown that *will* is acquired before *going to* by native speakers of English.

Another important reason to introduce *will* before *going to* is the difference in syntactic behaviour of *will* and *going to*. *Will* combines more freely with individual verbs and classes of verbs than *going to* (Mindt 1992: 71f.). Equally, *will* combines more freely with classes of subjects than *going to* (Mindt 1992: 111). The use of *will* is obviously less restricted than that of *going to*.

In spite of all these observations the two textbooks introduce *going to* and *will* in the following order:

1	*going to*	GOS2: Unit 5	LEOL2: Unit 4
2	*will*	GOS2: Unit 8	LEOL2: Unit 7

This grading clearly contradicts the relative frequency of the two constructions in spoken English. It is at variance with the order of acquisition in the mother tongue of the two constructions. Given the grading adopted in the textbooks, the learner will tend to overuse a less frequent construction and apply it in contexts where it is rarely used by native speakers. Finally, learners will find it difficult to understand most sentences with future time orientation uttered by native speakers before they have become acquainted with *will* at a later stage of the language course.

14.4.2 The use of shall

Most grammars used in German schools do not mention *shall* as an expression for future time orientation (Ungerer *et al* 1984: 138, Bald and Schwarz 1984: 55ff.). Consequently most German textbooks do not treat *shall* as a learning item for future time orientation, claiming that *shall* is only rarely used in spoken conversation and that it is restricted to formal language use. This may be true of American English. In British English, however, *shall* is more frequently found than these statements suggest.

Generally *shall* is compared with other expressions for future time orientation and found to be not very frequent. The figures for CEC are given in figure 14.3 (Mindt 1986: 143).

Figure 14.3 Relative frequency of expressions for future time orientation (percentages)

will + infinitive	52.7%
going to + infinitive	20.3%
present progressive	10.3%
simple present	8.2%
shall + infinitive	6.2%
will + prog infin	1.7%
going to + prog infin	0.6%

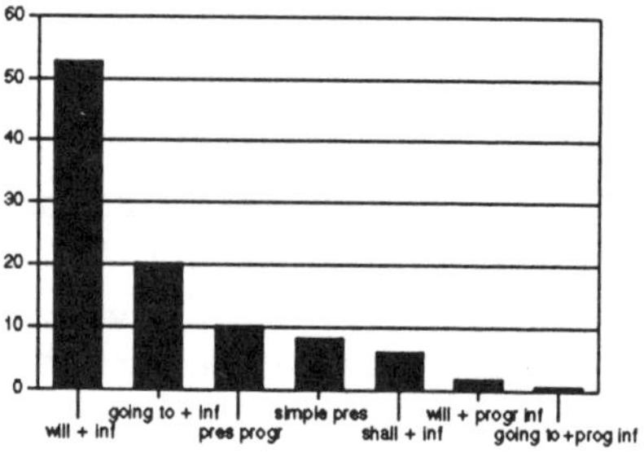

However, *shall* mainly occurs with the first person subject *I:*

I ***shall*** *not continue this*
if you argue with me ***I shall*** *just put this phone down.*

If we compare the use of *shall* with the first person subject *I* (see figure 14.4) the figures for *shall* look different (Mindt 1986: 146).

Figure 14.4 Relative frequency (percentages) of expressions for future time orientation with first person singular subject *I*

will + infinitive	53.4%
shall + infinitive	16.3%
going to + infinitive	14.4%
present progressive	9.5%
simple present	4.9%
will + progressive infinitive	1.5%
going to +progr infinitive	0.0%

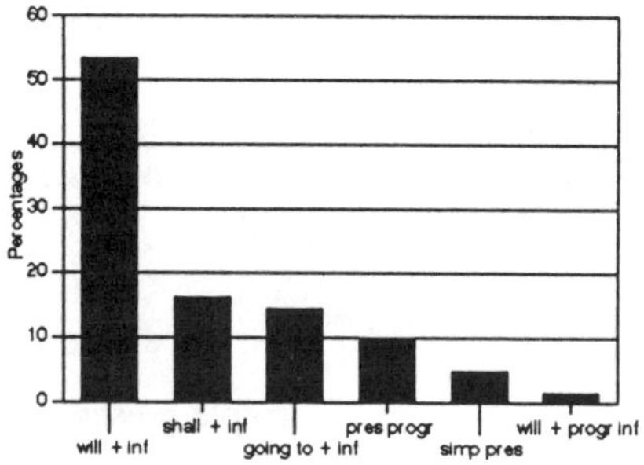

With first person subjects *shall* ranks even before *going to*. This begs the question of whether *shall* should be completely excluded from language courses. It is frequently used by native speakers with first person subjects and often encountered in spoken conversation. Corpus evidence suggests that the minimum requirement would be to teach it receptively so that the learner is able to understand *shall* when used for future time orientation by native speakers of British English.

14.5 Conditional clauses

14.5.1 Grammatical description

Conditional clauses are regarded as difficult for the foreign language learner for two main reasons:

- they belong to the class of complex sentences and
- the use of tenses differs from that in many other languages.

Grammars normally distinguish between two types of conditions:

Type I: real (or open) conditions and
Type II: hypothetical conditions.

Hypothetical conditions are further subdivided into conditions with:

(a) present or future time orientation
(b) past time orientation (cf. Quirk *et al* 1985: 1091 f.).

These distinctions result in three types of conditional clauses:

Type I: real (or open) conditions
The sequence of tenses in sentences expressing real (or open) conditions is very often:

subclause	main clause
simple present	simple present
if it ***happens***	*it* ***happens***
if we ***want to buy*** *anything at the moment*	*we* ***have to borrow*** *the money*

Another sequence of tenses in sentences expressing real (or open) conditions is:

subclause	main clause
simple present	*will* + infinitive
if we ***don't get*** *home soon*	*we* ***'ll be*** *barmy*
if she ***needs*** *anything*	*she'****ll have to wait***

Hypothetical conditions:

Type IIa (time orientation: present or future)
A very common sequence of tenses in sentences expressing hypothetical conditions with present or future time orientation is:

subclause	main clause
simple present	*should/would/might* etc + infinitive
if I ***had*** *a son like him*	*I* ***should be*** *happy*
if one ***went*** *up there*	*nothing* ***would*** *ever* ***be*** *quite the same again*

Type IIb (time orientation: past)
The sequence of tenses in sentences expressing hypothetical conditions with past time orientation is generally:

subclause	main clause
past perfect	*would/should/might* etc + perfect infinitive
*if they **had been** left there,*	*they **would have been ruined***
*if everything **hadn't been** quite in order*	*he **wouldn't have asked** her*

It is true that hypothetical conditions present learning problems for German students, because conditional clauses in German expressing hypothetical conditions differ with respect to the sequence of tenses.

14.5.2 Corpus data

Ingrid Haase (1988) has studied the frequency of the three types of conditional clauses and the sequence of tenses in the surreptitious part of the London-Lund Corpus (CEC). Figure 14.5 gives the distribution of the three types of conditional clauses (cf. Haase 1988: 71–75).

Figure 14.5 Absolute and relative frequency of the three types of conditional sentences

	absolute frequency	relative frequency
Type I	362	65.7%
Type IIa	154	27.9%
Type IIb	35	6.4%

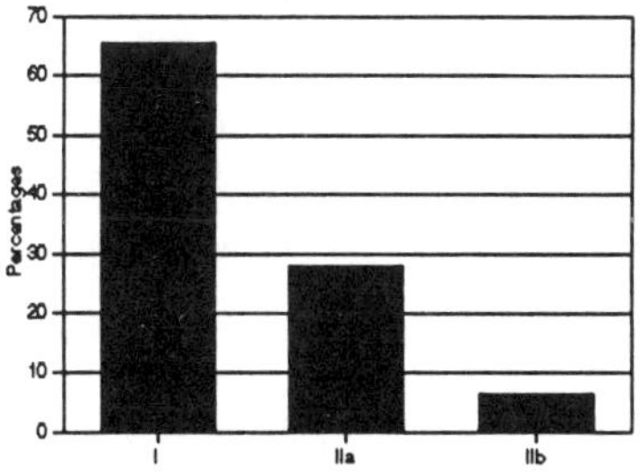

Type I (real or open conditions) is obviously the most frequent type and it would be natural to introduce this type as the first in a

foreign language teaching syllabus. Most textbooks proceed in this manner which is supported by corpus evidence.

If a textbook writer has decided to deal with real conditions first, the next decision would be on the sequence of tenses.

Figure 14.6 gives the distribution of the sequence of tenses for real conditions found by Haase (1988: 72f.).

Figure 14.6 Absolute and relative frequency of the sequence of tenses in Type I

	absolute frequency	relative frequency
simple present – simple present	119	32.9%
simple present – modal (present)	36	9.9%
simple present – *will*	22	6.1%
miscellaneous others	185	51.1%

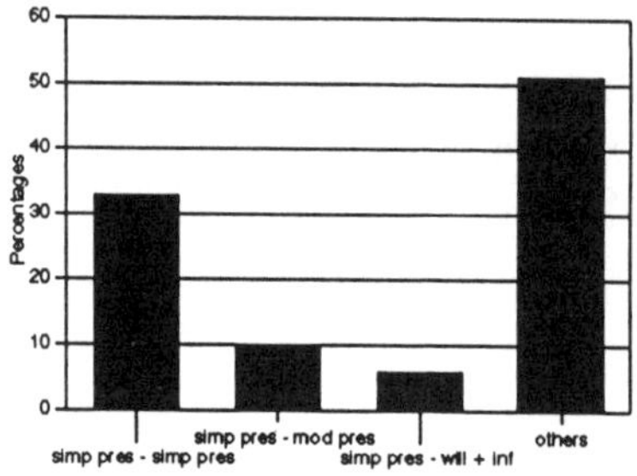

The 185 cases under 'miscellaneous others' are split up in the following way:

- 126 cases with 21 different sequences of tenses with a frequency which varies between 15 and 1 for each individual sequence of tenses
- 59 incomplete constructions where there is no main clause.

The three most frequent sequences of tenses are exemplified by sentences like:

subclause	main clause
simple present	simple present
*if you **fancy** them*	*you **need** them*
*if you **know** the person*	*it's all right*

subclause	main clause
simple present	modal verb (present form) + infinitive
if you ***want to do*** *philosophy and mathematics*	*[...] you* ***can do*** *those*
if you ***apply*** *that criterion*	*then surely you* ***must start to*** *rearrange your estimates*

subclause	main clause
simple present	*will* + infinitive
if we ***don't do*** *this*	*we'll never* ***improve*** *the accommodation*
if anybody ***rings***,	***I'll say*** *you're too busy to come to the telephone*

From the data presented by Haase 1988 the following grading of conditional clauses seems to be plausible:

1 Type I
2 Type IIa
3 Type IIb

All the three types should be clearly kept apart, because they differ not only with regard to type of condition but also with regard to the sequence of tenses.

When Type I is introduced as the first type, the next decision would be on the sequence of tenses within Type I. The data given by Haase 1988 suggest the following order:

1 simple present – simple present
2 simple present – modal (present form)
3 simple present – *will*

Having taken this decision, the next question would be at what stage in the curriculum the first type of conditional clauses should be introduced. This question can be answered by looking at the relative importance of conditional clauses in English. Francis and Kučera 1982 list *if* (the most frequent conjunction introducing conditional clauses) at rank place 42 (with an absolute frequency of 2199 in a one-million-word corpus). The importance of conditional clauses is clearly confirmed by the LOB-corpus, where the absolute frequency of *if* is 2209 in one million words.

The prominence of *if* in both corpora is a clear indication of the importance of conditional clauses in English. Since Type I (expressing real conditions) makes up more than 60% of all conditional clauses, it should be introduced at an early stage in the curriculum.

The corpus data on modals and future time orientation given above together with those for conditional clauses suggest the following grading:

1.	Type I: simple present - simple present	(1st year)
2.	Type I: simple present - modal (present form)	(1st year)
3.	*will* (for future time orientation)	(2nd year)
4.	Type I: simple present - *will*	(2nd year)

Types IIa and IIb should be clearly kept apart from Type I and neither should be introduced before the third year.

14.5.3 Conditional clauses in textbooks

LEOL3 introduces Type I in the third year with the sequence of tenses:

subclause	main clause
simple present	*will* + infinitive
If the sun ***shines*** *tomorrow,*	*we'****ll climb*** *Ben Bracken.*
And if it ***rains,***	*I'****ll catch*** *the next train home.*

There is no mention of other sequences of tenses for this type of condition (LEOL3: 31 and 94).

GA3 introduces two types of conditional clauses in the third year within the same teaching unit: Type I and Type IIa. For type I the following sequences of tenses are given in this order (GA3: 46):

subclause	main clause
1. simple present	*will* + infinitive
If you ***go*** *to a youth hostel,*	*you'****ll meet*** *lots of young people.*

2. simple present	*can, must* or other modal verb + infinitive
If you ***don't stay*** *at a hotel,*	*you* ***can save*** *a lot of money.*
*If you****'re*** *interested in music,*	*you* ***must go*** *to the festival in Llangollen*
3. simple present	imperative
If the sun ***shines***	***enjoy*** *it while you can.*

For Type IIa the following tense sequence is given (GA3: 47):

subclause	main clause
simple past	*would, could, might* + infinitive
If it ***was*** *Monday,*	*the girls* ***would go*** *by train.*
If they ***found*** *another telephone,*	*they* ***could phone*** *the youth hostel.*
If they ***had*** *enough money,*	*they* ***might*** *take a taxi.*

The grading in the textbooks is clearly at variance with the results of corpus analysis:

- Both in LEOL3 and in GA3 conditional clauses are introduced at a very late stage (third year) which contradicts their overall importance in English.
- Both in LEOL3 and in GA3 the prototypical sequence of tenses for conditions of Type I is given as: simple present — *will*.
- Both in LEOL3 and in GA3 the most frequent sequence of tenses for Type I (simple present — simple present) is not mentioned at all.
- In GA3 Type I is introduced together with Type IIa. The simultaneous introduction of two formally and semantically different types of conditional clauses violates the principle of isolation of difficult items in a syllabus.

14.6 Conclusions

Modal verbs, future time orientation and conditional clauses are interrelated areas of English grammar. The grading of grammatical items belonging to these areas of English grammar has been based on tradition and intuition rather than on empirical evidence. As a result, the order of these items in syllabuses very often does not correspond to what one might reasonably expect from corpus data of spoken and written English.

The textbooks postpone the first introduction of *will* (used to express future time orientation) to the middle or the end of the second year and instead introduce *going to* before *will*. This clearly contradicts the frequency of the two constructions in English and stands in contrast to the order of acquisition in the mother tongue of the two constructions. Given the grading adopted in the textbooks, learners will find it difficult to understand most sentences with future time orientation uttered by native speakers before they have become acquainted with *will* later in the language course.

The first introduction of real (open) conditions in the third year contradicts their overall importance in English. Real conditions should be introduced much earlier (preferably in the first year). The most frequent sequence of tenses for Type I (simple present — simple present) is not mentioned in the textbooks. Instead, the sequence of tenses simple present — *will* is assigned prototype character by the textbooks which clearly contradicts the findings in the corpus of spoken English. Corpus evidence suggests the following grading of the items studied in this article:

First year

- Simple present (for present time orientation and timelessness)
- Modals (present forms): *can, must*
- Conditional clauses Type I (open conditions) with the sequences of tenses:

simple present	simple present
simple present	modal (*can, must*)

Second year

- *will* (for future time orientation)
- conditional clauses Type I with the sequences of tenses:

simple present	*will*

Third year

- conditional clauses Type IIa

Corpus-based decisions on foreign language teaching syllabuses could help considerably to bring textbooks for teaching English as a foreign language into closer correspondence with actual English. Corpus linguistics could thus contribute to making foreign language learning more effective and to giving learners opportunities to communicate more successfully at earlier stages of the language learning process.

Notes

1 GOS1: Schwarz, Hellmut, Taylor, Carl and Vettel, Franz (1985), *English G - Neue Ausgabe - Band OS 1 für das 5. Schuljahr an Orientierungsstufen, Förderstufen, Gesamtschulen und anderen integrierten Schulformen*, Cornelsen, Berlin.

GOS2: Schwarz, Hellmut, Taylor, Carl and Vettel, Franz (1986), *English G - Neue Ausgabe - Band OS 2 für das 6. Schuljahr an Orientierungsstufen, Förderstufen, Gesamtschulen und anderen integrierten Schulformen*, Cornelsen, Berlin.

GA3: Schwarz, Hellmut, Taylor, Carl and Vettel, Franz (1987), *English G - Neue Ausgabe - Band A3 für das 7. Schuljahr an Gymnasien*, Cornelsen, Berlin.

2 LEOL1: Beile, Werner, Beile-Bowes, Alice, Reisener, Helmut *et al.* (eds.) (1984), *Learning English - Orange Line, Unterrichtswerk für Orientierungsstufen, Förderstufen, Gesamtschulen und andere differenzierende Schulformen*, Klett, Stuttgart.

LEOL2: Beile, Werner, Beile-Bowes, Alice, Reisener, Helmut and Speight, Stephen *et al.* (eds.) (1985), *Learning English - Orange Line 2, Unterrichtswerk für Orientierungsstufen, Förderstufen, Gesamtschulen und andere differenzierende Schulformen*, Klett, Stuttgart.

LEOL3: Amor, Stuart, Beile, Werner, Beile-Bowes, Alice, Hellyer-Jones, Rosemary *et al.* (1989), *Learning English - Orange Line 3, Erweiterungskurs, Unterrichtswerk für Gesamtschulen und andere differenzierende Schulformen*, Klett, Stuttgart.

15 Do corpora have a role in language assessment?

J CHARLES ALDERSON

15.1 Introduction

I owe the beginnings of my thinking about computer-based language testing to Geoff Leech. He invited me to give a talk on a British Council Specialist Seminar he was organizing at Lancaster in 1984 on Computers in English Language Education and Research. The result was an article published in the volume of papers from that seminar (Alderson 1986). Since then, I have devoted some time and thought to exploring ways in which computers can be used to innovate in language assessment. However, unlike many papers on language testing or on language corpora, this paper is speculative and programmatic. It is not data-based, it does not refer to experiments that have been carried out, nor does it describe the validation of assessment procedures. Although I shall briefly describe developments in the use of computers in language testing, for the most part I shall concentrate on exploring future possibilities for the application of computer-based language corpora (henceforth simply 'corpora') in language assessment, and will conclude by suggesting avenues for research and development work that might derive from such applications.

As this volume testifies, the advent of cheap and powerful computers is beginning to have a major impact on linguistics as on many other aspects of life. The ability to store large amounts of text and, more importantly, to retrieve parts of those texts more or less instantly has made possible a data-based approach to language analysis which was previously simply not practical. Linguists can now have recourse, not just to their intuitions, but also to others' language use which greatly facilitates activities like lexicography, the construction which greatly facilitates activities like lexicography, the construction of grammars, the testing of linguistic hypotheses, and the comparison of languages. In applied linguistics, corpora are beginning to impact on the development of language teaching materials, the study of interlanguage and learner productions in writing and speech, and even the analysis of translation. However, in the assessment of language learning and proficiency — language testing — corpora have yet to find an application.

Of course, one can argue that if corpora have not been used in language testing, that must be because there is no need for them. Language testing is centrally concerned with the validity of assessment, and it may be that the existence of corpora does not provide any form of solution to the problems that concern language testers; there may be no theoretical issue that corpora can enlighten. In which case, why speculate on their use?

The counter argument is twofold. Firstly, one may not know what corpora can offer language testing until one has at least thought through what they have to offer and speculated on how they might be used. The second argument is more pragmatic and says that since corpora exist, they will eventually be used, for better or worse, and therefore it makes sense to think about how best to use them in order to control their development rather than to suffer it.

15.2 Computers in language testing

The pragmatic approach suggested above has underlaid much of my own thinking and work to date in computer-based testing. As Alderson (1986) discusses, computers have been used in language testing for a long time, but more recent developments in the use of computers to deliver language tests threaten to compromise the validity of the instruments by encouraging users to employ test methods of questionable value. In particular, multiple choice questions and the cloze procedure have been given a new lease of life because they are easily adapted to computer-based testing, when their validity and value had begun to be questioned in testing research. The ease of the use of multiple choice and cloze in the computer age threatens to inhibit test developers from seeking new and more valid ways of assessing language proficiency and language learning. (But see Alderson 1987, Alderson and Windeatt 1991 and LUCAS 1992,[1] for an attempt to encourage innovation in test method and computer-based test research.)

Nevertheless, the use of computers in language testing is here to stay, for good or ill, and therefore it makes sense to seek to harness their potential for the benefit and improvement of tests, rather than either to ignore such developments or merely to decry them. And it is clearly the case that computers have much to offer language testing. In order to contextualize my discussion of the possible value of corpora in language testing, I first need to describe what computers do have to offer language testing. It should be noted, however, that much of what I describe below is only just beginning to happen: at present most tests and testing systems make minimal use of computers.

Computers can be used in language testing in various ways: for test construction, test compilation, test delivery, response capture, test scoring, result calculation and delivery, and test analysis. They can also, of course, be used for storing tests and details of candidates.

15.2.1 Test construction

Tests already exist which are constructed by computer. Computers can be programmed to delete words or parts of words randomly from text, or according to some algorithm, for example every *n*th word. Cloze tests are common forms of computer-based test, and C-tests are clearly also possible on computer. (A C–test is a variant of a cloze test in which the second half of every second word is deleted from selected passages, and the candidate's task is to restore the deleted letters.) Computers can randomly or otherwise insert material — words or non-words — into text, for learners to identify and remove (the cloze-elide technique is one such application). Computers can jumble words, parts of words, sentences, paragraphs or other language units and present them to learners for rearrangement.

15.2.2 Test compilation

Tests can be compiled by computer, either by reference to a computer based-item bank, or to a computer index of a paper-based bank. Computers can be instructed to create a test of given difficulty (by selecting only items of that difficulty level) or of particular content (by selecting only those items which test the desired ability, or which are based on texts on the required topic, or which employ a given method), or any combination of these.

15.2.3 Test selection

In adaptive testing, computers decide which items to present to test-takers, based upon their performance on the test to date. This is achieved by estimating the test-taker's ability level and presenting items whose difficulty most closely matches that level. This occurs iteratively until the best estimate of the ability level has been achieved.

15.2.4 Test presentation

Computers can be used to present the test to the candidate. In other words, the computer elicits the responses. This may be done entirely via the screen, keyboard and mouse, although it could also involve the use of multimedia, including video and sound. It can also be accompanied by computer-based support facilities which candidates can be allowed to request (help facilities, dictionary, clues, more than one attempt, feedback on one's response and so on — see Alderson and Windeatt 1991 for a discussion and exemplification)

15.2.5 Response capture

Computers can record the candidates' responses, again usually via the keyboard or mouse, but potentially also by capturing sound. Details of the response to be recorded can include latencies (time taken), use of support facilities, sequence of responses, number of attempts, and so on.

15.2.6 Test scoring

Computers can score responses, typically by matching candidate responses against a database containing correct or acceptable responses. These may be weighted in any number of ways, either according to degree of correctness, acceptability or difficulty, or depending upon the candidate's use of support facilities, the feedback they have received, or the number of attempts they have already made.

15.2.7 Calculation and delivery of results

Computers can also compute scores and deliver test results (including result sheets, individual profiles, test certificates, comparisons with national or local norms, previous attempts by individual or group, adjustments in scores for use of support, time taken, difficulty/ importance of items, severity of marker (if human) and so on.

15.2.8 Test analysis

Finally, data held by the computer (including response data, biodata, attitude data, learner characteristics, item characteristics) can be fed back into the testing system, (including the test data bank) for potential updating and modification of the test (for example, data on item difficulty, information on what sort of learner finds what sort of item easy/difficult, and so on).

In short, computers can be used at all stages in the test development and administration process. It should be pointed out that it is not NECESSARY for computers to be so used, and indeed it may be desirable for computers NOT to be used in some stages, especially perhaps that of test construction. However, it is not the purpose of this paper to discuss whether such uses are desirable or present an improvement on what can be done without computers, although I have suggested above that there are reasons for having reservations about their beneficial impact. It is important to guard against the danger of getting carried away by what the technology can do and how 'clever' it is, and to keep in mind the basic theoretical considerations (of the construct to be tested, of validity and reliability) as well as the results of empirical study, as the basis for test development and testing methodologies. In what follows, I shall accompany my speculations about uses for corpora in assessment with some discussion of their value.

15.3 Possible uses for corpora in assessment

In the context of this volume, it is unnecessary to define what is meant by a corpus. However, it will be important to keep in mind the difference between annotated and unannotated corpora. To avoid unnecessary repetition, I shall assume that by 'annotated' corpora, the reader will understand that I mean corpora which have been tagged for part of speech, and syntactically parsed. The possibility of other forms of annotation, such as semantic tagging, is not ruled out, but not assumed. Unannotated corpora do not contain such linguistic information.

Furthermore, I assume that both sorts of corpora can be accompanied by additional information which characterizes individual texts within the corpus. This would include things like: date of text production, author or originator, source, genre, nature of participants (especially if spoken text), topic(s) and so on; and possibly also information on text difficulty, length, number and nature of sections, and the like. I assume that such information is in any case necessary for judgements about the adequacy (representativeness, relevance, etc) of a corpus and for linguistic analysis, but we shall see that it is essential for some uses of corpora in language testing. However, I further assume that at the moment such additional information is not standardized, and varies considerably across corpora.

In any event, it may be the case that for the purposes of language testing, the information characterizing the corpus would need to be supplemented. For example, current language test research and development makes increasing reference to the so-called Bachman model of communicative language ability (Bachman 1990) and to his taxonomy of test method facets. Components of both the model and the taxonomy are used to describe what tests test and to validate and compare tests. It is likely to be extremely helpful to testers if corpora could be described in terms relevant to such criteria. However, the minutiae of test content and method characterization is extremely time consuming and difficult, and it is highly unlikely that any detailed corpus characterization will be available until such time as it can be generated by machine.

It is possible to conceive of different uses of corpora in testing: corpora might be used for test selection, or for test construction, but not for test delivery or test scoring. Or corpora could be used in the scoring process as well. I will therefore organize my speculations according to those stages of test construction used in section 15.2 above which appear particularly appropriate.

15.3.1 Test construction, compilation and selection

As a source of data for test construction, corpora clearly have enormous potential. Real language texts — spoken or written — which are classified according to relevant variables — source, genre, sociolinguistic variation, time, etc — are the basis of most language tests. Having such texts available on computer would save enormous amounts of time in text selection. Test constructors would simply specify the characteristics of the texts required, according to criteria set out in the test specifications. The computer could present all suitable texts for humans to select, or could automatically present a random sample of such texts.

For those corpora whose texts are characterized according to difficulty or suitability for levels of learner (one example that comes to mind are corpora of graded readers) it would be possible to select texts suitable for a given test population.

Lexical items could be selected from a corpus by computer according their frequency in the corpus. They could even be presented to learners in a computer-generated test, where the learner has to identify the words they know and those they do not, along the lines of Meara's Word Associates Test (see, for example, Meara and Buxton 1987).

None of these uses needs an annotated corpus. However, annotated corpora could be searched for particular structures, or sequences of parts of speech. Concordances could be compiled to produce sample sentences or texts with particular linguistic features. These could then form the basis of test items constructed by humans or machines, along the lines indicated in section 15.2. Computers could automatically construct test items by being required to select sentences according to particular linguistic criteria, and then to delete particular parts of speech or sequences of text. Such mutilated texts would then be presented to learners for restoration. Computers could conceivably also judge each restoration for its part of speech and assess performance accordingly.

Interlanguage corpora — corpora of language produced by learners — could be of considerable use in test construction. For example, corpora of scripts written by students taking particular tests, possibly stratified by achievement levels or test scores, could provide examples of language which particular learners find difficult. Such corpora could then form the basis of a test for such learners. If they were tagged according to part of speech or parsed for syntactic structure, then it would be possible to select examples of particular structures or sequences of parts of speech.

In 15.2.1 above I described how computers are already used to construct tests, by deleting, inserting or scrambling words in text. All these processes are applicable to corpora as well as to texts input by humans, and thus corpora expand the possibilities for computer generated tests. As in many such tasks, the response could be judged by humans, or by the computer making reference to the corpus from which the data had been taken.

Of these various possibilities, I consider the automatic generation of tests by computer, with or without reference to corpora, to be relatively undesirable and I would recommend its use only in circumstances where there are no negative consequences for the student of poor performance on the test. Clearly, however, the use of corpora to aid humans in test construction has interesting possibilities and is an area that should be pursued and developed energetically.

15.3.2 Test presentation

Corpora or concordances from corpora could be presented to learners for them to make judgements about the language data. For example, they could be asked to identify the likely source, genre of the text, the gender, regional origin or sociolinguistic status of the speaker, the deviance of the language. They could even be asked to identify the part(s) of speech of words or stretches of language, the meaning of words or phrases, the referents of anaphoric devices, lexical synonymy and so on. It would simply be necessary for the corpus to have previously been characterized according to the judgement being made by the student. The computer could then match learner response against the preclassified entry

Learners could be asked to make judgements about the probability of occurrence of particular bits of language in a given corpus. Responses could be compared against actual frequencies and the student would be judged accordingly. Alternatively learners could judge the acceptability or grammaticality of a given stretch, and this judgement could be automatically compared with a corpus based acceptability judgement based upon some computation relating to its frequency of occurrence in a relevant corpus.

Whilst attractive possibilities, these ideas would need careful trialling on competent users of a language before being used with non-proficient language users. Whilst not wishing to imply that native speakers can make such judgements about language uniformly well, I would certainly want to know much more about their ability to do so before recommending them as testing techniques. However, it may be that such techniques offer interesting possibilities for exploring the competence of competent language users even if they are not suitable for non-proficient users.

15.3.3 Response capture

Although it is difficult to see how corpora can be used to capture responses, they can certainly be developed as a result of response capture. A restricted form of corpus could be developed by the computer storing all responses by students to given test items. These can then be judged — usually by humans — for their correctness and/or appropriacy. The judgements can then be attached to the response. New responses produced by students can be matched against such a corpus, and evaluated accordingly. Responses not occurring in the corpus would be flagged for human judgement prior to being added to it. Note that such a corpus could be a very useful source of interlanguage data in its own right, and might even be usable for test construction in the ways outlined in 15.3.1 above.

15.3.4 Test scoring

Computer scoring of language tests presents possibly the biggest challenge to test designers, and is at present the most significant limitation in the type of test that can be administered completely by computer (rather than delivered by computer but scored by humans). The availability of corpora of naturally-occurring language offers the possibility of a reference point against which candidate responses could be compared. A response could be judged to be adequate if it occurred in similar contexts in a corpus. Alternatively a response could be weighted according to the frequency of its occurrence in the corpus. On-line taggers and parsers could be used in conjunction with an annotated corpus in similar ways: an improbable, highly infrequent or non-existent response would be judged to be unacceptable.

Reference has already been made above to some of the ways in which corpora could be used for scoring candidate responses. Some of these involve the computer in matching responses against pre-classified text in the corpus. Others require the responses to be tagged and/or parsed in some way before matching.

Clearly there would need to be a considerable amount of experimentation with such scoring techniques before they could be implemented. The absence of a stretch of language from a corpus does not necessarily mean that such language cannot occur and is therefore incorrect or unacceptable. The extent to which learners' responses can be tagged and parsed accurately by machine is also uncertain. In some cases, deviant language will not be capable of being tagged or parsed; but some will, and considerable test development effort might be needed to construct items the responses to which can be adequately annotated before scoring.

15.3.5 Calculation and delivery of results

It has already been suggested that the occurrence of language in a corpus could be used as a means of scoring or weighting candidate responses. Similarly, reference to corpus data could be made when norming the test, or when reporting results. Candidates' performances could be classified according to the extent to which they conformed to the 'norms' of given reference corpora. As a simple example, a learner's vocabulary could be estimated in terms of the frequency of occurrence of known words in a corpus, or according to the percentage of words in a corpus that the learner 'knew'. Quite what such 'norms' or results might mean is an important matter which would need exploration in its own right. Clearly, however, the existence of corpora makes such exploration possible.

15.4 Conclusions: validity

The above account represents an attempt to speculate on possible uses of corpora in language assessment. Some uses may be more attractive than others, or more practical, or more useful. Some may represent genuine advances in computer-based testing, some may even provide genuine advances in the assessment of language, whether or not it is computer-based.

As in all language testing, however, it is crucial to make sure that all attempts to innovate in test design or test use by involving corpora are fully justified. This might occur by offering the possibility of meeting a need that has not yet been met, by improving an existing measure or technique, by offering the possibility of assessing some aspect of language behaviour or proficiency that could not be measured before, or by offering the possibility of more convenient, economical, speedy or accurate assessment.

All corpus-based innovations and tests should be subject to the normal requirements of validity and reliability. Tests based on corpora should be demonstrated to have acceptable levels of reliability, especially but not only of scoring reliability. Evidence should also be available that the test measures what it is supposed to measure: by comparison with other equivalent measures, with teacher, learner and expert judgements, with appropriate predictor or criterion variables, with other perspectives on candidate proficiency. We would expect validity and reliability at least comparable to non-corpus based measures, but would hope for some evidence of increased validity or reliability.

I do not at present see how any of the uses suggested constitute theoretical breakthroughs in language test research, or offer the potential for increasing the construct validity of existing, non-computer based tests. What they DO offer is the potential for an increase in content validity to the extent that such tests would be based on naturally-occurring language, and judgements about candidates could relate to such language rather than to individual testers' intuitions.

To the extent that this is possible, corpora seem to offer the same sort of advantages to language testing as they have already been claimed to offer to language teaching. Nobody, I think, would want to claim that the use of corpora for the preparation of language learning activities or materials represents a theoretical breakthrough, or even contributes substantially to our knowledge of teaching or learning. What it does do, however, is make it possible for learners not only to have access to real (rather than contrived) language data, but also to explore language data on their own and to generate their own hypotheses and rules about the language. Similarly in language testing, the use of corpora may allow learners access to real language data and free them from the tyranny of the testers' judgements, allowing the exploration of corpus-based assessments of proficiency. In other words, learners may be enabled to compare their own performances with naturally occurring language, and to draw their own conclusions. Whilst perhaps not a theoretical advance, this may represent a significant benefit nevertheless.

The potential advantages of basing our tests on real language data, of making data-based judgements about candidates' abilities, knowledge and performance are clear enough. A crucial question is whether the possible advantages are born out in practice. Language testing offers the opportunity and challenge to corpus linguistics of a means of validating its claims to increased understanding of language and language use.

Notes

1 LUCAS (1992) *Lancaster University Computer-Based Assessment System.* Computer authoring program for language testing, for DOS systems. Available from J C Alderson, Department of Linguistics and Modern English Language, Lancaster University.

16 Computer lexicography: the importance of representativeness in relation to frequency

DELLA SUMMERS

16.1 Introduction

This paper describes how frequency influenced the presentation of phrases, the semantic description given in the definition, and the ordering of definitions in some entries in two recently published dictionaries. The two dictionaries are both for use by advanced foreign students of English. One, a dictionary of 80,000 words and phrases for general reference purposes, is the Longman Dictionary of Contemporary English (Third Edition, 1995). The other is a new type of dictionary, aimed at helping students to produce English themselves, using words and phrases in their appropriate meaning and context, the Longman Language Activator (1993), the first dictionary to be designated as a 'production dictionary'.

16.2 Representativeness

Both dictionaries were compiled by lexicographers using on-screen corpora which shared one central design principle — to be representative of general language. This is a bold ambition — some say one that is impossible to fulfil — yet we at Longman have always felt it essential to have a principled approach to corpus design, rather than following the more opportunistic path, which is usually overdependent on newspapers in electronic form or scripted or semiscripted radio broadcasts. For the purposes of designing these language' has been seen as being reducible into individually distinct text types, such as fiction, scientific writing, and educational books in written language, and conversation and business meetings in spoken communication. The text types are conceptualized as amalgams of:

- subject area in the written corpora (Fiction, Science, Politics, etc)
- medium (e.g. Books, Periodicals, or Unpublished in the written corpora),
- level (high, medium, or low in written corpora),
- context (Education, Leisure, Business, and Public or Institutional in spoken corpora)

This means that a work of literature such as *A Passage to India* has the features Fiction+ Book+ and High.

The demographic part of our spoken corpora are arguably the most representative of all, designed as they are to mirror statistically the demographics of the target group, be it in the US or Britain, in terms of age, gender, region and educational or social background. The design of such corpora, especially the Longman Lancaster Corpus of just under 30 million words and the British National Corpus of 100 million words, was much influenced by the work of Douglas Biber, and Geoffrey Leech was actively involved in advising on their creation, in his role as adviser on the Longman academic committee, Linglex, chaired by Lord Quirk, and as an academic partner in the British National Corpus[1] consortium.

The constitution of both these corpora is documented in detail elsewhere (Summers 1993, Crowdy 1994, etc.), but the question is: how does this influence dictionary compilation?

16.3 Frequency as an aid to the lexicographer

One of the main reasons for wanting the corpus to be representative was so that reliable frequency statistics could be generated and used to aid the lexicographers in making the many linguistic judgments that lie behind the final entry for a word in the printed dictionary. All aspects of lexicography are influenced by frequency, but perhaps the most important in relation to the new edition of LDOCE was that the dictionary would attempt to truly follow frequency ordering of definitions in the entries, a feature of dictionaries much vaunted in the past, but rarely carried through in any objective or consistent way, due to the lack of reliable, balanced corpora.

The principle of frequency ordering dictates that the most frequent definition should come first, but it is not a simple operation to decide which meaning is the most frequent. One of the great advances of the BNC is that it is reliably tagged grammatically, using the latest version of the CLAWS tagging system developed under Geoffrey Leech's guidance at Lancaster. This means that we can now produce frequency counts which split words with more than one part of speech such as *pull* the verb as opposed to *pull* the noun (see **Frequency marking**, section 16.7). However, no corpora are as yet tagged with meaning tags in the same way as they can be with grammatical tags (but see chapter 7, this volume). If we take the primary activity of lexicography to be the identification of the meanings of words, we can see that a parallel process is going on , with the lexicographer trying to base her analysis of the meanings of the word on frequency while at the same time framing the definitions and deciding on the meaning splits that she will eventually represent in the definitions in the dictionary.

Furthermore, experience has shown that even when working with corpora that are all based on the principle of representativeness, different corpora will present the lexicographer with different frequencies for words and repeated strings. There is therefore still a need to temper raw statistical information with intelligence and common sense. The corpus is a massively powerful resource to aid the lexicographer, which must be used judiciously. Our aim at Longman is to be corpus-based, rather than corpus-bound.

16.4 Frequency ordering and collocations in LDOCE

Because the users of the dictionary are advanced learners of English, collocation was an area of language that had been identified for special attention, but when we set out to make what we inelegantly term 'phraseology' into one of the predominant new features of LDOCE3, we had little idea of just how far-reaching this policy would turn out to be — for the look of the dictionary, for the organization of the entries, and for the form of the definitions themselves.

Preliminary work done by Penny Stock and Sheila Dignen into some of the most frequent words of the language, such as *day* and *eat,* alerted us to a fact that we should already have known: that is, that many such words were not just frequent by virtue of their single-word uses in the corpus,[2] but also because they often occur in so many set phrases or chunks of language, like *one day, the other day, some day* and so on. It is commonly opined by corpus workers that although things that are discovered from corpus analysis are 'obvious', they only become obvious once the corpus has revealed them to us, i.e. they are not reliably recovered from the lexicographer's innate knowledge and understanding of the language. The 'discovery' that collocations add to the frequency of some words is such a case.

It was decided to recognize the phraseological behaviour of many words by entering them in their phrasal form in the dictionary, although still retaining them under a single-word headword. We termed these phrases 'lexical units' or 'lexunits', believing that they function both semantically and grammatically as units. Quite often this resulted in the lexical unit being the first definition in the entry as the most frequent meaning. For example, under the headword **liable** you will find:

> **1 be liable to do something** to be likely to do or say something or to behave in a particular way, especially because of a fault or natural tendency: *The car is liable to overheat on long trips.* **2** [not before the noun] legally responsible for the cost of something: [+**for**] *Tenants have legal liability for any damage they cause.* **3** likely to be affected by a particular kind of problem, illness etc: [+**to**] *You're more liable to injury when you don't get regular exercise.* **4** *law* likely to be legally punished or forced to do something by law: [+ **to**] *Anyone found trespassing is liable to a maximum fine of $100.* [+**for**] *All males between 18 and 60 are liable for military service.*

The phrase is entered as the first definition because it was identified as the most frequent use on the corpus.[3] The frequency of the word *liable* is 2139 occurrences out of 88,361,710 in the written part of the BNC as accessed by our concordancing system. Nearly half of those occurrences are followed by the word *to*, either as an infinitive marker or as a preposition, with 460 uses being followed by the preposition *for*. Semantic and collocational analysis of the corpora produced the meaning splits as shown above, with the infinitival construction being shown to be the most frequent. This was borne out by the frequencies in the smaller Longman Lancaster Corpus, which unlike the BNC contains no newspaper material. (The BNC written part is made up of 31% news media.) The 10-million-word spoken component of the

BNC, which we access as a separate corpus, only provided 48 uses of the word liable, but of those 18 (or 37.5%) showed the infinitive complement. In this, as in other instances, the spoken corpus influenced the ordering of the senses in the entry and the lexical unit was given as the most frequent sense and therefore the first definition. Other cases of the phrase being shown as the first definition include **be on the lookout for, sectarian violence/ conflict/murder** (showing selection restrictions for an adjective), and **arouse hope/interest, expectations etc** (as an example of typical objects of a verb). Interestingly, the second sense of **arouse** is also a lexical unit with a different set of object preferences, **arouse anger/fear/dislike etc.**

16.5 Unitary definitions of lexical units

Presenting the thing to be defined (definiendum) as a lexical unit often radically alters the form of the definition, almost always with an increase of clarity and elegance. For example, these definitions:

> **miracle** *n* [C] **1** something lucky that you did not expect to happen or did not think was possible: *By some miracle, we managed to catch the plane.* **it is a miracle (that) ... 3 miracle drug/cure** a very effective medical treatment that cures even serious diseases **4 work/perform miracles** to have a very good effect or result: *Maybe you should try yoga — it worked miracles for me.* **5 a miracle of engineering/design etc** something that is produced or invented that is a very impressive example of a particular quality or skill: *This new electronic notebook is a miracle of miniaturization.*

16.6 Spoken phrases in the Activator

Very similar techniques to those described above were first used in the Longman Language Activator, the dictionary in which we first used the spoken corpus of the BNC. Spoken language was particularly relevant in this book, since its aim was to enable advanced students of English to 'activate' their passive knowledge of English and to use it more effectively in both speech and writing. The influence of the spoken corpus can be seen particularly, although not exclusively, in concepts with a functional or speech act aspect, such as PROMISE (**I promise, cross my heart,** and **I give you my word**), SOON (**as soon**

as possible, as soon as you can, and **the sooner the better),** and DON'T CARE **(not care, not give a damn, couldn't care less, be past caring, for all I care, who cares? so what?** and **shrug off).**

In the Activator, the individual semantic units are known as exponents, so that **for all I care** is an exponent of the concept DON'T CARE. All the above mentioned exponents would be covered in some form in dictionaries published before the Activator, but what is new is the inclusion of exponents made up mainly of delexical words such as **say what you like** under SURE or **you only have to ...** under OBVIOUS, which make their first appearance in a published dictionary due to our use of the spoken corpus:

> **you only have to ...** you say that you only have to look at something, read something etc when you think it is so obvious that anybody will notice it: *You've only got to look at the adverts for government jobs to realize that these people are paid too much. ...*

16.7 Frequency marking

I mentioned above the value of the CLAWS grammatical tagging in generating frequency information from corpora. In LDOCE 3, where different parts of speech are separate homographs, we have indicated the 3000 most frequent words of English in both spoken and written language, broken down by part of speech. This process will be described in detail at a later time, but what seemed to be a simple exercise — to identify the first one thousand, the next thousand, and then the third thousand — turned out to be a far more complex procedure than we envisaged at the beginning, involving a series of judgments, rather than taking raw frequency alone.[4] These judgments included deciding which categories of word to exclude from the count, for example we began by excluding all proper names and place names, and checking the corpus for the number of texts or contexts that a word appeared in. The word *bid* as a verb, for example, has a frequency of 226 in the 10-million-word spoken British corpus, which on raw frequency would have placed it in the top 3000 spoken words, earning it the S3 label in the dictionary. However, checking of the range of spoken sources showed that all the instances of this in the spoken corpus were from one source — an auction. There were no instances of the verb use in the 5 million words of general conversations in the demographically collected part of the spoken corpus —

and none at all in our American spoken corpus — so it was decided not to give the verb a spoken frequency tag at all. The noun for *bid*, on the other hand, with a frequency of 3144 in the 90 million words of the written part of the BNC, did receive a tag to indicate that it was within the 3000 most frequent words in written material, in examples like: *the highest bid for the house, rival bids for the contract,* and *a bid for power*.

16.8 Conclusion

Frequency is a powerful tool in the lexicographer's arsenal of resources, allowing her to make informed linguistic decisions about how to frame the entry and analyse the lexical patterns associated with words in a more objective and consistent way. However, in dictionary-making editorial judgment is of paramount importance, because blindly following the corpus, no matter how carefully it may be constructed to represent the target language type accurately, can lead to oddities. We expect our motto: 'Corpus-based, but not corpus-bound' to hold good for many years to come.

Notes

1 The British National Corpus is a collaborative initiative carried out by Oxford University Press, Longman, Chambers Harrap, Oxford University Computer Services, Lancaster University's Unit for Computer Research in the English Language (headed by Professor Geoffrey Leech), and the British Library. The project received funding from the UK Department of Trade and Industry and the Science and Engineering Research Council, and was supported by grants from the British Academy and the British Library.

2 At this point, the Longman Lancaster Corpus.

3 The corpus seen as a collection of corpora, including in this case the BNC and the Longman Lancaster Corpus.

4 For a comparison, see the frequency marking in the COBUILD Dictionary (2nd edition, 1995), which, perhaps due to its dependence on news media source material, gives *newscaster* as one of the 800 most frequent words of English and shows all nationality names, such as *Yemeni*, as being in the same band of frequency as *American*.

Appendix: Geoffrey N Leech Academic honours and publications

Academic Honours

Fil.Dr. (Honorary Doctorate) University of Lund
Fellow of the British Academy (1987–)
Member of Academia Europaea (1989–)
Fellow, University College London (1989–)
Member, Norske Videnskaps-Akademi (1993–)
Honorary Professor, Beijing Foreign Studies University (1994–)

Publications

Books

(1966) *English in advertising*. Longman, London
(1969) *A linguistic guide to English poetry*. Longman, London
(1969) *Towards a semantic description of English*. Longman, London
(1971) *Meaning and the English verb*. Longman, London
(1972) [with R Quirk, S Greenbaum and J Svartvik] *A grammar of contemporary English*. Longman, London
(1974) *Semantics*. Penguin, Harmondsworth
(1975) [with J Svartvik] *A communicative grammar of English*. Longman, London
(1978) [with S Johansson and H Goodluck] *Manual of information to accompany the Lancaster-Oslo/Bergen corpus of British English, for use with digital computers*. Department of English, University of Oslo, Oslo

(1979) [with S Greenbaum and J Svartvik] (eds) *Studies in English linguistics: for Randolph Quirk*. Longman, London
(1980) *Explorations in semantics and pragmatics*. Benjamins, Amsterdam
(1981) [with M H Short] *Style in fiction: a linguistic introduction to English fictional prose*. Longman, London
(1982) [with M Deuchar and R Hoogenraad] *English grammar for today: a new introduction*. Macmillan, London
(1983) *Principles of pragmatics*. Longman, London
(1985) [with R Quirk, S Greenbaum and J Svartvik] *A comprehensive grammar of the English language*. Longman, London
(1986) [with S Johansson, E A Atwell, R G Garside] *The tagged LOB corpus* Norwegian Computing Centre for the Humanities, Bergen
(1986) [with C N Candlin] (eds) *Computers in English language teaching and research*. Longman, London
(1987) [with R Garside and G Sampson] (eds) *The computational analysis of English: a corpus-based approach*. Longman, London
(1989) [in association with R Ivanič and B Cruickshank] *An A–Z of English grammar and usage*. Edward Arnold/Nelson, London
(1992) *Introducing English grammar*. Penguin, Harmondsworth
(1993) [with E Black and R Garside] (eds) *Statistically-driven computer grammars of English: the IBM/Lancaster approach*. Rodopi, Amsterdam
(1995) [with G Myers and J Thomas] (eds) *Spoken English on computer: transcription, mark-up and application*. Longman, London

Articles in journals

(1963) Disjunctive grammar in British television advertising. *Studia Neophilologica* **35**(2): 256–64
(1965) 'This Bread I Break': language and interpretation. *Review of English Literature* **6**(2): 66–75
(1968) Some assumptions in the metatheory of linguistics. *Linguistics* **39**: 87–102
(1969) On the theory and practice of semantic testing. *Lingua* **24**(4): 343–64
(1974) [with R Leonard] A computer corpus of British English. *Hamburger Phonetische Beiträge* **13**: 41–57
(1976) Being precise about lexical vagueness. *York Papers in Linguistics* **6**: 1–31
(1977) Natural language as metalanguage: an approach to some problems in the semantic description of English. *Transactions of the Philological Society*, 1–31

(1977) Literary criticism and linguistic description. *DQR* **7**: 2–22

(1980) [with J Coates] The meanings of the modals in British and American English. *York Papers in Linguistics* **8**: 22–34

(1980) Semantics and pragmatics; an example: interrogation and negation in English. *Reports from the Department of English, University of Jyväskylä* **8**: 19–30

(1983) [with R Garside and E Atwell] The automatic tagging of the LOB Corpus. *ICAME News* **7**: 110–17

(1983) Pragmatics, discourse analysis, stylistics and 'the Celebrated Letter', *Prose Studies* **6**(2): 141--57

(1983) [with R Garside and E Atwell] Recent developments in the use of computer corpora in English language research. *Transactions of the Philological Society*, 216–19

(1984) Music in metre: 'sprung rhythm' in Victorian and Georgian poetry. *DQR* **14**(3): 200–13

(1984) [with A Beale] Computers in English language research. *Language Teaching* **17**(3): 216–29

(1992) 100 million words of English: the British National Corpus (BNC). *Language Research* **28**(1): 1–13

(1992) [with R Fallon] Computer corpora: what do they tell us about culture?' *ICAME Journal* **16**: 1–22

(1993) 100 million words of English. *English Today* **9**(1): 9–15

(1993) [with A Wilson] Automatic content analysis and the stylistic analysis of prose literature. *Revue Information et Statistique dans les Sciences humaines* **29**: 219–34

(1993) Corpus annotation schemes. *Literary & Linguistic Computing* **8**(4): 275–81

Papers contributed to edited collections

(1966) Linguistics and the figures of rhetoric. In Fowler R G (ed) *Essays on style and language*. Routledge

(1969) Linguistic meaning, semantics. In *Encyclopedia of linguistics, information and control*. Pergamon Press

(1972) Foregrounding. In Fowler R G (ed) *Dictionary of criticism*. Routledge

(1972) Variation. In Fowler R G (ed) *Dictionary of criticism*. Routledge

(1972) [with W Pepicello] Semantic versus factual knowledge: an experimental approach. In Cohen D (ed) *Papers from the Symposium on Limiting the Domain of Linguistics*. Linguistics Department, University of Wisconsin-Milwaukee

(1976) Metalanguage, pragmatics, and performatives. In Rameh C (ed) *Semantics: theory and application, Georgetown University Round Table on Languages and Linguistics*. Georgetown University Press, Washington DC

(1980) [with J Coates] Semantic indeterminacy and the modals. In Greenbaum S, Leech G and Svartvik J (eds) *Studies in English linguistics: for Randolph Quirk*. Longman, London

(1981) Pragmatics and conversational rhetoric. In Parret H, Verschueren J and Sbisà M (eds) *Possibilities and limitations of pragmatics*. John Benjamins, Amsterdam

(1982) [with R Garside] Grammatical tagging of the LOB Corpus: general survey. In Johansson S and Hofland K (eds) *Computer corpora in English language research*. NAVF, Bergen

(1982) Pragmatics, discourse analysis and literature. In *Discourse analysis: theory and application*. Proceedings of the Second National Symposium on Linguistics and English Language Teaching, Faculty of Arts, Cairo University

(1984) [with E Atwell and R Garside] Analysis of the LOB Corpus: problems and prospects. In Aarts J and Meijs W (eds) *Corpus linguistics*, Rodopi, Amsterdam, pp 40–52

(1985) Stylistics. In van Dijk T (ed) *Discourse and literature: new approaches to the analysis of literary genres*. John Benjamins, Amsterdam

(1986) Varieties of English grammar: descriptive, pedagogical, communicative. In Efstathiadis S and Tryfona-Antonopoulou N (eds) *Proceedings of the Greek Applied Linguistics Association*. University Studio Press, Thessaloniki

(1986) Automatic grammatical analysis and its educational applications. In Leech G and Candlin C N (eds) *Computers in English language teaching and research*. Longman, London

(1987) General introduction. In Garside R, Leech G and Sampson G (eds) *The Computational analysis of English: a corpus-based approach*. Longman, London

(1987) Stylistics and functionalism. In Fabb N, Attridge D, Durant A and MacCabe C (eds) *The linguistics of writing*. Manchester University Press

(1988) Varieties of English grammar: the state of the art from the grammarian's point of view. In Bald W-D (ed) *Kernprobleme Englischer Grammatik*. Langenscheidt-Longman, Munich

(1989) Grammar and language learning. In *Actas del VII Congreso Nacional de Lingüística Aplicada*. Asociación Española de Lingüística Aplicada, Sevilla

(1989) [with J Thomas] Language, meaning and context: pragmatics. In Collinge N (ed) *An encyclopaedia of language.* Routledge

(1990) The value of a corpus in English language research: a reappraisal. In *Linguistic Fiesta: Festschrift for Professor Hisao Kakehi's Sixtieth Birthday.* Kuroshio, Tokyo

(1991) Corpora. In Malmkjær K (ed) *The linguistics encyclopaedia.* Routledge

(1991) [with R Garside] Running a grammar factory: the production of syntactically analysed corpora or 'treebanks'. In Johansson S and Stenström A-B (eds) *English computer corpora: selected papers and research guide.* Mouton de Gruyter, Berlin & New York

(1991) The state of the art in corpus linguistics. In *English corpus linguistics: linguistic studies in honour of Jan Svartvik.* Longman, London

(1991) [with L Taylor and S Fligelstone] A survey of English machine-readable corpora. In Johansson S and Stenström A-B (eds) *English computer corpora: selected papers and research guide.* Mouton de Gruyter, Berlin & New York

(1992) Corpora and theories of linguistic performance. In Svartvik J (ed) *Directions in corpus linguistics: proceedings of Nobel Symposium 82.* Mouton de Gruyter, Berlin and New York

(1992) [with S Fligelstone] Computers and corpus analysis. In Butler C S (ed) *Computers and written texts.* Blackwell

(1992) Corpus processing. In Bright W (ed) *Oxford international encyclopaedia of linguistics.* Oxford University Press, New York

(1992) Pragmatic principles in Shaw's *You never can tell.* In Toolan M (ed) *Language, text and context: essays in stylistics.* Routledge

(1993) [with R Garside and M Bryant] The large-scale grammatical tagging of text: experience with the British National Corpus. In Oostdijk N and de Haan P (eds) *Corpus-based research into language.* Rodopi, Amsterdam

(1993) [with L Eyes] Progress in UCREL research: improving corpus annotation practices. In Aarts J and de Haan P (eds) *English language corpora: design, analysis and exploitation.* Rodopi, Amsterdam

(1993) [with L Eyes] Syntactic annotation: linguistic aspects of grammatical tagging and skeleton parsing. In Black E, Garside R and Leech G (eds) *Statistically-driven computer grammars of English: the IBM/Lancaster approach.* Rodopi, Amsterdam

(1994) [with R Garside and M Bryant] CLAWS4: the tagging of the British National Corpus. In *Proceedings of the 15th International Conference on Computational Linguistics (COLING 94).* Kyoto, Japan, 5–9 August 1994

(1994) [with A McEnery, M Oakes, R Garside and J Hutchinson] The exploitation of parallel corpora in Projects ET 10–63 and CRATER. In *Proceedings of NewLAP*. UMIST, Manchester

(1994) [with A McEnery and M Oakes] Multilingual corpus resources and tools developed in CRATER. In *Proceedings of the International Workshop on Sharable Natural Language Resources*. Nara, Japan, 10–11 August 1994

(1994) Students' grammar — teachers' grammar — learners' grammar. In Bygate M, Tonkyn A and Williams E (eds) *Grammar and the language teacher*. Prentice Hall International

(1994) [with B J Francis and X Xu] The use of computer corpora in the textual demonstrability of gradience in linguistic categories. In Fuchs C and Victorri B (eds) *Continuity in linguistic semantics*. John Benjamins, Amsterdam

(1995) [with Lu Li] Indeterminacy between noun phrases and adjective phrases as complements of the English verb. In Aarts B and Meyer C F (eds) *The verb in contemporary English: theory and description*. Cambridge University Press

Reprints

(1984) Literary criticism and linguistic description. *DQR* **7**: 2–22 [1977] reprinted in Aarts F *et al* (eds) *The best of DQR*, Amsterdam

(1986) Music in metre: 'sprung rhythm' in Victorian and Georgian poetry. *DQR* **14**(3): 200–13 [1984] reprinted, with additions, in de Haan T (ed) *Linguistics and the study of literature*. Rodopi, Amsterdam

Miscellaneous

(1964) Advertising's grammar. *New Society* 108, 8 October, 16–17

(1970) The linguistic and the literary. *Times Literary Supplement*, 23 July, 805–6

(1977) Grammar and rhetoric within a functional approach to language. Inaugural lecture delivered 2 February 1977, University of Lancaster

(1977) *Language and tact*. Linguistic Agency University of Trier, Series A, Paper No. 46

(1985) Grammar, pragmatics and politeness. *The rising generation*. Tokyo, May 1985, 54–60

Electronic text databases

(1978) *Lancaster-Oslo/Bergen Corpus of British English*
1 million words of British English, consisting of 500 text samples subdivided into 15 categories of written language.

(1986) *Lancaster-Oslo/Bergen Corpus of British English*
The grammatically-tagged version of the Lancaster-Oslo/ Bergen Corpus.

(1987) *Lancaster/IBM Spoken English Corpus*
53,000 words of formal English speech, including a number of parallel versions: sound recording, orthographic transcription, prosodically-transcribed version, grammatically-tagged version, and skeleton-parsed version. Chief editors: G Knowles and P Alderson.

(1992) *Lancaster Parsed Corpus*
A representative subcorpus of the Lancaster-Oslo/Bergen Corpus, consisting of 144,000 words of syntactically-analysed sentences sampled from the 15 text categories.

(1994) *The British National Corpus*
A corpus of 100 million words of British English (90 million written and 10 million spoken), grammatically tagged at Lancaster University.

Editorships

Joint General Editor of the *Longman Linguistic Library*, 1970–1982
Joint General Editor of the Longman series *Learning about Language*, 1982–
Joint General Editor of the Longman series *Studies in Language and Linguistics*, 1982–

References

Adamson G W, Boreham J 1974 The use of an association measure based on character structure to identify semantically related pairs of words and document titles. *Information Storage and Retrieval* **10**: 253–60

Aijmer K 1985 The semantic development of will. In Fisiak J (ed) *Historical semantics — historical word-formation*. Mouton, Berlin, New York and Amsterdam, pp 11–21

Aijmer K 1987 Principles of semantic change and lexical variation. In Rosén V (ed) *Papers from the 10th Scandinavian Conference of Linguistics. Vol. 1*. Department of Linguistics and Phonetics, University of Bergen, Bergen, pp 21–36

Aitchison J 1994 *Language joyriding*. Clarendon Press, Oxford

Alderson J C 1986 Computers in language testing. In Leech G N, Candlin C N (eds) *Computers in English language teaching and research*. Longman, London, pp 99–110

Alderson J C 1987 *Innovation in language testing: can the micro-computer help?* Language Testing Update. Special Report Number 1, Lancaster University

Alderson J C, North B (eds) 1991 *Language testing in the 1990s: the communicative legacy*. Macmillan, London

Alderson J C, Windeatt S 1991 Computers and innovation in language testing. In Alderson J C, North B (eds) *Language testing in the 1990s: the communicative legacy*. Macmillan, London, pp 226–36

Allen R 1994 The presentation of speech and thought in popular fiction. Unpublished MA dissertation, Department of Linguistics and Modern English Language, Lancaster University,

Arnfield S 1994 Prosody and syntax in corpus based analysis of spoken English. Unpublished PhD Thesis, School of Computer Studies and Psychology, University of Leeds

Arnfield S, Atwell E 1993 A syntax based grammar of stress sequences. In Lucas S (ed) *Grammatical inference: theory, applications, and alternatives.* Colloquium Proceedings 1993/092, Institution of Electrical Engineers, London, pp 71–7

Atwell E S 1983 Constituent Likelihood Grammar. *ICAME Journal* **7**: 34–67

Atwell E S 1987a How to detect grammatical errors in a text without parsing it. In Maegaard B (ed) *Proceedings of the Third Conference of European Chapter of the Association for Computational Linguistics.* Association for Computational Linguistics, New Jersey, pp 38–45

Atwell E S 1987b A parsing expert system which learns from corpus analysis. In Meijs W (ed) *Corpus linguistics and beyond: proceedings of the ICAME 7th International Conference.* Rodopi, Amsterdam, pp 227–35

Atwell E S 1988 Transforming a parsed corpus into a corpus parser. In Kyto M, Ihalainen O, Risanen M (eds) *Corpus Linguistics, hard and soft: proceedings of the ICAME 8th International Conference.* Rodopi, Amsterdam, pp 61–70

Atwell E S 1993a Linguistic constraints for large-vocabulary speech recognition. In Atwell E (ed) *Knowledge at work in universities.* Leeds University Press, Leeds, pp 26–32

Atwell E S 1993b Introduction and overview of the HEFC Knowledge Based Systems Initiative. In Atwell E (ed) *Knowledge at work in universities.* Leeds University Press, Leeds, pp 1–5

Atwell E S 1993c Corpus-based statistical modelling of English grammar. In Souter C, Atwell E (eds) *Corpus-based computational linguistics.* Rodopi, Amsterdam, pp 195–215

Atwell E S 1994 *Speech-oriented probabilistic parser project: final report to MoD*. School of Computer Studies, Leeds University, Leeds

Atwell E S, Arnfield S, Demetriou G, Hanlon S, Hughes J, Jost U, Pocock R, Souter C, Ueberla J 1993 Multi-level disambiguation grammar inferred from English corpus, treebank and dictionary. In Lucas S (ed) *Grammatical inference: theory, applications, and alternatives*. Colloquium Proceedings 1993/092, Institution of Electrical Engineers, London, pp 91–7

Atwell E S, Churcher G, Souter C 1995 Developing a corpus-based grammar model within a commercial continuous speech recognition package. In Collingham R (ed) *Papers for the Institute of Acoustics Speech Group meeting on integrating speech recognition and natural language processing, Durham University, March 1995*, pp 5–6

Atwell E S, Drakos N 1987 Pattern recognition applied to the acquisition of a grammatical classification system from unrestricted English text. In Maegaard B (ed) *Proceedings of the Third Conference of European Chapter of the Association for Computational Linguistics*. Association for Computational Linguistics, New Jersey, pp 56–63

Atwell E S, Elliot S 1987 Dealing with ill-formed English text. In Garside R G, Sampson G R, Leech G N (eds) *The computational analysis of English: a corpus-based approach*. Longman, London, pp 120–38

Atwell E S, Hughes J, Souter C 1994 AMALGAM: automatic mapping among lexico-grammatical annotation models. In Klavans J (ed) *Proceedings of ACL workshop on the balancing act: combining symbolic and statistical approaches to language*. Association for Computational Linguistics, New Jersey, pp 21–8

Atwell E S, Leech G N, Garside R G 1984 Analysis of the LOB Corpus: progress and prospects. In Aarts J, Meijs W (eds) *Corpus linguistics: proceedings of the ICAME 4th International Conference*. Rodopi, Amsterdam, pp 40–52

Atwell E S, McKevitt P 1994 Pragmatic linguistic constraint models for large-vocabulary speech processing. In McKevitt P (ed) *Integrating speech and natural language processing: AAAI94 workshop proceedings*. American Association for Artificial Intelligence, Washington USA, August 1994, pp 58–64

Atwell E S, Souter C, O'Donoghue T 1988 Prototype Parser 1. *Communal Report No. 17 to MoD*. School of Computer Studies, Leeds University, Leeds

Bachman L 1990 *Fundamental considerations in language testing*. Oxford University Press

Bald W-D, Schwarz A 1984 *Active grammar*. Langenscheidt-Longman, München

Bally C 1912a Le style indirect libre en Français moderne I. *Germanisch-Romanische Monatsschrift* **4**: 549–56

Bally C 1912b Le style indirect libre en Français moderne II. *Germanisch-Romanische Monatsschrift* **4**: 597–606

Banfield A 1982 *Unspeakable sentences: narration and representation in the language of fiction*. Routledge and Kegan Paul, Boston

Barcus F 1969 Appendix: education in content analysis — a survey. In Gerbner G, Hosti O R, Krippendorff K, Paisley W J, Stone P J (eds) *The analysis of communication content*. Wiley, New York, pp 539–54

Beale A 1989 The development of a distributional lexicon: a contribution to computational lexicography. Unpublished PhD Thesis, Department of Linguistics, Lancaster University

Beaman K 1984 Coordination and subordination revisited: syntactic complexity in spoken and written narrative discourse. In Tannen D (ed) *Coherence in spoken and written discourse*. Ablex, Norwood, N.J., pp 45–80

Biber D 1988 *Variation across speech and writing*. Cambridge University Press, Cambridge

Billig M 1988 Methodology and scholarship in understanding ideological explanation. In Antaki C (ed) *Analysing everyday explanation: a casebook of methods*. Sage, London, pp 199–215

Billot S, Lang B 1989 The structure of shared forests in ambiguous parsing. In *Proceedings of the 27th Meeting of the Association for Computational Linguistics*. Vancouver, Canada, pp 143–51

Black E, Garside R G, Leech G N 1993 *Statistically-driven computer grammars of English: the IBM/Lancaster approach.* Rodopi, Amsterdam

Blackwell S 1987 Syntax versus orthography: problems in the automatic parsing of idioms. In Garside R G, Leech G N, Sampson G R (eds) *The computational analysis of English: a corpus based approach.* Longman, London, pp 110–19

Bloomfield L 1935 [1933] *Language.* Allen and Unwin, London

Brill E 1992 A simple rule-based template tagger. *Proceedings of the 3rd International Conference on Applied Natural Language Processing, Trento, Italy.* Association for Computational Linguistics, New Jersey. 152–55

Brill E 1993 A corpus-based approach to language learning. Unpublished PhD Thesis, Department of Computer and Information Science, University of Pennsylvania

Briscoe E 1994 Prospects for practical parsing of unrestricted text: robust statistical parsing techniques. In Oostdijk N, de Haan P (eds) *Corpus-based research into language.* Rodopi, Amsterdam, pp 97–120

Briscoe E, Carroll J 1993 Generalised probabilistic LR parsing for unification based grammars. *Computational Linguistics* **19**(1): 25–60

Briscoe E, Carroll J 1994 *Parsing (with) punctuation.* Rank Xerox Research Centre, Grenoble, MLTT-TR-007

Briscoe E, Grover C, Boguraev B, Carroll J 1987 A formalism and environment for the development of a large grammar of English. In *Proceedings of the 10th International Joint Conference on Artificial Intelligence.* Milan, Italy, pp 703–8

Brown P, Della Pietra V, Della Pietra S, Mercer R 1993 The mathematics of statistical machine translation: parameter estimation. *Computational Linguistics* **19**(2): 263–301

Burnard L 1995 *Users' reference guide to the British National Corpus.* Oxford University Computing Services, Oxford

Caldas-Coulthard C R 1994 On reporting reporting: the representation of speech in factual and factional narratives. In Coulthard M (ed) *Advances in written text analysis*. Routledge, London, pp 295–308

Carroll J 1993 *Practical unification-based parsing of natural language*. Cambridge University, Computer Laboratory, TR-314, Cambridge

Carroll J 1994 Relating complexity to practical performance in parsing with wide-coverage unification grammars. *Proceedings of the 32nd Meeting of the Association for Computational Linguistics*. Las Cruces, NM, pp 287–94

Carroll J, Grover C 1989 The derivation of a large computational lexicon for English from LDOCE. In Boguraev B, Briscoe E (eds) *Computational lexicography for natural language processing*. Longman, London, pp 117–34

Catizone R, Russell G, Warwick S 1989 Deriving translation data from bilingual texts. In Zernik U (ed) *Proceedings of the First Lexical Acquisition Workshop*. Detroit

Chafe W L 1982 Integration and involvement in speaking, writing and oral discourse. In Tannen D (ed) *Spoken and written language*. Ablex, Norwood, N.J., pp 35–53

Chomsky N 1957 *Syntactic structures*. Mouton, The Hague

Chomsky N 1965 *Aspects of the theory of syntax*. MIT Press, Cambridge, MA

Chomsky N, Halle M 1968 *The sound pattern of English*. Harper and Row, New York

Church K 1988 A stochastic parts program and noun phrase parser for unrestricted text. In *Proceedings of the 2nd Conference on Applied Natural Language Processing*. Association for Computational Linguistics, Austin, Texas, pp 136–43

Collins COBUILD English language dictionary. 1987 Collins, London and Glasgow.

Crowdy S 1993 Spoken corpus design. *Literary and Linguistic Computing* **8**(4): 259–65

Crowdy S 1994 Spoken corpus transcription. *Literary and Linguistic Computing* **10**: 25-28

Crowdy S 1995 The BNC Spoken Corpus. In Leech G N, Myers G A, Thomas J A (eds) *Spoken English on computer: transcription, mark-up and application.* Longman, London, pp 224–34

de Haan P 1989 *Postmodifying clauses in the English noun phrase: a corpus-based study.* Rodopi, Amsterdam

de Marcken C 1990 Parsing the LOB Corpus. In *Proceedings of the 28th Annual Meeting of the Association for Computational Linguistics.* New York, pp 243–51

de Roeck A, Johnson R, King M, Sampson G R, Varile N 1982 A myth about centre-embedding. *Lingua* **58**: 327–40

Demetriou G 1992 Lexical disambiguation using constraint handling in Prolog (CHIP). Unpublished MSc Thesis, School of Computer Studies, Leeds University

Demetriou G 1993 Lexical disambiguation using CHIP (Constraint Handling in Prolog). In *Proceedings of the sixth European Conference of the Association for Computational Linguistics.* Association for Computational Linguistics, New Jersey, pp 431–36

Demetriou G, Atwell E 1994 Machine-learnable, non-compositional semantics for domain independent speech or text recognition. In *Proceedings of 2nd Hellenic-European Conference on Mathematics and Informatics (HERMIS).* Athens University of Economics and Business, Athens, 103–4

Dice L R 1945 Measures of the amount of ecologic association between species. *Ecology* **26**: 297–302

Dodgson M 1995 *Computer recognition of speech presentation in text.* unpublished B.Sc. project report, Computing Department, Lancaster University

Elworthy D 1993 *Part-of-speech tagging and phrasal tagging. Acquilex-II Working Paper 10.* Cambridge University Computer Laboratory, Cambridge

Elworthy D 1994 Does Baum-Welch re-estimation help taggers? In *Proceedings of the 4th Conference of Applied Natural Language Processing*. Stuttgart, Germany, pp 293–98

Eyes E, Leech G N 1993 Progress in UCREL research: improving corpus annotation practices. In Aarts J, de Haan P, Oostdijk N (eds) *English language corpora: design, analysis and exploitation*. Rodopi, Amsterdam, pp 123–44

Fabricius-Hansen C 1975 *Transformative, intransformative und kursive Verben*. Niemeyer, Tübingen

Fairclough N L 1993 *Discourse and social change*. Polity Press, Cambridge

Fligelstone S D 1992 Developing a scheme for annotating text to show anaphoric relations. In Leitner G (ed) *Proceedings of the 11th International Conference on English Language Research on Computer Corpora*. Berlin, Mouton de Gruyter, pp 153–70

Fligelstone S D in preparation JAWS: using lemmatisation rules and contextual disambiguation rules to enhance Claws output. *UCREL Technical Papers*

Fludernik M 1993 *The fictions of language and the languages of fiction*. Routledge, London

Francis W N 1980 A tagged corpus — problems and prospects. In Greenbaum S, Leech G N, Svartvik J (eds) *Studies in English linguistics — for Randolph Quirk*. Longman, London, pp 192–209

Francis W N, Kučera H K 1979 *Manual of information to accompany a Standard Sample of Present-day Edited American English, for use with digital computers. Rev ed.* Department of Linguistics, Brown University, Providence RI

Francis W N, Kučera H K 1982 *Frequency analysis of English usage: lexicon and grammar*. Houghton Mifflin Company, Boston

Gale W A, Church K W 1993 A program for aligning sentences in bilingual corpora. *Computational Linguistics* **19**(1): 75–102

Garside R G 1985 A grammatical tagging system for text corpora. In *Proceedings of the 11th International Conference of the Association for Literary and Linguistic Computing 2–6 April 1984*. Slatkine, Geneva, pp 195–207

Garside R G 1993 The marking of cohesive relationships: tools for the construction of a large bank of anaphoric data. *ICAME Journal* **17**: 5–27

Garside R G 1995 Grammatical tagging of the spoken part of the British National Corpus: a progress report. In Leech G N, Myers G A, Thomas J A (eds) *Spoken English on computer: transcription, mark-up and application*. Longman, London, pp 161–7

Garside R G, Leech G N, Sampson G R (eds) 1987 *The computational analysis of English: a corpus-based approach*. Longman, London

Garside R G, McEnery A M, Rayson P 1993 *Argument frame extraction using corpora*. ET10-63 Working Paper

Gaussier E, Langé J-M, Meunier F 1992 Towards bilingual terminology. In *Proceedings of ALLC/ACH Conference, Oxford*. Oxford University Press, Oxford, pp 121–24

Gazdar G, Mellish C 1989 *Natural language processing in Pop-11: an introduction to computational linguistics*. Addison-Wesley, Reading

George H V 1963a A verb-form frequency count. *English Language Teaching* **18**: 31–7

George H V 1963b A verb-form frequency count — application to course design, grammatical implication. *Monograph of C.I.E.* **2**, Hyderabad

Givón T 1993 *English grammar: a function-based introduction. Vol II*. Benjamins, Amsterdam

Goldfarb C F 1990 *The SGML handbook*. Clarendon Press, Oxford

Grabowski E, Mindt D 1994 Die unregelmäßigen Verben des Englischen: eine Lernliste auf empirischer Grundlage. *Die Neueren Sprachen* **93**: 334–53

Grainger K 1989 Care and control: interactional management in nursing the elderly. In Clark R, Fairclough N, Ivanič R, McLeod N, Thomas J, Meara P (eds) *Language and power. Papers from the 22nd Annual Meeting of the British Association for Applied Linguistics.* CILT/BAAL, London, pp 147–56

Greenbaum S, Nelson G 1995 Clause relationships in spoken and written English. *Functions of Language* **2**

Greene B B, Rubin G M 1971 *Automatic grammatical tagging of English.* Department of Linguistics, Brown University, Providence, R. I.

Grishman R, Macleod C, Meyers A 1994 Complex syntax: building a computational lexicon. In *Proceedings of the International Conference on Computational Linguistics, COLING-94.* Kyoto, Japan, pp 268–72

Gros J, Mihelič F, Pavesič N 1994 Sentence hypothesization in a speech recognition and understanding system for the Slovene spoken language. In Evett L, Rose T (eds) *Proceedings of AISB workshop on computational linguistics for speech and handwriting recognition, Leeds University.* Leeds, pp 91–6

Grover C, Carroll J, Briscoe E 1993 *The Alvey Natural Language Tools Grammar (4th Release).* Cambridge University Computer Laboratory, TR-284, Cambridge

Guadagnin M 1994 A corpus-based analysis of speech and thought: presentation categories in 20th Century British prose fiction. Unpublished M.A. dissertation, Department of Linguistics and Modern English Language, Lancaster University,

Haase I 1988 Temporafolge und Bedingungstyp im konditionalen Satzgefüge. In Mindt D (ed) *EDV in der Angewandten Linguistik: Ziele — Methoden — Ergebnisse.* Diesterweg, Frankfurt am Main, pp 69–76

Haigh R, Sampson G, Atwell E 1988 Project APRIL — a progress report. In *Proceedings of the 26th Annual Meeting of the Association for Computational Linguistics (ACL).* Association for Computational Linguistics, New Jersey, pp 104–12

Hakuta K 1974 Prefabricated patterns and the emergence of structure in second language acquisition. *Language Learning* **24**(2): 287–98

Hall P A V, Dowling G R 1980 Approximate string matching. *Computing Surveys* **12**(4): 381–402

Hanlon S 1994 A computational theory of contextual knowledge in machine reading. Unpublished PhD Thesis, School of Computer Studies, Leeds University

Harrison P, Abney S, Black E, Flickenger D, Gdaniec C, Grishman R, Hingle D, Ingria B, Marcus M, Santorini B, Strzalkowski T 1991 Evaluating syntax performance of parser/grammars of English. In *Proceedings of the Workshop on Evaluating Natural Language Processing Systems.* Association for Computational Linguistics

Heritage J 1988 Explanations as accounts: a conversation analytic perspective. In Antaki C (ed) *Analysing everyday explanation: a casebook of methods.* Sage Publications, London, pp 127–44

Hindle D 1989 Acquiring disambiguation rules from text. In *Proceedings of the 27th Annual Meeting of the Association for Computational Linguistics.* Vancouver, Canada, pp 118–25

Hockett C 1954 Two models of grammatical description. *Word* **10**: 210–31

Hornby A S 1959/1961 *The teaching of structural words and sentence patterns. Stages 1 and 2.* Oxford University Press, Oxford

Howarth P 1995 A computer-assisted study of collocations in academic prose, with special reference to grammatical structure and stylistic value. Unpublished PhD Thesis, School of English, University of Leeds

Huddleston R D 1976 Some theoretical issues in the description of the English verb. *Lingua* **40**: 331–83

Huddleston R 1984 *Introduction to the grammar of English.* Cambridge University Press, Cambridge

Hughes J 1989 A learning interface to the Realistic Annealing Parser. Unpublished BSc Project Report Thesis, School of Computer Studies, Leeds University

Hughes J 1994 Automatically acquiring a classification of words. Unpublished PhD Thesis, School of Computer Studies, Leeds University

Hughes J, Atwell E 1994 The automated evaluation of inferred word classifications. In Cohn T (ed) *Proceedings of European Conference on Artificial Intelligence (ECAI)*. John Wiley, Chichester, pp 535–39

Hughes J, Souter C, Atwell E S 1995 Automatic extraction of tagset mappings from parallel-annotated corpora. In Tzoukermann E, Armstrong S (eds) *From text to tags: issues in multilingual language analysis. Proceedings of ACL-SIGDAT workshop, University College Dublin, March 1995*. Conference Proceedings, pp 10–17

Hutchins J, Somers H 1992 *An introduction to machine translation.* Academic Press, New York

ICAME collection of English language corpora. Norwegian Computing Centre for the Humanities, Bergen.

Jackendoff R 1977 *X-bar syntax.* MIT Press, Cambridge, MA

Jelinek F 1990 Self-organized language modeling for speech recognition. In Waibel A, Lee K-F (eds) *Readings in Speech Recognition.* Morgan Kaufmann, San Mateo, Ca., pp 450–506

Johansson S 1986 *The tagged LOB Corpus, user's manual.* Norwegian Computing Centre for the Humanities, Bergen

Johansson S, Atwell E S, Garside R G, Leech G N 1986 *The tagged LOB Corpus.* Norwegian Computing Centre for the Humanities, Bergen

Johansson S, Hofland K 1989 *Frequency analysis of English vocabulary and grammar, based on the LOB Corpus.* Clarendon Press, Oxford

Johansson S, Leech G N, Goodluck H 1978 *Manual of information to accompany the Lancaster-Oslo/Bergen Corpus of British English, for use with digital computers.* Department of British and American Studies, University of Oslo, Oslo

Jones B 1994 Can punctuation help parsing? In *Proceedings of the International Conference on Computational Linguistics Coling94.* Kyoto, Japan, pp 421–25

Jost U 1994 Probabilistic language modelling for speech recognition. Unpublished MSc Thesis, School of Computer Studies, Leeds University

Jost U, Atwell E 1993 Deriving a probabilistic grammar of semantic markers from unrestricted English text. In Lucas S (ed) *Grammatical inference: theory, applications, and alternatives.* Colloquium Proceedings 1993/092, Institution of Electrical Engineers, London, pp 91–7

Karlsson F, Voutilainen A, Heikkilä J, Anttila A 1995 *Constraint grammar: a language-independent system for parsing unrestricted text.* Mouton de Gruyter, Berlin

Keenan F 1992 Large vocabulary syntactic analysis for text recognition. Unpublished PhD thesis. Department of Computing, Nottingham Trent University

Kelly A, Sime A 1990 Language as research data: application of computer content analysis in nursing research. *Advances in Nursing Science* **12**(3): 32–40

Kirsten H 1972 Gibt es im Englischen ein Futur? In *Zeitschrift für Anglistik und Amerikanistik.* pp 229–36

Knowles G 1994 Annotating large speech corpora: building on the experience of Marsec. *Hermes* **13**: 87–98

Knowles G in preparation The design of historical corpora.

Knuth D E 1984 *The TeXbook.* Addison-Wesley, Reading, Massachusetts

Kučera H, Francis W N 1967 *Computational analysis of present-day American English.* Brown University Press, Providence, R.I.

Labov W M 1973 The place of linguistic research in American society. In Hamp E P (ed) *Themes in Linguistics: the 1970s.* Mouton, The Hague, pp 97–129

Labov W M 1975 Empirical foundations of linguistic theory. In Austerlitz R (ed) *The Scope of American Linguistics.* Peter de Ridder Press, Lisse, pp 77–133

Labov W, Fanshel D 1977 *Therapeutic discourse: psychotherapy as conversation.* Academic, New York

Larsen-Freeman D E 1976 An explanation for the morpheme acquisition order of second language learners. *Language Learning* **26**: 125–34

Larsen-Freeman D E 1978 An explanation for the morpheme accuracy order of learners of English as a second language. In Hatch E M (ed) *Second language acquisition: a book of readings*. Newbury House, Rowley, Massachusetts, pp 371–79

Leech G N 1966 *English in advertising: a linguistic study of advertising in Great Britain*. Longman, London

Leech G N 1969 *A linguistic guide to English poetry*. Longman, London

Leech G N 1983 *Principles of pragmatics*. Longman, London

Leech G N 1985 Stylistics. In van Dijk T A (ed) *Discourse and literature*. John Benjamins, Amsterdam, pp 39–57

Leech G N 1986 Automatic grammatical analysis and its educational applications. In Leech G, Candlin C (eds) *Computers in English language teaching and research: selected papers from the British Council Symposium*. Longman, London, pp 204–14,

Leech G N 1987 *Meaning and the English verb, 2nd ed.* Longman, London

Leech G N 1991 The state of the art in corpus linguistics. In Aijmer K, Altenberg B (eds) *English corpus linguistics: essays in honour of Jan Svartvik*. Longman, London, pp 8–29

Leech G N 1992a Corpora and theories of linguistic performance. In Svartvik J (ed) *Directions in corpus linguistics. Proceedings of Nobel Symposium 82, Stockholm, 4–8 August, 1991*. Mouton de Gruyter, Berlin and New York, pp 105–22

Leech G N 1992b Pragmatic principles in Shaw's *You Never Can Tell*. In Toolan M (ed) *Language, text and context*. Routledge, London, pp 259–78

Leech G N 1993 100 Million Words of English. *English Today* **33**: 9–15

Leech G N, Fligelstone S D 1992 Computers and corpus analysis. In Butler C (ed) *Computers and written texts*. Basil Blackwell, Oxford, pp 115–40

Leech G N, Garside R G 1991 Running a grammar factory: the production of syntactically analysed corpora or 'treebanks'. In Johansson S, Stenström A-B (eds) *English computer corpora: selected papers and research guide*. Mouton de Gruyter, Berlin

Leech G N, Garside R G, Atwell E S 1983a Recent developments in the use of computer corpora in English language research. *Transactions of the Philological Society* : 23–40

Leech G N, Garside R G, Atwell E S 1983b The automatic grammatical tagging of the LOB corpus. *ICAME Journal* **7**: 13–33

Leech G N, Garside R G, Bryant M 1994a Claws4: the tagging of the British National Corpus. City, 622–28

Leech G N, Garside R G, Bryant M B 1994b The large-scale grammatical tagging of text: experience with the British National Corpus. In Oostdijk N, de Haan P (eds) *Corpus-based research into language*. Rodopi, Amsterdam, pp 47–63

Leech G N, Short M H 1981 *Style in fiction*. Longman, London

Leech G N, Smith N 1995 *A brief users' guide to the grammatical tagging of the British National Corpus*. UCREL, Lancaster University

Levinson S C 1983 *Pragmatics* Cambridge University Press, Cambridge

Ljung M 1990 *A study of TEFL vocabulary*. Almqvist and Wiksell International, Stockholm

Longman Dictionary of Contemporary English 1995 Summers D, Rundell M, (eds). Longman, London

Longman Language Activator 1993 Summers D, Rundell M (eds) Longman, London

Louw B 1993 Irony in the text or insincerity in the writer? — The diagnostic potential of semantic prosodies. In Baker M, Francis G, Tognini-Bonelli E (eds) *Text and technology: in honour of John Sinclair*. John Benjamins, Amsterdam, pp 157–76

Lyons J 1991 *Chomsky (3rd edition)*. Fontana, London

McArthur T 1981 *The Longman lexicon of contemporary English.* Longman, London

McEnery A M, Oakes M P, Garside R G, Hutchinson J, Leech G N 1994 The exploitation of parallel corpora in Projects ET10/63 and CRATER. In Jones D, Somers H (eds) *Proceedings of the NEMLAP Conference.* UMIST, Manchester, pp 108–15

McEnery A M and Wilson A 1994 *Corpora in language education and research. A selection of papers from Talc94.* UCREL Technical Papers Volume 4. Unit for Computer Research on the English Languae, Lancaster University

McIllmurray, M B, 1992 Psychosocial, behavioural and communication research in oncology. *Lancaster and Westmorland Medical Journal* **1**(8): 220–22

McHale B 1978 Free indirect discourse: a survey of recent accounts. *Poetics and Theory of Literature (PTL)* **3**: 249–87

McKenzie M 1987 Free indirect speech in a fettered insecure society. *Language and Communication* **7**(2): 153–59

McKevitt P 1991 Analysing coherence of intention in natural-language dialogue. Unpublished PhD Thesis, Department of Computer Science, Exeter University

Magerman D 1995 Statistical decision-tree models for parsing. In *Proceedings of the 33rd Annual Meeting of the Association for Computational Linguistics.* Boston, MA

Marks L E 1968 Scaling of grammaticalness of self-embedded English sentences. *Journal of Verbal Learning and Verbal Behavior* **7**: 965–7

Marshall I 1983 Choice of grammatical word-class without global syntactic analysis: tagging words in the LOB Corpus. *Computers and the Humanities* **17**: 139–50

Matthews P H 1981 *Syntax.* Cambridge University Press, Cambridge

Meara P, Buxton B 1987 An alternative to multiple choice vocabulary tests. *Language Testing* **4**(2): 142–51

Miller G A, Chomsky N 1963 Finitary models of language users. In Luce R D, Bush R R, Galante E (eds) *Handbook of mathematical psychology, vol. ii.* Wiley, New York.

Mindt D 1986 Futurisches *Shall* für den Hauptschüler? In Harks-Hanke I, Zydatiß W (eds) *1945 – 1985: Vierzig Jahre Englischunterricht für alle: Festschrift für Harald Gutschow.* Cornelsen, Berlin, pp 140–51

Mindt D 1987 *Sprache — Grammatik — Unterrichtsgrammatik: Futurischer Zeitbezug im Englischen I + Darstellungen.* Diesterweg, Frankfurt am Main

Mindt D 1992 *Zeitbezug im Englischen: Eine didaktische Grammatik des englischen Futurs.* Gunter Narr Verlag, Tübingen

Mindt D 1995 *An empirical grammar of the English verb: modal verbs.* Cornelsen, Berlin

Modd D, Atwell E 1994 A word hypothesis lattice corpus — a benchmark for linguistic constraint models. In Evett L, Rose T (eds) *Proceedings of AISB workshop on Computational Linguistics for Speech and Handwriting Recognition, Leeds University.* Leeds University, pp 191–98

Nespor M, Vogel I 1986 *Prosodic phonology.* Foris, Dordrecht

Noonan M 1985 Complementation. In Shopen T (ed) *Language, typology and syntactic description, vol. II: complex constructions.* Cambridge University Press, Cambridge, pp 42–140

Nunberg G 1990 *The linguistics of punctuation. CSLI Lecture Notes 18.* Stanford, CA

O'Donoghue T 1993 Reversing the process of generation in systemic grammar. Unpublished PhD Thesis, Department of Computer Studies, University of Leeds

Oakes M P, Taylor M J 1992 Clustering of thesaurus terms using ART, FCMs and approximate string-matching techniques. In Beale R, Findlay J (eds) *Neural networks and pattern recognition in human-computer interaction.* Ellis Horwood, Chichester, pp 246–63

Ogilvie D M, Stone P J and Kelly E F 1989 [1982] Computer-aided content analysis. In Züll C, Mohler P and Weber R P *Computer-assisted text classification for the social sciences: The General Inquirer III*. ZUMA, Mannheim, pp 199–228

Oksefjell S 1994 GET — towards a unified syntactic and semantic description. Unpublished Unpublished 'hovedfag' thesis, Department of British and American Studies, University of Oslo

Papageorgiou H, Cranias L, Piperidis S 1994 A new approach to automatic sentence alignment (Abstract). In *Conference Handbook, 1st International Conference on Teaching and Language Corpora (TALC 94), Lancaster University*. Department of Linguistics and Modern English Language, Lancaster University, Lancaster, pp 27–8

Pascal R 1977 *The dual voice: free indirect speech and its functioning in the Nineteenth Century European novel*. Manchester University Press, Manchester

Pawley A 1994 Beyond the grammar-lexicon model: the central role of speech formulas in linguistic competence. Paper presented at the International Symposium on Phraseology, University of Leeds, 18–20 April, 1994

Pawley A, Syder F H 1983 Two puzzles for linguistic theory: nativelike selection and nativelike fluency. In Richards J C, Schmidt R W (eds) *Language and communication*. Longman, London, pp 191–226

Perebejnos V I, Chidekel S S, Vajner L R, Volkova N O, *et al* 1986 *Spravocnik naibolee upotrebitel'nych anglijskich slovosocetanij [A deskbook of most frequent English collocations]*. Prosvescenie, Moscow

Pereira F, Warren D 1980 Definite clause grammars for language analysis — a survey of the formalism and a comparison with augmented transition networks. *Artificial Intelligence* **13**(3): 231–78

Perkins M R 1983 *Modal expressions in English*. Frances Pinter, London

Peters P in press Macro- and macro-linguistics. In Wichmann A, Fligelstone S, McEnery A M, Knowles G (eds) *Teaching and Language Corpora*. Longman, London

Phillips J D and Thompson H 1987 A parsing tool for the Natural Language theme. *Software Paper 5*. Department of Artificial Intelligence, Edinburgh University

Pocock R, Atwell E 1993 Treebank-trained probabilistic parsing of lattices. In *Technical Report 93.30*. School of Computer Studies, Leeds University

Quirk R, Greenbaum S, Leech G N, Svartvik J 1972 *A grammar of contemporary English*. Longman, London

Quirk R, Greenbaum S, Leech G N, Svartvik J 1985 *A comprehensive grammar of the English language*. Longman, London

Rayson P 1994 MATRIX: Automatic linking of key relations in tagged text. ACAMRIT Project Technical Report CS-3. Lancaster University, Computing Department, Lancaster

Reich P A 1969 The finiteness of natural language. *Language* **14**(4): 831–43

Reich P A, Dell G S 1977 Finiteness and embedding. In Pietro R J D, Blansitt E L (eds) *The Third LACUS Forum, 1976*. Hornbeam Press, Columbia, South Carolina, pp 438–47

Richards J C, Platt J, Platt H 1992 *Longman dictionary of language teaching and applied linguistics*. Longman, London

Rissanen M, Kyotö M, Palander-Colin M 1993 *Early English in the computer age: explorations through the Helsinki Corpus*. Mouton de Gruyter, Berlin and New York

Robins L S, Wolf F M 1988 Confrontation and politeness strategies in physician-patient interactions. *Social Science and Medicine* **27**(3): 217–21

Robins R H 1959 In defence of WP. *TPS*: 116–44

Roeh I, Nir R 1990 Speech presentation in the Israeli radio news: ideological constraints and rhetorical strategies. *Text* **10**(3): 225–44

Rundell M, Stock P 1994 The corpus revolution. *English Today* **8**(4): 45–51

Sampson G R 1975 *The form of language.* Weidenfeld and Nicolson, London

Sampson G R 1980 *Making sense.* Oxford University Press, Oxford

Sampson G R 1989a Language acquisition: growth or learning? *Philosophical Papers* **18**: 203–40

Sampson G R 1989b How fully does a machine-readable dictionary cover English text? *Literary and Linguistic Computing* **4**: 29–35

Sampson G R 1994 Susanne: a Doomsday book of English grammar. In Oostdijk N, de Haan P (eds) *Corpus-based research into language.* Rodopi, Amsterdam, pp 169–88

Sampson G R, Haigh R, Atwell E 1989 Natural language analysis by stochastic optimization: a progress report on Project APRIL. *Journal of Experimental and Theoretical Artificial Intelligence* **1**: 271–87

Schabes Y, Roth M, Osborne R 1993 Parsing of the Wall Street Journal with the inside-outside algorithm. In *Proceedings of the Meeting of European Association for Computational Linguistics.* Utrecht, The Netherlands, pp 341–46

Schmidt K 1986 Concept versus meaning: the contribution of computer-assisted content analysis and conceptual text analysis to this disputed area. In *Hommage à Charles Muller: méthodes quantitatives et informatiques dans l'Etude des textes.* Slatkine, Geneva, pp 779–93

Sell R D 1991 *Literary pragmatics.* Routledge, London

Shastri S V in collaboration with Patilkulkarni C T, Shastri G S 1986 *Manual of information to accompany the Kolhapur Corpus of Indian English, for use with digital computers.* Department of English, Shivaji University, Kolhapur, Kolhapur

Short M H 1988 Speech presentation, the novel and the press. In van Peer W (ed) *The taming of the text.* Routledge, London, pp 61–81

Short M H 1994 Understanding texts: point of view. In Brown G, Malmkjaer K, Pollitt A, Williams J (eds) *Language and understanding.* Oxford University Press, Oxford, pp 170–90

Simard M, Foster G, Isabelle P 1992 Using cognates to align sentences in bilingual corpora. In *Proceedings of the Fourth International Conference on Theoretical and Methodological Issues in Machine Translation (TMI92)*. Montreal, Canada, pp 67–81

Simpson P 1993 *Language, ideology and point of view*. Routledge, London

Sinclair J 1991 *Corpus, concordance, collocation*. Oxford University Press, Oxford

Sinclair J M, Coulthard M 1975 *Towards an analysis of discourse*. Oxford University Press, Oxford

Slembrouck S 1992 The parliamentary Hansard 'verbatim' report: the written construction of spoken discourse. *Language and Literature* **1**(2): 101–19

Snow C, Meijer G 1977 On the secondary nature of syntactic intuitions. In Greenbaum S (ed) *Acceptability in language*. Mouton, The Hague, pp 163–77

Souter C 1993 Harmonising a lexical database with a corpus-based grammar. In Souter C, Atwell E (eds) *Corpus-based computational linguistics*. Rodopi, Amsterdam, pp 181–93

Souter C, Atwell E 1992 A richly annotated corpus for probabilistic parsing. In Weir C, Grishman R (eds) *Proceedings of AAAI workshop on Statistically-Based NLP Techniques*. American Association for Artificial Intelligence, San José, California, July 1992, pp 28–38

Souter C, Atwell E 1994 Using parsed corpora: a review of current practice. In Oostdijk N, de Haan P (eds) *Corpus-based research into language*. Rodopi, Amsterdam, pp 143–158

Stone P J, Dunphy D C, Smith M S, Ogilvie D M 1966 *The General Inquirer: a computer approach to content analysis*. M.I.T. Press, Cambridge, MA.

Summers D 1993 Longman Lancaster English Language Corpus: criteria and design. *International Journal of Lexicography* **6**(3): 181–208

Svartvik J (ed) 1990 *The London-Lund Corpus of Spoken English: description and research*. Lund University Press, Lund

Svartvik J, Quirk R 1980 *A corpus of English conversation.* Lund University Press, Lund

Swan M 1980 *Practical English usage.* Oxford University Press, Oxford

Sweet H 1910 *The sounds of English.* Clarendon Press, Oxford

Taavitsainen I 1994 Subjectivity as a text-type marker in historical stylistics. *Language and Literature* **3**: 197–212

Tannen D 1989 *Talking voices: repetition, dialogue, and imagery in conversational discourse.* Cambridge University Press, Cambridge

Taylor L, Knowles G 1988 *Manual of information to accompany the SEC corpus: the machine-readable corpus of spoken English.* University of Lancaster, Lancaster

Taylor L, Leech G N, Fligelstone S D 1991 A survey of English machine-readable corpora. In Johansson S, Stenström A-B (eds) *English computer corpora.* Mouton de Gruyter, Berlin, pp 319–54

ten Have P 1991 Talk and institution: a reconsideration of the 'asymmetry' of doctor-patient interaction. In Boden D, Zimmerman D H (eds) *Talk and social structure.* Polity Press, Cambridge, pp 138–63

Thomas J A 1994a The effectiveness of communication within the Lancaster Cancer Support System. Report to ESRC.

Thomas J A 1994b A comparative study of patient satisfaction with cancer treatment in rural and urban practices within the Lancaster District Health Authority. Report to Lancaster District Health Authority.

Thomas J A 1994c *Communication between cancer patients and their carers: a comparative study of surgical and medical patients at the Royal Lancaster Infirmary. Report to Lancaster Health Authority.*

Thomas J A 1995 *Meaning in interaction: an introduction to pragmatics.* Longman, London

Trager G L, Smith H L 1957 [1951] *An outline of English structure.* American Council of Learned Societies, Washington

Ungerer F, Meier G E H, Schäfer K, Lechler S 1984 *A grammar of present-day English.* Ernst Klett, Stuttgart

Visser F T 1973 *An historical syntax of the English language. Part III: 2.* Brill, Leiden

Wekker H C 1976 *The expression of future time in contemporary British English: an investigation into the syntax and semantics of five verbal constructions expressing futurity.* North Holland Publishing Company, Amsterdam, New York

Wells G 1979 *Learning and using the auxiliary verb in English Language development.* Croom Helm, London

Wilson A 1991 'No', 'not' and 'never' negation in a corpus of spoken English transcripts. *Lancaster papers in linguistics* **73**, Department of Linguistics and Modern English Language, University of Lancaster

Wilson A 1993 Towards an integration of content analysis and discourse analysis: the automatic linkage of key relations in text. *Unit for Computer Research on the English Language Technical Papers* **3**, University of Lancaster

Wilson A, Leech G N 1993 Automatic content analysis and the stylistic analysis of prose literature. *Revue: Informatique et Statistique dans les Sciences Humaines* **29**: 219–34

Wilson A, Rayson P 1993 The automatic content analysis of spoken discourse. In Souter C, Atwell E S (eds) *Corpus-based computational linguistics.* Rodopi, Amsterdam, pp 215–26

Yngve V H 1960 A model and an hypothesis for language structure. *Proceedings of the American Philosophical Society* **104**: 444–66

Young S 1995 The state of the art in speech recognition. In *Papers for the Institute of Acoustics Speech Group meeting on Integrating Speech Recognition and Natural Language Processing*, Durham University, March 1995.

Zimin W, White J D 1990 Computer processing of Chinese characters: an overview of two decades research and development. *Information Processing and Management* **26**(5): 681–92

Index of Authors

Index of Subjects